Producing New and Digital Media

Producing New and Digital Media is your essential guide to understanding new media. Diving deeply into such topics as cultural and social impacts of the web, the importance of digital literacy, and creating in an online environment, this text provides an introductory, hands-on approach to creating user-generated content, coding, cultivating an online brand, and storytelling in new and digital media. Integrating media studies aspects with production and design tutorials, key features include:

- Coverage of up-to-date forms of communication on the web: memes, viral videos, social media, and more pervasive types of online languages.
- A companion website with research resources and links for further investigation.
- Online instructor materials, including lecture slides, sample syllabus, and instructor's manual.

In showing you how to navigate the world of digital media and complete digital tasks, this book not only teaches you how to use the web, but also helps you understand *why* you use it.

James Cohen is the program director for the Molloy College New Media Program. He was formerly the director of web and digital media at the Hofstra University School of Communication. He has been published several times on media literacy and digital curation.

Thomas Kenny has co-authored both the new media minor and major programs at Molloy College, designing both production and studies courses. Since 2008, Tom has held the position as television studio and media facilities manager for the Communications Department at Molloy.

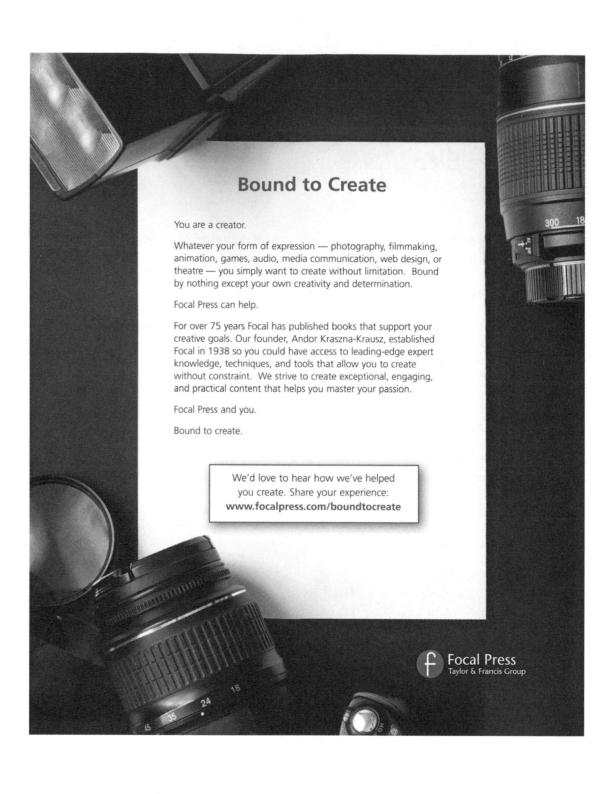

Bound to Create

You are a creator.

Whatever your form of expression — photography, filmmaking, animation, games, audio, media communication, web design, or theatre — you simply want to create without limitation. Bound by nothing except your own creativity and determination.

Focal Press can help.

For over 75 years Focal has published books that support your creative goals. Our founder, Andor Kraszna-Krausz, established Focal in 1938 so you could have access to leading-edge expert knowledge, techniques, and tools that allow you to create without constraint. We strive to create exceptional, engaging, and practical content that helps you master your passion.

Focal Press and you.

Bound to create.

We'd love to hear how we've helped you create. Share your experience:
www.focalpress.com/boundtocreate

Focal Press
Taylor & Francis Group

Producing New and Digital Media

Your guide to savvy use of the web

James Cohen and
Thomas Kenny

Focal Press
Taylor & Francis Group

NEW YORK AND LONDON

First published 2016
by Focal Press
70 Blanchard Road, Suite 402, Burlington, MA 01803

and by Focal Press
2 Park Square, Milton Park, Abingdon, Oxon OX14 4RN

Focal Press is an imprint of the Taylor & Francis Group, an informa business

Library of Congress Cataloging in Publication Data
Cohen, James, 1981 – A practical introduction to new and digital media: your guide to savvy use of the Web/by James Cohen and Thomas Kenny.
    pages cm
    Includes bibliographical references.
    1. Internet—Popular works. 2. Digital media—Popular works. 3. Social media—Popular works. 4. Internet users—popular works. I. Kenny, Thomas, 1983–. II. Title.
    TK5105.875.I57C636 2015 004.67'8—dc23 2015009537

ISBN: 978-1-13883-010-3 (pbk)
ISBN: 978-1-13883-009-7 (hbk)
ISBN: 978-1-31573-742-3 (ebk)

Typeset in Giovanni and Serifa
by Florence Production Ltd, Stoodleigh, Devon, UK

Printed and bound in the United States of America by Sheridan Books, Inc. (a Sheridan Group Company).

The authors wish to thank their wives, Nicole Samartino and Holly Kenny, for affording them the love and the time to write the book they've always wanted to read.

Contents

Acknowledgments

First and foremost, we would like to thank our students at Molloy College and Hofstra University, who inspired us, encouraged us, and supported us with their ideas, creativity, and participation in new and digital media.

We would also like to thank our colleagues and co-workers who offered us the time to write this book. We are lucky to have such great mentors, Paul Mihailidis and Deidre Pribram, for teaching, advising, and navigating us toward our goals anytime we need advice.

We would especially like to thank Kathryn Morrissey for giving us the opportunity and guiding us throughout the process. Additionally, we'd like to thank our colleagues, especially Brian Cogan, for his honest thoughts and feedback on our project.

This book has been made possible by the generous contributions from Steven Tsapelas, Ok Go, Rob Barnett, Veronica DeSouza, Melissa Grebe, Becky Arnzen, Alyssa Reynolds, Jess Schaefer, and especially to Bob Samartino for his excellent illustrations. Additional thanks to Ehlayna Napolitano, Rebecca Kern, Mike Schultz, Lauren Zafonte, Brianne Catalano, Raymond Mantoura, Craig Knittle, Laura Amante, Jess Falcone, and the rest of our Communications majors at Molloy College.

In closing, we want to thank our parents, Tom, Sharon, Jerry, and Joanna, and sisters, Meghan and Katy, who have been nothing but supportive of all of our dreams and aspirations.

This book would not have been possible without the love, support, and confidence given to us by our wives, Nicole and Holly.

CHAPTER 1

Introduction

WHAT IS NEW AND DIGITAL MEDIA?

The word media, the plural term for medium, covers a broad spectrum describing communications through television, film, radio, and print. Media require a viewer, a listener, a reader, or a spectator to carry any effect whatsoever. In our rapidly advancing hypermedia landscape of the present, where all traditional media have become singular on the screen-based Internet, the reader, viewer, and listener can participate as well and truly use media as communication. Technology has inevitably transformed our traditional media into a multitude of interactive platforms, now read and listened to on mobile devices, tablets, e-readers, flat screens, and wearable devices. Whether it's media consumption, the form of the content, or the interaction with the media, the Internet changed the habits of citizens globally. We are now ever connected, ever participating, and consuming film, television, music, news, radio, and millions of native websites.

In many ways, new and digital media are distinct from traditional media. New media are any emerging technologies that affect you both socially and culturally. Like traditional media, new and digital media allow for media consumption; however, new media make participation imperative in order to be useful. Users may use an existing platform, but they can create the content. Coders and developers working for their respective companies design Facebook and YouTube, but it's the millions of users worldwide who create and participate to enhance their growth and reach. The citizens of the web create the additional media in pictures, videos, text, artwork, and sound, among other forms of rapidly developed communication formats and data on the platforms.

New and digital media are unique because of the addition of the World Wide Web and how it connects users to a plethora of stimulating, user-generated amateur and professional, textual and visual content. New and digital media also include web design and site creation, as users can simply read and consume the web while also creating and designing their own digital environment. In the last two decades, the web has increased, from blogging

Figure 1.1

Welcome to the Internet, we'll be your guide.

Source: Photo by Jonathan Leung

and web platforms, to fully produced website design and access to code and gaming. Where traditional media were based on a consumption model, new media encourage online communities and many users to form them, with Twitter, Reddit, Vine, and Facebook acting as places to bring users together to interact, create, and have daily conversation and interactivity with one another.

New and digital media are simultaneously production and design for those who consume and participate in the content. Digital media creation has invented new ways of communication, and there have been various unique forms of that where users send messages and express themselves digitally and creatively. New media can be accessed online through memes, short-form videos on Vine, and looping animated GIFs, to name a few. In the digital media environment of the web, media can be watched, as well as altered and disseminated, by participants. Your outlet on the web can be a particular website or social media platform, among others. New and digital media prosper because you create and participate.

How Do You Use This Book?

The main purpose of this book is for you to become savvy in new and digital media. In order to become savvy, you have to understand the theories and cultural significance of the pieces of technology, some of the platforms, and the web as a communication device. Once you have an understanding of the reasons why you participate in online communities, how viral videos work, and the influence of web television and memes on the digital landscape, it is up to you to join and take part in the medium as a more savvy, responsible web citizen. Being a savvy user of new and digital media means having the knowledge and background information of how and why the technology and platforms in which you participate and create work. After you have read each chapter, we want you to join us online and take a chance. After you read about online communities in the following chapter, we would like for you to join one yourself; if you have never created a meme before, try making one; if you have never produced a vlog before, record one. In order to take advantage of digital media, you have to take chances and jump right in. Once you become a participant and content creator, with an understanding of the purpose or meaning of digital media, you will experience its benefits.

Another aspect and purpose of this book is, once you have the knowledge of how to use particular platforms, technology, and communication and digital media tools, we want you to become a storyteller. Whether it's through textual or visual formats, we want you to be a storyteller in whichever area of digital media you plan to participate in. After reading the chapter on web television, you may want to start your own web channel on YouTube to create your first series. After reading the chapter on online branding, you may want to start producing your own podcast or blog to promote yourself. Regardless of which chapter affects you, share your story and content with participants connected all over the world. We hope this book organizes and advances your techniques for online storytelling to your audience. You may be inspired to become a storyteller on digital platforms through tools you will be learning in this book. It can be as simple as tweeting on a daily basis or having a voice through your blog, posted once a week. You have the ability to reach millions with digital media, and your story can be unique, creative, and motivational for all to enjoy.

This book is not only your guide, but also a step-by-step reference for how to complete your digital tasks. We want this reference to be your one-stop shop to inform you of new and digital media theory, creation, and participation in the web, all in one place. We understand you can find this information in many places on the vast web, but we offer this as a practical introduction to new and digital media and hope it serves as a valuable tool and guide by your side as you become empowered.

We have included sidebars throughout this book that offer additional insight into and awareness of a given topic. The sidebars are designed to increase your media literacy perception in relation to the information we are discussing at the time. These sidebars are meant to start a discussion, build your knowledge, and encourage you to participate and learn more. The sidebars also fill in some of the blanks and quirky questions left unanswered by the growing environment online. These will help you build your mental skills and knowledge area in a specific topic.

To Keep in Mind While Reading

The Internet and the web are a hugely open media platform accessible from anywhere at anytime. Your participation is required for the evolution of the media, and we encourage you to be curious and try everything. We offer one phrase of advice we wish you to keep in mind when using the web: If you do not pay for it, *you* are the product.

These are strong words to associate with digital media platforms, but paramount for all users to keep in mind. Before we delve deeper into the book, you have to remember that, although these media are accessible and open and for the most part "free," someone, somehow, is always making money and a profit. In Chapter 2, we will be discussing online communities based on many different social media platforms, such as Facebook, Twitter, YouTube, and many more. Building communities with other users will be the main focus of the chapter, but keep in mind that the material and content you create regularly are bought and sold to advertisers in order to support the storage and delivery costs of the platforms. For every platform you join where you do not have control of the design of the system, there is a professional team that regulates, monitors, and controls your access. Participate, but be responsible and read your terms of service on each platform. We know that most terms of service are boring to read, but they offer you information on your rights and usage of any given technology. We will do our best to explain how you can use the web in the most responsible and creative way and as safely as possible, but, with the nature of the web, this information regularly changes and updates. It is your responsibility to read the "rules" every time they update, for the best experience you can have using new and digital media.

Why We Wrote This Book

Recently, while at a traffic light, four construction workers were identifying the underground lines of either electricity or gas with their technical gauge. While one of the construction workers waved the device around, two of the other three were listening to a story about a remote-control drone copter outfitted with a Halloween costume that flew near joggers, who were frightened into an all-out sprint. The storytelling worker was laughing hysterically at the memory, while the other three looked confused. This is the idea of visual memes and viral videos, which we'll be talking about in chapters 4 and 5. What the storytelling construction worker failed to realize was that memes are considered a "selfish gene" of culture. It's hysterical to the one with the memory of the visual, but those without the image feel a bit lost.

The construction worker had seen a video called "Epic Halloween Prank by Tom Mabe." The video, posted in October 2013 by comedian Tom Mabe, has been seen by over 7 million people. It's clearly a viral video that has made its rounds. The flying skeleton doesn't just involve scaring joggers half to death: It also scares some basketball players and frightens some relaxing kids. The video, just over 2 minutes in length, sits right in the sweet spot of virality. The way the video is composed and created helps make the theme very meme-like in quality and begs for it to be shared.

New and digital media are ubiquitous, that is certain. When we sought to approach this book, we knew that we'd have to explain the culture surrounding the omnipresent media. The web, the Internet, and social media are becoming supersaturated, with almost half the world with access to the Internet[1] and nearly 2 billion people with some sort of social media account.[2] Our approach in this book concerns the ever-pervasive need to control your intentions in the digital space. You can see and hear the need consistently. When we are asked to do talks and workshops, we often find the same thing asked by some of our audience members: "Why isn't there a book on this topic?" This is what we aim to achieve.

The variety of ways the web plays into our lives often go unnoticed. We have started taking the essence and ambience of the web for granted. In Alfred Hermida's essay, "Twittering the News: The emergence of ambient journalism,"[3] he explains that Twitter has become background noise and, in the case of journalism, it takes on the qualities of information as having nearly ethereal qualities. This so happened recently, when the Associated Press announced that algorithm bots would now write financial news stories.[4] In this book, we break down some of the immense amounts of information flow and, more importantly, separate the quality signal from the growing noise.

In respect to understanding the power of using the web for something much deeper and more pronounced than ambient information, we turn to users who utilize the web's tools, such as YouTube, to enhance their daily lives in ways unimaginable just over a decade ago. In Chapter 6, we will discuss how YouTube can be utilized as a learning tool, and how the user can get involved as a teacher to those who may be in need of their specific information.

Savvy users of the web are far beyond those who use it for frivolous updates or posting pictures of their pets, and they participate by creating quality content. Digital media have no sense of time or place. We understand time linearly, but time is always the same to digital media. Understanding that, we start to recognize that thousands of new users are logging on daily, and people are discovering new parts of the web all the time. We ourselves, as a people, are very similar to the construct of the web.

The web is a replicating entity that continues to grow, creating content out of every subject as each new member joins. If there is something that exists, you can most likely find it online. To paraphrase Clay Shirky, you can see the immense use of the web and the power of its users by going to *Harry Potter and the Sorcerer's Stone* on Amazon and checking the reviews—most likely a new review was added very recently. (Go check!) Additionally, Shirky adds an important note to those who are looking for answers on any topic. His example was going to YouTube and checking Gothic-style makeup advice, a search query that yields nearly 20,000 results (and continues to grow).

If you are seeking information or advice on any subject, from changing tires to cooking, someone has created a video of that happening, and, if they haven't, someone will very soon. To sift through this information to become a savvy user of, and participant in, this media landscape involves a process of understanding how we use the web and how we can get involved. Take, for example, Christine McConnell, a woman who is a self-taught baker who learned all of her techniques from YouTube. She is a savvy user of the web and a phenomenal participant in new and digital media.

McConnell loves the style of the 1950s. A makeup artist and stylist by career, McConnell practices her work on herself. While expanding her skills, she watched YouTube videos on how to bake interesting pastries and desserts. She created a niche when she started baking desserts in the form of monsters and characters from horror movies from the 1980s. She started an Instagram account to show off her work, and, very soon, online publications such as BuzzFeed ran profiles on her. She is now a web darling, among many others, who developed their persona online and use the web to continually increase their knowledge and expand their skill set.

Many average web users feel overwhelmed when they learn about Christine McConnell or other users who have created personas from their own expertise. If you are reading this book, then you have already taken steps toward advancing your identity online and becoming a better user of the vast amount of free tools available.

In Marc Prensky's article, "Digital Natives, Digital Immigrants,"[5] he explains we are in an era of youth growing up to understand digital media as a natural tool. This was later corrected, when Prensky realized his article was a bit too ahead of its time: The digital natives are really those born after the rise of the World Wide Web and, more specifically, touch-screen media. Although many readers of Prensky's article felt insulted by the insinuation that, if you were not savvy with digital media you were relegated to immigrant status, it opened a conversation about what it means to be truly native in a landscape of 1s and 0s.

Prensky explained that a fair amount of the backlash to his article comes from users who felt insecure about their web usage and experience. He further explained that the next language to be mastered is the language of programming.[6] We will spend Chapter 3 focusing on understanding how to identify several online languages and further focus on basic writing skills of the web languages HTML5 and CSS3. This will come with examples and learning tools for being a better reader of website data and functionality and will hopefully encourage the reader to modify and write websites on their own.

We recognize that website media constitute a changing landscape and that trends quickly change, and we hope that our practical introduction to code and website literacy focuses strongly enough on the construct to work with all of the trends that are evolving. In the last several years alone, we've seen websites go from multipage database sites to flat responsive design to card-type sites. It's hard to predict what trend will be considered the most aesthetically pleasing in the coming years, but we can be sure that HTML and CSS will be widely used.

In the near future, more than half the population of the planet will have access to media creation in the online digital space. Being a savvy user does not mean to be a YouTube creator or Instagram star; what it means is to *understand* why people are using the web and how important it is to be a citizen of the planet and online environment. Web users now have more potential than ever before to be more connected and knowledgeable; it is important to recognize the web as a large tool made up of hundreds of important tools, all working together.

The online companion website for this book also provides you with additional digital learning material to enhance your reading experience. You are encouraged to follow along with it as you read.

Remember to always be the authentic you online, because the web is an exciting, growing, and amazingly weird place. We're here to guide you and we hope you enjoy!

NOTES

1   ITU global ICT statistics. Retrieved from www.itu.int/en/ITU-D/Statistics/Pages/stat/default.aspx (accessed April 22, 2015).

2   *eMarketer* (2013). "Social Networking Reaches Nearly One in Four Around the World." Retrieved from www.emarketer.com/Article/Social-Networking-Reaches-Nearly-One-Four-Around-World/1009976 (accessed April 22, 2015).

3   Hermida, A. (2010). "Twittering the News: The emergence of ambient journalism." *Journalism Practice*. Vol 4. No. 3, pp. 297–308. Retrieved from http://papers.ssrn.com/sol3/papers.cfm?abstract_id=1732598 (accessed April 22, 2015).

4   Greenfield, D. (2014). "AP Turns Over the Tedious Business of Writing News Stories to Automated Bots." *Frontpage Magazine*. Retrieved from www.frontpagemag.com/2014/dgreenfield/ap-turns-over-the-tedious-business-of-writing-news-stories-to-automated-bots/ (accessed April 22, 2015).

5   Prensky, M. (2001). "Digital Natives, Digital Immigrants." Retrieved from www.marcprensky.com/writing/Prensky%20-%20Digital%20Natives,%20Digital%20Immigrants%20-%20Part1.pdf (accessed April 22, 2015).

6   Prensky, M. (2008). "Programming Is the New Literacy." Retrieved from www.edutopia.org/literacy-computer-programming (accessed April 22, 2015).

CHAPTER 2

Creativity in the Online Environment

Traditionally, communities are a group of people living together in one place, thereby creating a feeling of fellowship as a result of sharing common attitudes, interests, and goals. The group of people has to include multiple citizens interacting with a vast amount of individuals in the same place, such as a municipality, city, or state. Communities are also groups of people with common (and especially professional) interests within a larger society.

In our hypermedia landscape, communities belong, no longer solely to the physical space, but to the new and digital environment. According to Lee Rainie and Barry Wellman, communities online are a new social operating system that gives rise to "networked individualism," because, when you are in a community online, it is personal and individual and for multiple simultaneous users multitasking in the environment.[1] Online communities also allow both experts and information seekers to coexist and contribute equally.[2] This is not possible in most physical communities, and the web offers thousands, if not millions, of new places to participate.

"Every web page is a community," says media theorist Clay Shirky in the book *Here Comes Everybody* (2008), "Each page collects the attention of people interested in its contents and those people might well be interested in conversing with one another."[3] Online databases, message boards, and social media sites provide digital interaction with one other, but it's the content or material discussed through text, displayed through visuals, or heard through sound that captures the imagination of the you, the web user.

If you have created a presence on a social media platform, you have cultivated an online world where you have a group of individuals who are friends, followers, or fans. Your audience has turned into a community over time, where you gather with others in the digital space to share common interests such as discussing film, television, books, or other interests. How you interact within those communities can be your own unique experience. It is important to note that users of a social media community can define each platform as a different community. For example, in her book, *It's Complicated: The social lives of networked teens* (2013), danah boyd discusses that teenagers have different communities for different platforms and audiences. While explaining how a young woman uses Facebook with her actual name and Twitter with a nickname, boyd describes this act as "choosing to represent herself in different ways on different sites with the expectation of different audiences and different norms."[4] Online communities are places to locate a common audience and discuss your interests with others. The content being discussed, with interests shared with other users, may affect which platform you decide to join or start a community with others.

How do you find an online community to join? How do you find others who share a common interest with you? Whether on a laptop, smartphone, or tablet, you are always connected to a community and you are able to be a part of a group of creative individuals in your area of interest. You are part of a community no matter what, but it is up to you to decide which community to be a part of by selecting the platform and content of choice. In Shirky's *Cognitive Surplus* (2010), he describes the connection to the web as a place that "allows you to find other people who like building model trains and doing macramé, designing paper airplanes or dressing up as anime characters."[5]

If you are interested in being creative with a group of similar users, whether it may concern fictional characters or serious topics, you are looking for a community. And, like a community in physical space, your contribution and participation become consistent and attractive. Some may perceive your attachment to the community as an addiction, because you are always on Instagram or Facebook or Reddit, but it's most likely just a desire to be part of your community. It is where the community is built, and where your social interactions take place day to day. Communities are both digital and in your physical environment.

Communities provide outlets for you to meet with other users who have similar opinions on particular cultural issues. If you want a platform to discuss topics and issues you truly care about, there are outlets for that, and you will participate and create content within the community once you acclimate to the platform. Online communities offer new ways for you to discuss issues that affect your daily life that you traditionally wouldn't discuss with your physical community. A vast majority of digital media users use online communities for creative purposes, to discuss and share and create content such as memes, videos, and messages with others. Online platforms can also be used to start a community of change to influence opinions and for all users to have a voice, such as discussing political views on a blog or participating in a social activity such as the "ALS Ice Bucket Challenge." With this activity, you have used the community to raise awareness on a particular topic that affects our culture. As media theorist Henry Jenkins describes, in the book *Convergence Culture* (2006):

> New communities are defined through voluntary, temporary and tactical affiliations, reaffirmed through common intellectual

enterprises and emotional investments. Members may shift from one group to another as their interests and needs change, and they may belong to more than one community at the same time. These communities, however, are held together through the mutual production and reciprocal exchange of knowledge.[6]

Communities are built so that members can learn and exchange ideas with one another. Whether you are a part of a fan-fiction community or a community discussing political issues, you are exchanging experiences, ideas, and information with each other while learning things that will enhance your passion for the topic within the community or professional theme. By sharing your knowledge and information, you are participating in a community. Digital media communities can easily become larger, owing to their ability to have a farther societal reach. It is easier to gather a group of individuals to your community, owing to the connectivity of society as a group.

PARTICIPATION IN THE ONLINE ENVIRONMENT

In order to be a part of a community, you have to participate; in order to be a savvy user of digital media, you should understand your role as a creator to complete the interaction within the community. The ability to consider creativity in the online space will allow you to become a better citizen online and make your use of the web more valuable. The web is a boundless and limitless environment for creativity, and the only way you can use the web incorrectly is by not using it at all. There are millions of communities in which to get involved. To never participate in the online environment would keep you from advancing in society, learning new technologies, and seeking new ways to connect with others. The web is a vast landscape of small communities, inside larger communities, inside massive communities. If you participate passionately, you will be seen as a valuable community member.

In order to participate on your platform, you have to understand how it works and how to become involved with one another. In *Cognitive Surplus*, Clay Shirky explains, "a group has to do more than understand the things its members care about. Its members also have to understand each other in order to share or work well together."[7] If you are to join Twitter, you have to realize it is different than other communities. Where a community on BuzzFeed may read articles about quirky topics to be read any time, Twitter's community is more immediate and short form. You can update Twitter in real time, whereas other communities post information to be read later.

In *It's Complicated: The social lives of networked teens*, danah boyd adds, "teens connect to people they know, observe how those people are using the site, and then reinforce or challenge those norms through their own practices."[8] Digital media users take a step back and understand their community. Once you have an understanding of how to be involved within the community and learn to communicate with other users, you can then participate on the platform in your own unique way. Take the time, once you locate a community, to understand its features, who the other users are, and whether the community creates content that would encourage you to participate.

Once you have understood how your community works, it is time to participate and create. What makes online communities grow and prosper is that anyone has the ability to publish content, because platforms and tools are easy for non-technical users. To participate in a community, it is both easy to join and easy to create content. You carry the tools with you at all times to capture moments that can be published to the web, instantly transforming yourself into a content creator. But what is important to note is that you are creating content with the sense that it's purposely created for the specific community. Communities vary, so the content you post differs from platform to platform. For instance, creating a photo album of family photos is for your Facebook audience of family and friends, whereas your short Vine video tribute to the *Hunger Games* shared on Twitter is for a completely different audience. Both communities describe your personality, but you have intent of creating different content for multiple communities.

Later in this chapter, we will discuss the four key forms of content: writing, pictures, video, and sound. Once you have found the community, platform, and audience, it is time to create your content using one or more of the forms. For example, BuzzFeed community pages incorporate all four forms of content into their stories. Shirky states that if:

> people can share their work in an environment where they can also converse with one another, they will begin talking about things they have shared. The conversation that forms around shared photos, videos, weblog posts and the like is often about how to do it better next time—how to be a better photographer or better writer.[9]

When one participates in an online community and creates content, especially when posting on social media sites, the nature of those sites means instantaneous feedback from the audience. For instance, your WordPress blog post has a comments section for readers to respond; your Twitter feed allows for replies; and your Reddit post has a thread. Although the material may be negative at times, the feedback will mostly be valuable, allowing you to perfect and enhance your future content that will be added to the community. If you write fan fiction of your favorite television show, the feedback received from the audience will involve shared interests, providing ways for you to take your story to another place or the next post. This feedback helps you enhance your content, motivates your participation in the community, and improves the material within the community as well.

The Rules of Participating in Various Communities

As you explore the many communities on the web, you'll find that each has its own method of participation and communication with other users. BuzzFeed community posts allow flexible methods of posting, but are restricted to only a few styles of posting; on Reddit, you can participate anonymously with text or images; on Tumblr, to communicate you need to reply or reblog. You may find a community of users who share similar interests, but the platform may not encourage your personal creativity. Sometimes, you should observe the community and how other users are participating before creating an account. You have to remember that, although you may have a creative idea, it might not fit into the format of the digital environment. The benefit is that you do not have to pay to play in the space, but you do not have much of a say over how the platform works or how your content is used. Make sure you read the terms of service before committing to full participation.

What cultivates participation is the fact that stories are created on multiple platforms instantaneously. The content you create to participate in your community may appear on several different digital media sites. This is what Henry Jenkins describes as transmedia storytelling and the convergence of media: "Transmedia stories unfold across multiple media platforms, with each medium making distinctive contributions to our understanding of the world."[10] For example, the AMC television series *The Walking Dead* premieres new episodes weekly during its season run. Each week, fans of the show are able to interact with the show online with an application on their phone or tablet. The story continues on multiple platforms. Also, during the show's off-season, producers have created a web series on the AMC website for fans of the show to watch original content. Additionally, there are communities for *The Walking Dead* on Facebook, Twitter, and YouTube, where fans can create their own content pertaining to the show. This is an example of convergence, which is where "multiple media systems coexist and where media content flows fluidly across them."[11] You have the ability to post your video on YouTube and tweet to your community of followers on Twitter. If the subject of your communities is the same, your two platforms have converged, which is why you publish the content on each. This also helps to build and grow your community. By creating this type of content, communities are very much intertwined with fandom, where users create content and want to participate with television, games, film, and anime, and other media where users have a passion for an area of interest and wish to connect with others who share the same. Fan-fiction communities are just as important as non-fiction communities, and they can be outlets where users who are fans of a television series can be creative with digital media tools. Online communities provide you with ways to interact with others who share your interests, whom you may have had a hard time finding in physical space.

Keep in mind that users want to be noticed on communities, but at points want to remain private. Young adults have flocked to many different social media sites throughout the years. When those sites have become populated with their parents, young adults view it as being an invasion of their privacy when adults ask too many questions. Thus, users tend to move to a new social media platform as yet undiscovered by parents. As danah boyd points out, "teens aren't looking to hide, they just want privacy."[12] This theory can be applied to several developments in online communities. Although communities are meant to be found by all using digital devices and have users added to them regularly, if it's an invasion of your privacy, you want to move on to a community where you are not judged and can discuss, debate, participate, and create your topics of interests with your cultivated audience.

DIGITAL ENVIRONMENTS AND COMMUNITIES

In Dan Simmon's *Hyperion* (1990),[13] a science fiction novel that takes place nearly a millennium into the future, there are references to the early information age of humanity, a time that spans the first 100 years of the Internet. If we are yet to be through that first century, it is hard to imagine the history of the vastly changing landscape. In order to be a savvy user of the web and become an empowered user, one must go beyond website literacy into participation in some of the most valuable experiences of the World Wide Web itself. As far as we can tell, the users themselves make up the early information age. Much like the people who, by sharing knowledge, made the Age of Enlightenment, those who create and share information make the information age. Each user is responsible for their part, and, in order to increase our awareness of each other, our issues, and our culture, we must participate in the online environment.

In this section, we hope to cover the basics of some of the most popular communities in the new and digital space. Although we cannot predict the future and what platforms may exist, the communities discussed will almost certainly be present for many more years in the future. There is a good chance you are already part of most of these communities, but, if you are not, we recommend you participate—the web benefits from your involvement.

SOCIAL MEDIA COMMUNITIES: THE BEGINNINGS OF FACEBOOK

When looking at the advancement of communities in the digital space, you need to look at the start of Facebook. When Mark Zuckerberg and his team launched Facebook (originally Facemash and thefacebook.com) in 2004, its purpose was providing a community-driven environment to bring Harvard University students together by giving them a platform to find out basic information about their classmates and view photographs of each other. Facebook offered students a way to find new friendships, build relationships, and discover people with similar interests among classmates at their school. Facebook was the start of the largest digital community that would occur online. Once Facebook was opened to the general public in 2006, the online community was open for all to join (at least if they were a minimum of 13 years old). Bonds were quickly formed with users with whom you already had prior connections, such as friends, family, and fellow classmates. Users were finding connections through Facebook's recommendations and friend algorithms, leading to the discovery that they might share common interests, such as movies, books, or politics, with other users. Facebook has always used the word "friend" to describe connected users, and the term "friending" appeared in our vernacular. Now, a friendship can be completely online, without a face-to-face meeting. Connections were built primarily through shared hobbies, pictures, and having conversations through Facebook posts, messages, and comments.

Facebook Friend Algorithms

One of the features of Facebook that has made it the most popular and most populous social networking site is its proprietary code and algorithms. Facebook's algorithms are like other algorithms: They do computations to solve problems. Facebook's code is much more advanced, however, and the data you provide solves the problem of having to seek out other users, products, and communities on your own. Facebook helps you connect. The more you use Facebook, the better and more refined the algorithm is at finding something specific for you. However, you should be aware that the data used in the algorithms is also sold to advertisers, to make the ads on the page more pertinent and specific to you. Additionally, Facebook is a publicly traded company, and the majority of its value comes from the data you create while participating on the platform.

Whereas traditional communities were built on social settings, Facebook did not anticipate how users of the social media site would build communities that focused on interests or connections and use the platform for personal reasons. In the 2011 CNBC documentary *The Facebook Obsession*, a young woman named Jennifer Kolb was featured because she was adopted as a child and was looking to find her birth mother using Facebook. When she typed her mother's name in the search box, no results were coming up. She came up with the idea to start a Facebook group titled, "Looking for My Biological Mother." One of the 1,500 users in the group happened to be a social worker whose hobby is to help children find their birth parents. Using online people searches, the social worker found Jennifer's match and even found her biological mother's Facebook profile. Jennifer was united with her biological mother and she used the online community on her Facebook group to help her with a personal goal.

Facebook Groups, Games, and Pages

Today, Facebook still provides plenty of ways to build a community. Facebook groups bring members together to discuss topics in animation, television, sports, and technology, or any specific interest. You can join groups with users who share the same interest in software such as Adobe Photoshop or Illustrator and use the group to ask questions and discuss new techniques and tools. There are location-based groups where you can connect with others who may live in the same town as you to discuss issues affecting the area as a way to build your local community and connect it to your digital community.

Facebook groups have been a resource for colleges and universities, as professors can connect with their students to discuss course issues and answer questions, and students can discuss the main topics in the class, without the faculty member friending the student. In addition to using Facebook groups, you can use Facebook's mobile games to start communities. Mobile games enable interactivity and entertainment with your friends who are also playing the game and lead you to engage in this form of social interaction with other users of the platform.

Pages are another great way to build communities on Facebook, because users can connect to a product or corporate brand and communicate their questions, comments, and passion directly to the brand by interacting and connecting with the same fans on the page. For instance, fans of Starbucks can like the page and connect with the brand more personally. If you have had a positive or poor experience with Starbucks, you can discuss it by commenting on their page and carrying on a conversation with fellow users. Brands have taken to Facebook to build community by asking their fans to post what's on their mind.[14] This helps other users get a sense of the people who share their similar interest. This builds brand trust and online community engagement through the page, as other members of the community may comment on the post.

Active Facebook Use

Facebook has over 1 billion users, and many people use it without reading the directions of the platform or considering the terms of service. Facebook is a publicly traded company growing in multiple tech industries that profits from selling user data to advertisers to make a better user experience. When using the platform actively, check the privacy settings on your images and your posts. If someone is a member of Facebook, they can see anything you post publicly. Facebook allows you to control what other members may see of the content you post, but you must manually control the visibility settings.

You can be a positive community member on Facebook and a user who is seen as a good influence by controlling your posts. Sometimes you want everyone to see a post, and you should post publicly, and sometimes you should change the custom settings so only your closest friends see what you are posting. Facebook uses sharing algorithms to post your content on your friends' feeds, so the more interaction your post has, the more the post shows up.

To post and be a leader, you should add photos to a status update, as people are more likely to interact with the content. If you post a link, Facebook will populate the post with the link's information, so you can delete the hyperlink before you post. You also have the ability to edit posts on Facebook, but remember that users can see the edits you made—sometimes it's better to delete the post and post again.

TWITTER

Twitter is a platform containing hundreds of communities where users tweet in short form, reply, or retweet, to engage the various users on the platform. Whether you are on your phone or on your desktop or on a Twitter app such as TweetDeck or Hootsuite, you invest in your community by reading the feed that is streamed in real time. When you read any type of Twitter user, either by following them or researching a hashtag, you gain a sense of a community by getting an insight into an individual's or group's thoughts, comments, and activities. What binds the community together is the communication of topics and issues to fellow and new followers.

To participate in the community of Twitter, you should have constant contact with other users in your interest area and post tweets on a consistent basis to those users. In fact, to be a part of any social media platform, you should become literate in the platform in order to fully grasp its full use. It is important to understand how to connect with other users by using hashtags, retweets, and all forms of communication on Twitter. When you first join Twitter, you should research which communities you want to participate in and follow the people and brands who fit your interests. There are plenty of interest communities to follow relating to your favorite television shows, musicians, anime, books, and politics. At first, you may follow too many users, and you will soon learn to reorganize whom you like to see in your feed consistently.

Twitter and Corporate Engagement

Some communities you may join on Twitter may be based on a sponsored hashtag or promoted trending topic. Although these hashtags show a cohesive communicating environment, you should make sure that the brand sponsoring or promoting the tweet also fits in with your general interest. Companies looking to promote their brand sometimes try to form communities. For example, the hashtag #HelloFuture may be a common response to something cool and futuristic or technical, but it is used by BMW as a promotional tag. Participating in these promoted communities can be just as fun as in user-created communities; just be aware that your activity also helps the brand.

When you follow users, some may follow back, some may not; the way to increase followers is by consistently tweeting. You want your tweets to be read by as many followers as possible to build a community. To do so, you have to tweet, not only regularly, but also directly to the users. For instance, if you are a part of *The Walking Dead* community, you may tweet directly to a fan or a show character (using the @twitterhandle) to start a conversation others will find. Another way to build your community on Twitter is by retweeting content in your area of interest. This will help other users in your community who, when researching topics through the hasthags, come across your feed, thereby increasing the connectivity between the two. Speaking of hashtags, the Twitter trending topics play a part in building community. A trending topic means that something is popular or being discussed simultaneously by thousands of users at that moment in time, using the hashtag or keyword. If the Twitter user comes across your page, a connection can be made when the interaction begins, and a community member is located in the process.

As Dhiraj Murthy points out in his book, *Twitter: Digital media and society series* (2012), there are more than interest communities (television, film, and anime) for users to follow, such as disaster or health communities.[15] If natural disasters occur, communities are developed through social media sites such as Twitter for those affected to gather information, locate missing persons or materials, and figure out their next course of action. Twitter becomes a community when fellow users in the digital space help those who need to find information by seeking specific pages, profiles, and sites built for information about the particular event. These communities are built around those who share similar situations.

Twitter as a Creative Platform

When Twitter started in March of 2006, little did the creators realize that they would start a trend of short-form storytelling and creativity with those who wanted to participate in the platform and as a way to attract new users. This form of storytelling influenced many future applications such as Vine and Instagram, which will be discussed in further sections. Because they were only given 140 characters, users had a limit to the way that they could express themselves with their words and the text on the screen. Whereas Facebook provides users with an unlimited platform to write a post in as many words as they wanted, users are forced to be creative and to come up with new ways to communicate a sentence on Twitter. Each 140-character tweet could be its own chapter of your story, with your entire Twitter profile feed as the whole book for your visitors to read, sharing your life story.

There are many tools for users to be creative on Twitter. Although the community builds on your tweets and your interactions, it's the way that you write your tweets that will engage new followers and allow you to be interactive within the community you wish to be a part of, whether it's your own friends or fandom, such as a television community on Twitter. You should include a statement as well as a mix of links and pictures to connect to others. For instance, you have to use someone's handle when talking directly to a friend or to someone you wish to answer your tweet, beginning a back and forth discussion. Users who use hashtags to participate in a specific conversation on Twitter may also realize that the hashtag can be beneficial as a research tool.

HISTORY OF THE HASHTAG

Organizing content on the web was not beneficial to the average digital media user. Locating and organizing content was in the hands of those who created the social platforms on the web and supplied the content. Chris Messina, who was a consultant and regular user of Twitter, serendipitously created the now ubiquitous hashtag back in 2007. Liz Gannes researched the history in her article "The Short and Illustrious History of Twitter #hashtags" (2010) and found that Messina made the discovery when he inserted the pound symbol

Figure 2.1

Chris Messina posted the first ever tweet using the hashtag to propose Twitter groups. Chris's tweet stated, "How do you feel about using # (pound) for groups. As in #barcamp [msg]?"

Source: Photo by Kat Borlongan

after typing in a word or a phrase, and it automatically became a hyperlink that would take the connected word to the organized search results on Twitter. This allowed Messina to place all of his keywords into particular groups.[16] The hashtag was born, and it became a way to place a label on a subject in categorizing content on Twitter. This form of tagging became a tool for users on Twitter to research an array of topics, from words to brands to news to events. It opened up a full database of information never before attainable by the regular user of social media or the Internet as a whole.

HOW IS THE HASHTAG USED?

Murthy explains, "Hashtags are an integral part of Twitter's ability to link the conversations of strangers together."[17] The use of the hashtag brings users together who may not have conversed before, but are brought into the community together by discussing a topic being researched. For instance, if you are researching #worldseries, not only will it bring you information on players, teams, and games, but it will enable you to connect with others, opening up a possible new line of communication. Although you can see other users and their tweets on the subject, it is more of a flow of information coming through your feed. Many Twitter users have used the hashtag to be incorporated into trending topics for what is currently happening in pop culture or at that very moment. If you incorporate the hashtag, there is a better chance for your tweet to be read by other followers or potential new followers.

As the hashtag has evolved, it has become a necessary requirement for users to place the symbol on Twitter content, and it is also attached to videos, blogs, and other forms of multimedia in order to organize content on the web and

Figure 2.2
#Jan25 hashtag used in the Egyptian protests.

Source: Photo by Essam Sharaf, Creative Commons license

to help users looking to organize and collect data. The reach and importance of the hashtag have moved beyond Twitter, as other social media sites have used the utility, such as Instagram, Vine, YouTube, and Facebook, all incorporating it to allow their users to search their interests.

The hashtag has even been incorporated as an online community tool to organize information for the masses. In 2011, the Arab Spring used the hashtags #Jan25 and #PrayforEgypt to gain supporters looking to rebel against the Egyptian government, to raise awareness of the movement outside of Egypt, and so that online users could distribute content and find information.[18] When Occupy Wall Street occurred in the fall of 2011, #occupy, #OWS, or #99percent were used to gather citizens to protest in New York about economic and income inequalities. Later, hashtags were used around the world, helping to spread the message, such as #OccupyLondon. Supporters of the Occupy movement used the hashtag to find those who wished to come out and protest with them, find donations to their cause, and spread their message globally. The hashtag became a constant news source for new daily information.

Hashtags generate new information in real time, and it becomes a task for the digital user to sift through all of the content and connect the information together. It can be quite the undertaking for a user to go through multiple social media sites to put together information on movements or actions to make a story. Look to the next presidential election. As each presidential candidate will use social media to display their goals, tasks, and outlines for the country, it is up to the user to put the puzzle pieces together to understand the full circle of issues each candidate is bringing to the table. With Twitter and all social media sites using the hashtag, it has made digital research easier and placed the role of researcher on each digital user looking to be a part of the social good. Looking at the themes of the Occupy Wall Street movement, it may have started as an angry protest toward the US financial district, but it also showcased problems in American culture including student debt and, later, became a worldwide symbol of youth protest. Through the social conversation, the hashtag provided this movement, new awareness of these issues became national and world news and topics for discussion in all communities.

Hashtags and Society

Although the hashtag helped protestors gather together for the Occupy movements worldwide and attract attention to the protests during the Arab Spring, the public nature of the hashtag allowed those opposed to the movements also to see the information. Hashtags are essential pieces of new and digital media production and can be used in a variety of ways, from gathering people together, to analyzing an event, or even managing a brand. As a community member, you have the added fun of choosing to participate in the use of hashtags, knowing that you can be aiding powerful activist movements and showing support for causes you care about. Do your best to help the community, knowing that users of all types can see your tweet.

YOUTUBE

Whereas some online video distribution outlets rose, fell, merged, corporatized, and otherwise faded away, YouTube succeeded by being the most efficient method of sharing stories. Much of the content was created traditionally, with larger cameras and desktop editing software. With the advent of the iPhone in 2007, YouTube saw an influx of video, as users began to use their cellphones to record higher-quality video (480p, the equivalent of standard definition television) and upload them to the site. YouTube prevailed as the ultimate destination of videos, and thousands of users became vloggers on the site. YouTube was simultaneously the place to create and broadcast yourself to the world and the place to watch content. In late 2011, the iPhone upgraded once again to the iPhone 4s, offering a front-facing camera and a main camera that recorded 1080p, high definition, and video capture. Now, a professional video acquisition tool was available in anyone's pocket.

It's easy to see why YouTube became a community. With many social networks centered on text and pictures and with the vast amount of conversations centered on television, a distribution site where users can participate, engage, and discuss videos is engaging to the online world. In chapters 5 and 6, we will be discussing the effects of viral video and creating channels with web television through video-sharing sites such as YouTube.

THE COMMUNITY OF YOUTUBE

The powerful community built through the video-sharing site is now considered a competitive outlet to television channels. In Lev Grossman's *Time* article "The Beast with a Billion Eyes" (2010),[19] he explained how YouTube has features that make it the go-to outlet for digital video media. First is the ease of uploading recorded video: The fact that everyone with a smartphone or tablet can record video instantly, thus capturing any moment that happens in their life. Video-acquisition technology is continually becoming cheaper to purchase and use. Second, when YouTube was created, it made a platform for users to watch any video, at any moment they wanted. YouTube is a distribution platform for all video content, whether produced by independent content creators or by professional businesses. If you want to watch the latest viral video, you go to YouTube. When you want to watch your favorite music videos, you go to YouTube. If you want to see the latest in sports bloopers, you go to YouTube. If you want to watch hours of cat videos, again: YouTube. At a moment's notice, you can use your phone, laptop, or tablet, whether it is to spend hours watching videos of your desire or to pull up a video to discuss with friends. Thus, when the platform was built, it turned into a community because, not only did users want to consume media, they were also participating and creating content.

"More video is uploaded to YouTube every month than has been broadcast by the three big TV networks in the past 60 years", Grossman notes.[20] Before YouTube, there was no place to go to view the vast amount of video uploaded every second, minute, hour, and day. Once created, it became a platform for millions of users to join, watch, and create, to post video to some form of platform, because we have a need to share our content for instant feedback, comments, and community building.

YouTube hopes to be a platform where those who visit will be inspired to create videos, learn from the videos and channels, and connect with those on the web. YouTube is a community because a user can find videos instructing how to put on a tie, change a tire, build a table, learn a basic foreign language, or solve a math equation. Users are willing to share videos to help others who come across them, provide knowledge, and inspire users to new skills. According to YouTube's community guidelines, the site is made for participation and for you to get the most out of its videos, to be creative, and to learn, and you must join in the variety of ways to interact with the users. Whether it is just by rating a video, leaving a comment, or building up to creating your own videos, it's a simple way to connect with a video that affects you or has some form of meaning, so that it fulfills the desire to engage with the online world.

What is a community on YouTube? The main goal of being a part of the YouTube community is to participate with the content creator. If you visit their channel regularly and incorporate their videos into your daily life by viewing the videos at work, discussing the vlog with friends, and writing comments on the video on the channel while interacting with other fans, you are part of the community. You also should take the initiative to become a creator and producer of your own channel. The entire site is a platform, but content creators need a channel where they can post or collect their videos. Each channel is its own community, and within that community may be one particular subject or a channel devoted to multiple playlists of curated video content, such as if you are a film producer creating a channel for your short films, commercials, or interviews to show to your fans. The minute you sign on to YouTube, you are welcomed to its vast amount of possible communities. Through browsing channels or searching in categories that the site recommends, such as music, sports, gaming, education, news, and spotlight, it is easy for those who love to watch videos to find a community to be a part of on the social site. Once you find the community, you can subscribe to the channel as a way to easily click on your favorite channels to view the latest vlog or web series post. Your YouTube feed comes from the channels you subscribe to, and, if you post your videos or create compelling playlists, you can find yourself with more subscribers than some traditional television channels.

If you wish to cultivate a community on YouTube, it is good to have a few videos created before you design your channel. Whether it's vlogging, creating a web series, or posting funny videos of your friends doing stunts in the style of MTV's *Jackass*, you need content. Once several videos have been posted to your channel, subscribe to other channels that coincide with your content. This will bring other members of the YouTube community to your channel, who may then promote your channel by subscribing to it. Additionally, you can use the featured channels posted to your site and promote others in your community that post similar videos, in the same genre. Everything matters in getting others to join your community on YouTube. From the channel name, to the videos, to the description and comments from your audience, the channel creator has to look at each piece of the puzzle and turn to the analytics to understand its audience.

Google Purchased YouTube in 2007

When Google bought YouTube, it bought a community full of vloggers, web series creators, and users looking to post their most recent video captures. They bought a YouTube search engine of videos that look raw, real, and have professional or amateur styles. It gave creators a quality outlet to post videos, because Google's technologies are limitless. Through the ability to create and edit videos, your latest vlog can look professional enough that it is of a standard that would appear on national television. Grossman describes how the average user spends 15 minutes a day on YouTube, whereas 3 hours is the average use for television.[21] Although this may seem small, this is a huge number, as the community grows, and all forms of video content are added daily to the platform. More so than any other community, YouTube has had excessive amounts of copyright issues on the social site. YouTube has been proactive in this area by placing ads on videos or having the videos pulled down, among other forms of infringement action. But why would Google want to purchase YouTube? It could have easily invented a similar version, with its resources. Well, just as the search engine understands and takes notice of your search results, it is now able to understand which videos you desire to watch. Through analytics and bookmarking your Internet history, YouTube and Google understand which videos engage its everyday users. Just open up YouTube on your mobile device and you will quickly see, "What to watch", which is YouTube recommending videos to you from your latest searches. Google purchased the community of active users.

The site has successfully built a community for those who enjoy watching cat videos or such funny moments as "David After Dentist" (2009), where new and digital media users enjoy watching these videos just as much as they do watching the latest sitcom on television. Video is the same to the online community and, whether it is a web television series or a viral video, it's just content for users to enjoy as entertainment. Google and YouTube:

> will notice if you watch the whole video or give it up in the middle, and which video you watch right after it, whether you post that video on your blog, and if you leave the site after you watch it or hang around for a while.[22]

If you are a user on YouTube, it will feed to your interests and help you cultivate your community by featuring videos relating to your interests. It knows exactly what you want to view; therefore it will bring the videos to you, hoping that you will be engaged and will share the videos with others of your community to help with clicks toward raising the number of views of the video.

TUMBLR

Created in 2007 by a young developer named David Karp, Tumblr was bought by Yahoo! in 2013. This social media platform offers a sense of community similar to Facebook's and Twitter's and offers the additional ability to have anonymity, together with motion graphics such as GIFs and videos. Tumblr is an interesting hybrid social network that is somewhere between Twitter and Instagram. It allows microblogging and picture posting, as well as video and audio embedding. Tumblr is often considered the most creative social network, with thousands of artists and photographers posting continually.

The Tumblr community is an extremely engaged group of users who feel they have the insider view of the web. Like Twitter, anyone can be on the platform and communicate with one another, and users have to create their feeds by following similar or interesting people. Also, like Twitter, you can use hashtags to organize your content into categories of information. Making your own Tumblog is easy: You just sign up and start posting. To make posts popular, you can add notes by liking the post or reblogging the post to your own feed and adding commentary.

The Tumblr community is very welcoming to a variety of fandoms and special interests ranging from photography, to books, to houses, to television shows such as *Sherlock, Dr Who*, and *Supernatural*. Users find each other through their interests and create tight communities of creative participants. Tumblr thrives on savvy user interaction and witty responses. The savvier and more knowledgeable of the web and culture you are, the more your posts can get reblogged or liked. Adding commentary is helpful as well, as you can contribute and enhance someone else's post. The low-risk, easy-to-approach use of Tumblr makes it welcoming to all users, including celebrities and authors such as John Green and Neil Gaiman. Additionally, memes can come from Tumblr owing to pranks and misunderstandings. There was once a post about a missing woman named Becky, and the user happened to post a picture of a young Taylor Swift. Someone replied, "I think that's Taylor Swift," and the original user reblogged and said, "No it's Becky." Several weeks later, Taylor Swift was seen in LA wearing a shirt that said, "No it's Becky," and the Tumblr community reblogged that image hundreds of thousands of times. We highly recommend participating in the Tumblr environment—you never know who you may also be participating with.

WORDPRESS

WordPress is the most advanced open-source blogging platform on the web. Digital media users flock to the site to create their own blog in hopes of having a voice, with their words and subject as their community. WordPress is a community platform, and, if you are to use WordPress.com, you will be using the content management system (CMS) as a contributor to the blogging environment. For many new and digital media users taking part in WordPress with the hopes of building a community around their written stories, you can use the WordPress open-ware free version, which is WordPress.com.

This means the URL of your blog will have WordPress.com on the site (blog.wordpress.com). This does not require you to purchase a domain name or hosting, as WordPress will host it for free, with ads that show up on your page.

The WordPress CMS is utilized by many organizations and business websites that we visit daily, such as CNN, Reuters, GigaOm, and Mashable. Still, even with all of its HTML features, plug-ins, and tools, WordPress is still community driven by bloggers. To start your community on WordPress.com, create a blog with some pictures and text that fit within your chosen theme. We recommend that, when you create your blog, you chose a theme and be consistent. Find something you enjoy and write about it at length and consistently. If you like fashion, create a fashion blog. Like sports? Create a commentary blog that helps fellow fans see your point of view. The great part about each time you create a new post in WordPress is that you are able to put your blogs into categories, so that the reader of your blog can quickly come across or research the subject they are interested in. Although you are only using posts to create your blogs (rather than pages), the categories feature means that you are placing your blogs into topics. For example, if you are writing a blog about pumpkin picking, your categories will be Halloween or holiday, to help it appear in topic listings.

Your community grows because of how you take action to promote your blog via social media or using a nice theme for your blog. When readers and fellow bloggers visit your site, it is a two-way interaction within the community, because you are discussing topics, issues, and reactions to those commenting on your blog. Those comments that appear at the end of each blog will encourage regular conversation with your audience, thereby improving your blog and impacting you personally, encouraging growth and maturity, which are what communities should do. Whether your blogs are about your daily activities of being a college student, love of video games, or playing music, your built community helps drive a desire to continue writing, improving skills, but willing to share your stories with the world and connect with others.

USER-GENERATED COMMUNITIES: REDDIT

Reddit is a user-based forum website that curates content of events, images, and news currently affecting those in the world. Information and posts appear on the page when participants find a pertinent or interesting link they want to share with the rest of the community. Think of Reddit as a news site, with content updated so quickly that it has been referred to as "the front page of the Internet." Reddit users submit links to Reddit in categories such as space, DIY, old-school cool, and Photoshop battles. The other Reddit users vote on those links to move them upward or downward on the page. The community on Reddit is turning the links into a list of what all users on the Internet are currently reading, viewing, or watching at that very moment in time. As users read the links, the post goes lower down the page, which is where the site got its name.

Reddit doesn't edit the posted content or filter out information, and there is minimal moderation; therefore, what you see on the pages is important to the entire community. When new links are added, they either push toward the top if they are important and pertinent, or, if not, the links will be pushed quickly down the page. Any posted content has the opportunity to go viral, be it informational or entertainment. On any Reddit link, you will find the number of votes a link has received from the Reddit community.

Reddit has hundreds of different, very specific categories made by the community, called subreddits, where you can find links to politics, sports, history, and science, or even obscure and quirky categories such as fatbirds and Earthporn. Subreddit pages are made by the community and work exactly the same way as the main page of the website. There are subreddits specifically geared toward where you live or to things that have happened in the past that you still wish to discuss, and, if a topic does not exist, you are able to create a subreddit in the category you wish to post links for. The great feature of subreddits is that, not only can you see the number of users subscribed, but you can also see how many of those users are using the subreddit community at that moment, giving you an indication of whom you are interacting with.

Offering the possibility to join subreddits, Reddit becomes geared toward your interests, and they appear on your main page to encourage you to continue participating. As Reddit is forum-based, the comments appear as a thread, branching away from the main link. Users can reply to a single commenter or to the direct link. Because some subreddits are very specific discussion topics about politics or technology, Reddit provides a debate forum for users. When debating topics, authority users on Reddit write "I am a police officer" or "I am a science teacher" or "I am a runner," and users can ask those members any question they wish on that topic. This has lead to the very popular "Ask Me Anything" (AMA) discussions on Reddit, where you can ask an authority figure anything. People using the AMA feature range from Barack Obama[23] to Daniel Radcliffe[24] to Glitter manufacturers.[25]

Like in the Tumblr community, Reddit users can remain anonymous, and, whereas other communities such as Facebook and Google require the majority of users to use some form of their given name, it's refreshing to comment and post from a pseudonym. However, keep in mind that Reddit's anonymous environment is optional, as there are many occasions where celebrities, musicians, and authors use the site to open up a community to answer questions from fans. Although anonymous users could cause an issue on

Reddit owing to material some may deem not appropriate for the web, the site trusts the new and digital media users to push that material down the page, as the power is in their hands.

Reddit Activists

As discussed in the hashtag section, the communities built on Reddit have been used for activist movements. For instance, users have used the site to raise money for charities or to raise awareness on issues affecting the world, such as, when the Stop Online Piracy Act (SOPA) was being brought to the U.S. government, users on Reddit flocked to explain how this Act could harm the web. Reddit users encouraged a "blackout" protest on the site to show their anger against a poorly proposed law.[26] Another way that Reddit performs as an activist group is the subreddit Secret Santa at /r/secretsanta and Reddit Gifts. The Secret Santa subreddit was started in 2009, when Reddit users each got a Secret Santa and had to give another reddit user a gift. Inspired by JetBlue's gift-giving challenge, Reddit users created a similar process of anonymous gift giving. The response was an instant hit, and a set of rules was created where, if you sign up, you will actually send a gift and you won't be a jerk by promising something you can't deliver, there is a spending cap of $15 (including shipping), and you should try to be creative by doing something such as a handmade gift. In 2009, almost 5,000 users joined Reddit Gifts. In the reddit gift exchange site, those joining create a profile page with their likes, dislikes, and interests, where they can be matched with someone to give them a gift. Users then have 2 weeks to research a gift and go back to the site to let it know that they have purchased one, providing tracking information. Once the user receives the gift, he/she posts a picture of him/herself with the gift, as a thank–you note to the reddit user who provided the gift. Several extraordinary gifts were given, such as $1,500 dollars a broke college student received from another Reddit user, and others sent gifts that matched users' interests. After the first success, over 96 percent of the users who signed up actually sent gifts. The 2010 Secret Santa grew to over 17,000 participants; in 2011, it grew to over 38,000; and 2012 saw it grow to 60,000 participants. It has continually broken the Guinness Book of World Records with the number of exchanges.[27]

With the success of Secret Santa and Reddit Gifts, the site began topic exchanges, such as a book exchange, board-game exchange, calendar exchange, or the Marvel superhero exchange. There are even programs for Reddit users to give and not receive anything in return, such as gifts for teachers providing school supplies for a class. It's a true online community, because people are sending gifts to a complete stranger, but sharing the Reddit community in common.

How Do Communities Get Funded?

Venture capitalism is an investment system where investors and major corporations provide money to start-up companies, with the potential for it to grow into a long-term money-making investment. This is very common for technological endeavors by creators who are looking to start social media companies, mobile applications, websites, or devices. For small companies, agreeing to partner with investors is pivotal in helping the long-term growth of their business, assisting with paying for staff, materials, products, etc. An example of a venture capital firm is Sequoia Capital, which has worked with, and made millions of dollars from, technology companies such as Google, particularly when the company purchased YouTube.

Peter Thiel is an entrepreneur, co-founder of PayPal, and one of the first investors in Facebook and he started the Founder's Fund, among other investment projects. Thiel invested approximately $500,000 in Facebook and, when he sold off most of his share, netted $1 billion in profit. He is always on the lookout for creative ideas for innovating, not only in tech start-ups out of Silicon Valley, but also in areas that affect culture, society, and global issues. Thiel has run a program called 20 under 20, where that number of college students are asked to take a "break" or "stop" out of college to pursue their dream innovation, and Peter invests in their venture. Thiel has stated in previous interviews that he believes that college is too expensive, causing major debt, and takes away from the time period for young adults to innovate with their ideas. Past fellows have been chosen to innovate in areas such as information technology, robotics, education, business, energy, and space. Students chosen for the opportunity are able to create a new technology, leading into a future business or start-up, and, as for Peter Thiel, he finds the next new talent and venture to invest in and make a profit.

IMAGE FORUMS: 4CHAN

Chris Poole, who goes by the name of "moot," created 4chan in 2003. 4chan is a bulletin board and forum for digital media users to post comments and share photographs and images with the database. Discussion boards include topics on Japanese animation, comic books, television, and origami. This site and community are completely anonymous, with Internet users not having to even register. All they have to do is select their interest and they can participate in the site. Each category has a short code that it uses, such as /p/ for photography, /jp/ for otaku culture, or /vr/ for retro games. A word of warning: It is an adult-oriented board, and users will find material that is not safe for work (NSFW). As the bulletin board is anonymous, each picture posted, for example, is given an identification number. If users share identities, the post will be moved off the site to a chat. The 4chan bulletin boards have started many popular web memes and happen to be the birthplace of lolcats and Rick Rolling.

With more than 20 million views per month, this site has built quite a large gathering of Internet users. One of the most visited and controversial discussion boards is /b/, which means random. The board has very few policy rules on posts (except for explicit illegal activity), and it is commonly linked with the trolls of the web, who have the freedom to post any sort of information online, but do so in destructive ways, posting anything that they want by doing pranks. 4chan is also the origin of the Anonymous "hacktivist" group that uses technology and connective networks to promote political issues, protests, and human rights. One example of hacktivist movements was a protest against the Church of Scientology called "Project Chanology" in 2008, where 4chan users protested and prank-called Scientologists—all organized on the boards. During these protests, the use of Guy Fawkes masks became associated with the group, as they were worn to the public protests. As the group was going to be protesting in public, members had to hide their faces, because the use of 4chan is anonymous.

Deep and Dark Communities

A word of warning: As responsible authors, we must warn that communities such as 4chan's /b/ board are not for the faint of heart. You cannot "unsee" things, and, unfortunately, users of the random board post images that are unfit for your consumption. Although many users of the rest of the 4chan boards are often well behaved, be careful of trolls and illicit behavior on these sites. Some of the darker communities lead to pirate sites, viruses, and dubious content.

GAMING COMMUNITIES

When traditional arcade and console games became connected on the web, users found that their previously limited approach to gaming expanded into a community. Traditional games may have had multiplayer features, but they were still limited to the characters and the storyline provided by the game developer. Online gaming allows for a massive multiplayer experience, and the user can role-play as a customizable character of a game. Games such as *World of Warcraft*, an RPG game that dates back to the mid 1990s, entered the online realm on its tenth anniversary in 2004. The game is open to any user with an Internet connection and the software provided.

The massively multiplayer online role-playing game (MMORPG) *World of Warcraft* encourages web users to join guilds and teams with other players in order to win battles against other teams. As on social media, friendships form in the digital space, without the need for face-to-face meeting. The games require dedication and involvement to such an extent that some MMORPGs have created their own digital currency. It's actually possible to earn real money playing games if your team becomes good enough to win and collect enough digital commodities to sell to fellow users.

There are hundreds of MMORPGs for you to play,[28] and we recommend you locate a community of players with similar interests and time involvement. With a little bit of experimenting within the game, you can navigate a digital landscape that entertains, encourages community, and uses strategy.

USER CREATIVE EXPRESSION

There are thousands of places to express yourself on the web, and our recommendation is you pick what you like best. With the web changing so rapidly, it's up to you to find your place of comfort and creativity within a community that appreciates your work.

WRITING

If you really like something passionately, you should make that your muse and create as much as you can. There are fandoms on every platform, and you should participate in them, whether that means writing fan fiction about *Harry Potter*, *Supernatural*, or *The Walking Dead*. Whether you use Tumblr, Twitter, or a subreddit, there is a community where you can write. Writing also means being a really good reader, so follow your community's various posts and progress and play along with them. If you are a sports writer, make sure you write for the community, not the general, wide audience. Everyone can write about sports, but only you can write about it in your personal style, for your specific audience.

The web is a fairly new medium for writers, and bloggers, especially those who have been writing for over a decade, take a lot of pride in their online platform. The BradLand Manifesto (1999),[29] written near the turn of the century, explains why the web is a great platform on which to create, and we believe Brad Graham's thoughts are still just as important today. Graham wrote that he writes for his need to publish and see his words in print and his desire to control the information he knows well—to minimize "fram," in his words. Blogging gives an opportunity to learn and grow as a writer and web participant, and the web is there to explore. When you write online, you are given a ticket to explore the web and find information and points of view that increase your overall awareness. And think of it this way: Never before in history has the opportunity to publish, join a community, and share your ideas been so available.

You are encouraged, not by the platform, but by those reading your material online who become fans and followers of your stories. In online writing communities, you have the choice to write fiction or non-fiction. It doesn't matter what you choose, as long as you are writing. You'll find that most social media offer ways of adding creative writing on their platform. Check out R.L. Stine's horror fiction on Twitter[30] and follow comedians as they test their material on Tumblr. Join fandoms and follow people who interest you and try to find new insight into pop-culture ideas.

The BuzzFeed platform allows users to create community posts where you have the same access to the tools the professionals use to create articles. The more platforms you learn to write on, the more likely you have mastered the style of writing on each platform. Remember that you should be creative and authentic when you write, because the web is a platform for people to enjoy each other's work. Look for communities that showcase your individuality and creativity on the web. Writing online should be looked at as an art form, whether it's writing on blogs, Twitter, or even a status update. The words you post online, whether fiction or non-fiction, provide the audience with a glimpse of your voice. Today, there are thousands of "bots" writing articles about any information available, and you have to separate yourself from the machines. After you write your material, be sure to share it on Reddit, post it on Facebook and Tumblr and Twitter, and be proud of your work. This is the best time in history to be a writer—you have the audience immediately available to help you out.

On Fandoms

A fandom is a group of online users who are fanatic to the point of creating a community that acts as a small kingdom of a shared common interest. The fandom usually creates related media and writing that is an extension of the media. Fandom isn't new to the web and has been around since fiction authors published and changed readers' lives. It's rumored that Johann von Goethe had a huge fandom surrounding his *Sorrows of Young Werther* (1774) and *Faust* (1808) books. If his fans had had access to the Internet, they probably would have created a fandom on Tumblr and written additional fan fiction.

Fan fictions are stories created by the community that follow the "canon" of material made by the original creator. Some of the biggest fandoms not only create fan fiction, but go a step farther, creating alternative expository sequences that border (if not cross into) erotica. Fan-fiction writers become so passionate about some of the characters that they may "ship" the characters, creating an "OTP" story that is completely fan made. To "ship" means to create a relationship between two existing characters who were not intentionally paired in the original concept and make them a "One True Pairing," or OTP. For example, the Sherlock fandom may create an OTP out of Sherlock and Watson and write shipping stories about that new subculture plotline. If the fandom collectively agrees the story is good enough and plausible in relation to the original plotline, it may get accepted as fandom canon.

If you like something, there is most likely a fandom already out there for you to join. You should write for it, because you only have something to gain in new friends and writing skills.

PHOTOS

The aim in creating and sharing photos in communities is for you to try, not to duplicate classical work, but to be an innovator. It is up to the user to incorporate their own style when taking photos and become an artist through using photos as creative expression. Taking photos has never been easier in today's digital environment, owing to mobile technologies providing users with the ability to take photos instantaneously. Photography online is a work of art to be looked at, as well as a communication tool. Since the inclusion of hashtags on images, your photography communicates to various users in a way that printed photographs originally could not. You know the adage that a photo is worth a thousand words: Well, in the age of new and digital media, a thousand people may take the same photo.

Whether you post on Flickr, DeviantArt, Instagram, Imgur, or Twitter, you should promote your style. Join photography communities and be sure to hashtag your images on Twitter with #photog or #photo to have other photographers take a look at your work and start a discussion.[31] Whatever photography platform you choose, pay close attention to the comments that people leave, because they will help you develop and appreciate your style. No one likes looking at the same photo over and over; people like to see new and interesting photography.

Our world is a beautiful place, and images of it you capture with your DSLR or your camera phone should be shared with the online audience. Follow Brandon Stanton's "Humans of New York" to see a great example of photography and community engagement using Facebook as a photography platform.[32] Brandon has photographed over 6,000 people and takes quotes from each subject and adds them as captions on the photos to inspire viewers, from New Yorkers to the rest of the world, with the experience of the New York lifestyle. Some professional photographers and photojournalists have taken to Instagram to show and share their work as well. NowThisNews occasionally features photojournalists' work on their Instagram feed. Photo-journalist Ashley Gilbertson captured images of returning troops struggling with PTSD, and his work was featured on NowThisNews in order to show the horrors of war and display Gilbertson's work.[33]

There are too many apps to name them all, and you should find the photography app that works best for you and your phone. It should allow cropping, color saturation changes, and the ability to post to social media from the app. You should be photographing and sharing as much as possible—not just to make your friends jealous of what you are doing and where you are going, but to help users experience parts of the world and points of view at their fingertips.

Photo Quality and Sharing

When deciding on a photo community to join, consider how well that community preserves your photos online. The web is not kind to photo quality, because it only works with certain file formats. Some sites, such as Flickr, allow you to upload full-resolution photos that can be downloaded in various sizes. This can be helpful if you are storing your portfolio online and you want your client to see the photos properly. You also want to look for an embedding feature, so that users can embed your photo on their site while keeping the important photography data of the original. Web-based photo communities such as Imgur allow embedding and sharing for the sake of driving users back to the community to continue the conversation.

VIDEO

Video communities are ones to be experimented with by all users. To participate with video is to both produce video content in a variety of creative ways and share it on video-based platforms, along with personal environments that can utilize media content. There are many ways to produce video content that will help you be creative and entice you to participate. The video content you produce can either be long form or short form, depending on the community you join. For example, a user can post a 10-minute vlog on YouTube or a 15-second clip on Instagram. Opportunities are available to produce video anywhere.

Chapters 5 and 6 will cover in depth the use of video on digital media through the use of viral videos and web television. Those chapters will discuss how you can use video to your advantage to market an idea, while generating revenue and building an online audience. Before you reach that point, understand that you are a producer and, when you create video, let the type of content you want to create influence you. This means experimenting with different genres, styles, and editing. YouTube allows you to create a vlog with your mobile device or your web camera. With technology available and all platforms offering video tools, experiment creating a web series, a trailer, or fan fiction. Using a smartphone or tablet, you are able to capture those important moments each step of the way, such as vacations, graduations, birthdays, that you would want to remember for a lifetime and show to future generations. If you want to go more professional, you can use a GoPro camera or DSLR and you can experiment creating that short film you have always dreamed about.

Video communities, such as Vimeo, engage and inspire users to want to create web series or short films, particularly when indie filmmakers are using the site. By finding videos, you become part of a community to watch that video grow from a grassroots perspective.

As with writing, there is an audience for every type of video production. If you like playing video games, record yourself, make a "Let's Play" video, and post it on YouTube. Have an idea for an experimental film about dandelions blowing in the wind, record it, add music, and post it on Vimeo. If you want to dance in class to your friend playing "Chopsticks" on the piano, record a 6-second Vine. You can be a writer and share script ideas with your fans on Twitter or Tumblr. You can also be an editor: After filming your vlog, you can edit it through YouTube by adding filters, cuts, and effects. Digital media users have to experiment, and, if you create, you have the opportunity to build a gathering around your videos while finding a passion that you never knew existed before. There are now communities for you to create vlogs and talk to an audience, create your own web series, or share a moment with the world; those communities exist that thrive on viewing multimedia content.

SOUND

GarageBand and Audacity have allowed access to digital audio workstations, originally confined to audio facilities, on anyone's computer. Any creative individual with a nice microphone can create a mix album, a cinema score, or a podcast. If you are interested in what your friends are listening to, you can join Spotify and see their playlists. Besides being able to stream your favorite bands and artists, you are able to share what you are listening to at that very moment with your community on your social media platforms. You do not want to listen to your music alone, and digital music allows you to share your musical tastes with the world in order for others to discover these artists. Spotify also allows you to follow each other's music playlists, as well as to listen to the same music as each other. You are able to experience music more than ever before, even through video-sharing sites such as YouTube, as fans of artists have used the platform to post videos and tracks of their favorite artists. Apple streams music, and YouTube even created a streaming music service so users can access music through portable devices on the go.[34]

If you are a music creator, digital media give you a place to create and share your work globally on platforms such as SoundCloud, which is geared toward professional artists or anyone to create mixes for others to hear. There is now a community built around sound and audio in a way that makes it shareable, downloadable, and high quality. If you have ever wondered what a community thought of your sound, you are now able to post your track on SoundCloud and see what the community is saying about it through embedded messages on the SoundCloud player. Be more than a listener to music online: Be a creator.

THE CREATORS

The term user-generated content (UGC) has been around for many years, used to describe those who create a video, picture, or any form of media to post on the web. UGC can be anything that you make. It can be a meme, a GIF, or a podcast. Everything you create on social media, such as a tweet, an animation on Vine, or a picture on Instagram, is UGC. Although it was new to the generation of those who consumed media, we are now in one where we are constantly making our own content to supplement the consumption. Therefore, no longer are you just labeled as those who make UGC, but you are *creators*. You are creating material all over the web for distribution and personal use. Creating is commonplace and part of who you are as a person. After reading our book, we hope those who do not create take the next step and join those who create each day.

The Makers

The makers are people who are creators in the physical space, using new and digital media tools. As we move to a creators' world, the "Maker Movement" is occurring, where people are using computer programming to make open-source materials to help advance the way the web works and how we participate. Makers use digital media to print material on 3D printers, program little computers such as the Raspberry Pi, and program new virtual reality systems such as the Oculus Rift.

There is a gathering called the Maker Faire where makers and creators come from all over the world to celebrate new and digital media advancements and hands-on creativity. The slogan for the Maker Faire is "The greatest show and tell on Earth."[35] If there is one by you, try your best to attend!

GEEKS AND NERDS

This entire book would have been considered really geeky or nerdy years ago, and now the techniques learned on new and digital media are profitable and entertaining to a vast majority of people. The image of geeks and nerds is changing. When you look back at American culture, the classic use and image of the term nerd or geek is someone who wears high pants, glasses, and suspenders and has no sense of style. Think Steve Urkel in the 1990s television show *Family Matters* and every portrayal of the term in movies during that time period as well. Not only did nerds have a "style" they were labeled as having, even your personality could be associated with that term as well.

A nerd or geek was characterized as someone who played video games all day, read comic books, loved science, and was good with computers and technology. Today, those same traits are no longer looked down upon. The geeks and the nerds from yesterday are now the superstars of today. Learning code today is a superpower that anyone from Mark Zuckerberg to Chris Bosh appreciates.[36] Whereas, during the 1980s and 1990s, you might have been labeled a geek or a nerd for having a passion for any one of those hobbies, today, you are part of what is now trendy in American pop culture. As explained by the comic Chuck & Beans, nerds are academically inclined, whereas geeks are really passionate about their hobbies.[37]

The top movies of today are all superhero films from classic comic books, graphic novels are being turned into television shows, and technology is at the forefront. Those who understand how to code, create a social network, or design an app are now seen as the ones in vogue with society and successful. The subjects that were designated as "uncool" are now popular. Look at the success of Comic Con, held in San Diego and New York each year. Thousands of fans travel around the world to attend this weeklong convention, just to get a glimpse of meeting comic book artists and see the latest trailer for the next superhero movie, or sneak a peak at the new season in television. We want you to be a passionate geek or nerd and, more importantly, we want you to participate in communities that help you create.

KHAN ACADEMY

Khan Academy is an example of the consumer becoming a "prosumer." This means that a user, creating short-form video content and posting it on the web, intends to interact with the audience and community, but in turn creates a successful venture and turns their product into profit. Clay Shirky calls these users "the people formally known as the audience."[38] What he means is the audience is now producing and has the ability, with short-form creativity, to produce income as well. Salman Khan, who created Khan Academy in 2006, is one such example, as he provides educational resources to anyone on the web.

As the website boasts, it's free for anyone, providing lessons via video tutorials on math, science, history, computer science, and many other subjects. In 2006, Salman was using YouTube to post math tutorial videos for his cousin and other family members, to provide extra help for them learning the subject. He used YouTube as his teaching platform because Salman was working at a hedge fund in Boston, and his family members were in New Orleans. The videos became an instant hit with, not only his family, but also the community on YouTube wanting to learn the subject. Through engaging tutorial videos, Salman was able to provide what students would learn in the classroom to adults who desired to learn a subject or those who have never had the opportunity to learn.

Students can now use the video tutorials as a guide, playing, pausing, and stopping those videos at the their own pace of learning. The videos were receiving millions of views and so many positive comments that the Khan Academy quickly became a community on YouTube for those thirsting to learn. The success of what turned out to be a social venture is that the content never gets old, as users flock to digital media for productivity, research, and the enhancing of skills, just as much as entertainment, and it shows how a community can come together to help one another online. In his TED Talk from 2011, Salman theorizes how he has "humanized the classroom," because teachers are interacting with the students.[39] Teachers are using his video in their lessons in flipped-classroom-style pedagogy, because his video acts as the lesson, while the teacher is going around the room to help all of the students and work on the problems with them.

After quitting his job, Salman turned the Khan Academy into a non-profit organization. It is funded on donations, but it receives backing from the Bill & Melinda Gates Foundation and Google among many others, who continue to build its educational resources. The Khan Academy website includes, not only video tutorials, but also modules, assignments, and exercises for each subject area. The Khan Academy started as a community to change education and now it has proved successful, with self-paced learning and teachers using the program to see data on what videos their students are watching and what problems they are struggling with, among other analytics. With millions of subscribers and views and having changed the educational landscape, it comes back to community, as its short-form videos have captured millions around the world. Khan successfully created videos with ease, using technological tools that are available to anyone around the world, and he posted them to a platform where millions gather, not realizing that users are comfortable with the one-on-one interaction, not just with him, but also with the device they are using. Khan has built a successful venture, with 10 million students a month visiting the website, which has 60 employees and interns, and it all started with videos being posted to the community on YouTube.

SHORT-FORM CREATIVITY

The majority of savvy web users are now accessing creative spaces using smaller machines such as phones and tablets, rather than desktop computers. The main way that people produce content on these small devices is through apps such as Vine, Instagram, and Snapchat. Users of the short-form apps follow specific users relevant to their creative interests. Why do users enjoy this form of content? Not only is this short-form creativity, it is also short-form storytelling. Each Instagram photo or video or 6-second Vine is telling your visual story on your specific profile page. These are "lightweight" apps that instantly take a picture from your phone and post it, and, before you know it, content is up on your profile page, where the audience can be brought into your life. Instead of long-form narratives, a simple picture tells a story of a day in your life. It is a footprint of your personality and a collection of your life story.

Your story is assembled in visuals rather than text, enabling the audience to see your creativity. It is a challenge to tell a story using a simple picture or 6-second Vine. More so than anything else, short-form storytelling encourages creativity, and that is what attracts an online audience and builds community on these platforms. Users of short-form media truly have to think about what to produce before they hit the button. When a picture or video is posted on Instagram, you have the opportunity to be creative in how you take a picture and whether you use a filter. Short-form storytelling has established itself as a new narrative style for digital media.

INSTAGRAM

Mobile video, or video captured by digital appliances such as the iPhone or Android smartphones, has flooded video-sharing sites such as YouTube. Everyone has equal opportunity to share and create stories, and, once the outlets were established, users occupied the outlets even before corporations saw their positive uses. Before Instagram and Vine, if a user captured a video on their smartphone and wanted the world to see the product, the audience had to go to the distribution outlet, whether that was YouTube, Facebook, or Vimeo. The creator was an operator of several applications, made distant by digital mode application, and they severed the creator from a seamless integration with sharing.

In 2010, Kevin Systrom and Mike Krieger created the mobile photography platform Instagram. The Instagram application platform uses the aesthetic constraint of square photo capture. The user and content creator can no longer choose the way the camera is held: The application forces the user to hold vertical positioning in order to capture an image that is formatted properly. Additionally, Instagram allows users to capture images and share them in the same application where the capture takes place and, therefore, it is a one-stop shop for all users. The application allows the user to capture a constrained square image, apply a digital filter effect to the image to "enhance" the visual, and share it immediately. The digital filter allows everyone to be a professional photographer. You have the power to apply a plethora of enhancements, enabling the user to play editor to their photo and apply an artistic look to what would be a "normal" image. It brings the traditional Polaroid or Kodak camera into a digital form. When photos from those cameras were printed, photographers had to go into a darkroom and apply filters and edits. Instagram brings those aesthetics to people who want to create. The image appears in the timeline almost immediately after it has been captured, without leaving the creative space.

The users of Instagram are able to research photos and users (hoping to add them to their community) through hashtags, a technology implemented in 2011. Users can be creative with the pictures they are taking and with the text accompanying each picture attached. Many users have come up with creative hashtags to place on photographs for users to search in order to come across their pictures, but this has also sparked trends on Instagram too. Instead of a generic text below a photo, the use of hashtags on Instagram is creative and inspires additional creativity,. One of the big Instagram hashtag trends is "Throwback Thursday", or #tbt, which is used each week for users to post a

Figure 2.3
#foodporn.

picture from their past, such as from when they were a child, on recent vacation, or a personal past event. Other trends include users taking pictures of their breakfast, lunch, or dinner at home or at a restaurant and calling it #foodporn; Man Crush Monday, or #mcm; and Women Crush Wednesday, or #wcw. The most popular trend, the selfie, or #selfie, is used when you flip your camera around and take a self-portrait of yourself. There is style and expression in the way you take a selfie, such as how you hold the camera to create the image you wish to have of yourself. It's expressive for the user, giving an entryway into their emotions, personality and how they are feeling at that moment. The selfie trend has transformed itself into an art form and has spread into pop culture. It has become a popular trend because users have the ability to control how they present themselves on screen to their audience. It has became a shareable trend that celebrities, looking to connect to their audience, regularly use for their visual stories.

Instagram's Upgrade

On April 12, 2012, Facebook acquired Instagram for $1 billion in cash and stocks. There was immediate backlash from users concerned for their privacy when Facebook updated its terms of service after the acquisition. The new terms of service stated that it could sell your photos to third parties without telling you or compensating you for the photos used. Immediately, users were upset by this invasion of their privacy. Facebook had purchased an application that was used for creativity and art, and users were bothered and wanted their community to be left alone. After many users flocked to new photo-sharing applications that week, and negative feedback, Instagram had new terms of service created. Facebook is still generating income in the service, as sponsored posts were created in late 2013 as a way for advertisers to create specific photo and video posts in users' feeds.

VINE

The mobile aesthetic constraints were limited to photography until 2013, when Twitter announced the mobile video service Vine. Like Instagram, the videos had an aesthetic constraint of square capture, but, more importantly, Vine contained a temporal constraint that videos be 6 seconds or less. Twitter explained that the video was similar to tweets, and the brevity of the video would inspire creativity.[40] After the success of Vine, Instagram introduced short-form video capture, increasing the time to 15 seconds and adding filters to videos. The originality of Vine lay in the previously unconsidered concept of video capture: merging the micro blog and video. The message was to be short, and the shape was predecided.

Vine started quietly, used by a very small base of users who appreciated the speed with which video could be captured and shared. Like Instagram, the user can capture and share within the same environment. Originally, the user could not upload captured video material from their digital phone camera's library: The material had to be captured within the application itself. (Now the app allows for video to be uploaded from the camera's media library.)

Vine is a unique creation tool. In order to capture video, the user must hold their finger on the viewfinder, the screen of the phone. The electrical sensitivity of the smartphone user interaction is the standard operating procedure of the creation process. Once the finger is released from the screen, the recording stops. This means that Vine video can only be captured with phone in hand and operated with the application open. The application allows linear, in-camera editing, and the user can create 6-second linear narratives that allow for up to 100 edits (depending on how quickly the user can tap the screen). Vine has inadvertently reinvented a stop motion camera with a similar workflow to that of a Bolex film camera, where the user had to manually trigger the shot and was limited to the amount of "film" available in the camera— in this case, as much content as can fit into 6 seconds.

Before Vine, mobile video acquisition was a form without standards. The user's responsibility to capture utilizing a mobile device was completed when the user finished the entire video. The challenge for users on Vine is creating a 6-second storytelling with beginning, middle, and end, and thus using traditional film techniques on the platform will only engage the audience to your feed of Vines. With traditional techniques, after editing a wide shot of you opening the door, on action, the next shot would possibly be a close-up of a hand opening the door handle, and then back to a medium shot of you walking through. All edits were matched to actions. In Vine, temporal continuity still takes places, as time moves rather quickly in each video, so that the end of a story is quickly reached. You will see temporal continuity thoroughly achieved in stop motion videos, for example. In order for a three-act structure, with beginning, middle, and end, to happen on Vine, the point of the story has to be got across to the viewer immediately, with each section being its own specific camera angle or next point of the story.

Although Instagram Video has incorporated 15-second video, Vine tends to be the platform for artistic and creative stories. Instead of traditional videos, with someone holding up the camera and recording, you will find many forms of stories told with animation, Claymation, or Vine movies, owing to the stop motion effects built into the application making live editing interactive for all users. What Vine is doing for its users is teaching them how to edit video and tell a narrative story. It has allowed users to create stories in many short forms, and companies such as the Tribeca Film Festival have asked users to participate in its #6SECFILMS competition, where users can enter to post Vines in either the #Animation, #Drama, #Genre, or #Comedy categories. Many other companies and celebrities have since incorporated Vine into their marketing as a way to attract users' attention to short stories.

SNAPCHAT

Evan Spiegel, Bobby Murphy, and Reggie Brown created Snapchat in 2011 as a way to share photos and videos with a smaller online community. The difference is that the pictures or video you take within the application do not store any information on your phone or use up any memory according to amount of pictures or video you take daily. When a user takes a "snap," they take a photo or video in the Snapchat application, and then add filters and text captions or draw messages over the content. Each time you share a Snap with one of your contacts in the online community, the receiver only has up to 10 seconds to view it once it is opened. After the 10 seconds are over, the Snap is deleted.

Privacy and Snapchat

There have been some issues in the past with privacy and whether the photos are actually deleted. Many have questioned whether the photos are saved on Snapchat's servers. Also, many have taken screen shots on their phones when photos have come in. Although Snapchat will send users a notification, there have been ways around such alerts being sent. Snapchat made a deal with the Federal Trade Commission in 2014 because it was caught lying to its users. Although it bills itself as private, those who are not media literate or familiar with Internet technology might not realize that screen shots could be taken or that IP addresses were saved with the information. Also, Snapchat was collecting its users' information through its Find Friends feature, saving your personal and location information. The application is going to be monitored for the next 20 years.

Snapchat Creativity

You work with your phone's camera, and the screen becomes the viewfinder while your hand is on the record button. It is a constant interaction between the user and the screen. Within the application, you are able to focus just by tapping on the screen, which is acting as your lens and the f-stop of the camera. It offers creativity to online users, and fans of short-form storytelling navigate to this program because they see advantages in what they see as being private and helping tell stories that quickly fade away, without anyone else ever looking. When you tap on the screen and select the pencil, your finger becomes the paintbrush, and your cellphone screen becomes the canvas where you create a caption. You can always erase or change your design with a fresh coat of paint or new canvas. Private messages, funny notes, and symbols all add creativity to the content. Because users have control of how long someone can view the snap, they are made sure to feel that they are in control of the content, not the application. If it's no longer on your profile, newsfeed, or explore icon, then it must have never existed, or only happened in that particular moment. The fascinating thing about Snapchat is that users are engaged for only a few seconds and, in that short moment, are entertained enough to continue to interact with the device. Even when looking at a picture, the user, seeing that countdown number on the bottom of the screen, is forced to not multitask with their media, which is what occurs in modern times: The user is forced to focus on the picture or video, as the pressure to be engaged is on the recipient, not wanting to miss the interaction with their community after the content has been viewed. When the content is deleted, there is a sense of closure for the user.

Whereas Vine and Instagram posts are always on your profile, Snapchat gives users a comfort level that no one will ever see it again if you do not want them to, and your creativity has no limits to what it can do, opening up all forms of storytelling. There is a close-knit community on Snapchat, because users are in control over who sees their content.

Snapchat encourages users to create photo or video stories giving an insight into their last 24 hours, as that is how long the story will stay on their feed for. After the 24 hours, it is deleted, and they can post a new story to their feed. This has given users the creativity to tell a story as a "day in the life of me" aspect of its community. You have one image or one video to share with your followers that will convey your personality, wit, and emotions in that time frame. This has offered users many innovative ideas for expressing themselves, as, normally, someone tells their story in a book, a paper, or conversation. To have one image tell your story, it has to be original, clever, and representative of how you want to be viewed by the online audience. By incorporating conversations and live video into Snapchat and even deleting conversations once they are completed, unless saved, Snapchat is hoping to offer instantaneous access and be intimate and exclusive to you and your online community.

NOTES

1 Pew Internet (2012). "Networked Individualism: What in the world is that?" Retrieved from http://networked.pewinternet.org/2012/05/24/networked-individualism-what-in-the-world-is-that-2/ (accessed April 29, 2015).

2   Zhang, J., Ackerman, M.S., and Adamic, L. (2007). "Expertise Networks in Online Communities: Structure and algorithms." In *WWW '07: Proceedings of the 16th international conference on World Wide Web*, pp. 221–230, New York: ACM Press. Retrieved from www2007.org/papers/paper516.pdf (accessed April 29, 2015).

3   Shirky, C. (2008). *Here Comes Everybody: The power of organizing without organizations.* London: Penguin, p.108.

4   boyd, d. (2014). *It's Complicated: The social lives of networked teens.* Newhaven, CT: Yale University Press, pp. 38–39.

5   Shirky, C. (2010). *Cognitive Surplus: How technology makes consumers into collaborators.* New York: Penguin.

6   Jenkins, H. (2006). *Convergence Culture: Where old and new media collide.* New York: New York University Press, p. 27.

7   Shirky, C. (2010). *Cognitive Surplus: How technology makes consumers into collaborators.* New York: Penguin, p. 143.

8   boyd, d. (2014). *It's Complicated: The social lives of networked teens.* Newhaven, CT: Yale University Press, pp. 39–40.

9   Shirky, C. (2008). *Here Comes Everybody: The power of organizing without organizations.* London: Penguin, p. 99.

10   Jenkins, H. (2006). *Convergence Culture: Where old and new media collide.* New York: New York University Press.

11   Ibid.

12   boyd, d. (2014). *It's Complicated: The social lives of networked teens.* Newhaven, CT: Yale University Press, p. 59.

13   Simmons, D. (1990). *Hyperion.* New York: Random House.

14   Bullas, J. (2012). "10 Ways Leading Brands Use Facebook Ingeniously for their Marketing." Retrieved from www.jeffbullas.com/2012/09/12/10-ways-leading-brands-use-facebook-ingeniously-for-their-marketing/ (accessed April 29, 2015).

15   Murthy, D. (2013). *Twitter: Social communication in the Twitter age.* Cambridge, UK, and Malden, MA: Polity Press.

16   Gannes, L. (2010). "The Short and Illustrious History of Twitter #hashtags." GigaOM. Retrieved from http://gigaom.com/2010/04/30/the-short-and-illustrious-history-of-twitter-hashtags (accessed April 29, 2015).

17   Murthy, D. (2013). *Twitter: Social communication in the Twitter age.* Cambridge, UK, and Malden, MA: Polity Press.

18   Shonfeld, E. (2011, January 25). "Twitter Is Blocked in Egypt Amidst Rising Protests." Retrieved from http://techcrunch.com/2011/01/25/twitter-blocked-egypt/ (accessed April 29, 2015).

19   Grossman, L. (2012, January 30). "The Beast with a Billion Eyes." *Time Magazine.* Retrieved from http://content.time.com/time/magazine/article/0,9171,2104815,00.html (accessed April 29, 2015).

20   Ibid.

21   Ibid.

22 Ibid.

23 Graham, D. (2012). "Obama's Reddit AMA: The full questions and answers." Retrieved from www.theatlantic.com/politics/archive/2012/08/obamas-reddit-ama-the-full-questions-and-answers/261756/(accessed April 29, 2015).

24 Silman, A. (2014). "The Best Answers from Daniel Radcliffe's Reddit AMA." Retrieved from www.vulture.com/2014/10/best-answers-from-dan-radcliffes-reddit-ama.html (accessed April 29, 2015).

25 Reddit. (2013). "IamA Glitter Manufacturer AMA!" Retrieved from www.reddit.com/r/IAmA/comments/1nppaa/iama_glitter_manufacturer_ama/ (accessed April 29, 2015).

26 Savov, V. (2012). "The SOPA Blackout: Wikipedia, Reddit, Mozilla, Google, and many others protest proposed law." Retrieved from www.theverge.com/2012/1/18/2715300/sopa-blackout-wikipedia-reddit mozilla-google-protest (accessed April 29, 2015).

27 Klima, J. (2014). "Reddit Opens Secret Santa, Seeks New Guinness World Record." Retrieved from http://newmediarockstars.com/2014/11/reddit-opens-secret-santa-seeks-new-guinness-world-record/(accessed April 29, 2015).

28 Wikipedia list of MMORPGs. Retrieved from http://en.wikipedia.org/wiki/List_of_massively_multiplayer_online_role-playing_games/(accessed April 29, 2015).

29 Graham, B. (1999). "The BradLand Manifesto, or, Why I Weblog." *The Digital Manifesto Archive.* Retrieved from http://digitalmanifesto.omeka.net/items/show/121/ (accessed April 29, 2015).

30 Mazza, E. (2014). "R.L. Stine Writes an Entire Short Story on Twitter Called 'What's in My Sandwich?'." Retrieved from www.huffingtonpost.com/2014/10/29/r-l-stine-twitter-story_n_6065514.html (accessed April 29, 2015).

31 Creek, N. (n.d.). "Twitter Users, Hashtag Your Photography Tweets." Retrieved from http://digital-photography-school.com/twitter-users-hashtag-your-photography-tweets/ (accessed April 29, 2015).

32 "Humans of New York." www.humansofnewyork.com/ (accessed April 29, 2015).

33 NowThisNews. (2013). The acclaimed photojournalist who captures PTSD through his lens. Retrieved from www.ashleygilbertson.com/projects/bedrooms_of_the_fallen/

34 Flanagan, A. (2014). "YouTube's Music Streaming Service Launches." Retrieved from www.billboard.com/articles/business/6312376/youtubes-music-streaming-service-launches (accessed April 29, 2015).

35 MakerFaire. http://makerfaire.com/ (accessed April 29, 2015).

36 Code.org. (2013). "What Most Schools Don't Teach." Retrieved from www.youtube.com/watch?v=nKIu9yen5nc (accessed April 29, 2015).

37 Golijan, R. (2010, April 30). "This Is Why Im Not a Dork." *Chuck and Beans.* Shoebox. Retrieved from http://gizmodo.com/5528552/this-is-why-im-not-a-dork (accessed April 29, 2015).

38 Shirky, C. (2010). *Cognitive Surplus: How technology makes consumers into collaborators.* New York: Penguin.

39   Khan, S. (2011). "Let's Use Video to Reinvent Education." TEDTalks. Retrieved fom www.ted.com/talks/salman_khan_let_s_use_video_to_reinvent_education#t-266633 (accessed April 29, 2015).

40   Twitter blog. (2013). "Vine: A new way to share video." Retrieved from https://blog.twitter.com/2013/vine-a-new-way-to-share-video (accessed April 29, 2015).

CHAPTER 3

Web Literacy

You are a creator for the web, and your creative participation helps the web grow and become more advanced. In fact, your participation is exponentially increasing the Internet at a rate of over 40 percent per year. As more users create and more devices come online, the Internet has expanded from the browser and the World Wide Web to the "things" such as phones, wearables, and household items—basically anything with an Internet connection. The content you create is part of the future web, an immense database of everything we are all working on. It's estimated that, by 2020, the web will be 44 zettabytes (44 trillion gigabytes) big.[1]

This chapter advances the creative explorations you have initiated and teaches you how to understand the overwhelming amount of information that affects your use and your participation. We think the savvy user should have a working knowledge of how the web works and why. Understanding the basic functions of the systems of participation will help you speak the language and create on a higher cognitive level, enabling you to become a leader in the digital environment and make higher-quality work.

People often think that literacy means comprehending and reading information. Literacy means to read *and* write. This chapter will focus first on comprehension and reading of technical information and code, and then we will focus on how you can learn to write and create material. The first part of this chapter will focus on technical terms and general information about the web, file structure, information pathways, web language, data, and the physical technology of the online world. We will not overburden you, but we will encourage you to appreciate the technologies and science that most users take for granted every minute they are using the web. You will become far savvier by understanding the structures that make the web work. First, we offer a short history of the web itself and then delve further into the technical structure of the user environment. We will do our best for this not to overwhelm, but to inform.

This chapter will fill you up with knowledge of the web from head to foot. Or maybe we should say from "header to footer"! You use the web every day and interact with it on a consistent basis, but do you know how it works?

Figure 3.1

Empty monitor.

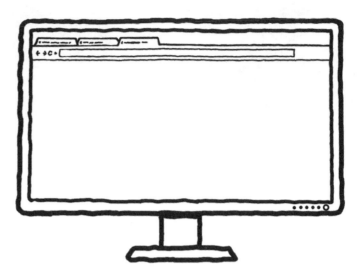

This chapter will start from the first visuals that appear when you open your browser to the very wires that carry blips of light across the oceans.

When you first open a new webpage template, it usually comes blank, with the boxes prepared and floating in space (in web terms, these are cascading style sheets (CSS)), and you have to fill the blocks with your specific information. By the end of this chapter, you'll know why the web works and why you can use it so freely and easily. The adage goes that you do not need to be a mechanic to drive a car—but it helps!

Welcome to the web!

It's not your fault you take the web for granted—it's because it works really well. But when you find out how it works, you'll be astounded. There was once a time, not long ago, that the entire World Wide Web ran off one computer in Tim Berners-Lee's office at CERN, in France. Within 30 years, it has grown to encompass the entire globe and functions as an everyday part of the lives of nearly 3 billion people.

When you get home and you turn on your computer, it runs on a micro version of the web itself. Your computer is a machine that processes data using dozens of microchips, a processor, and a hard drive. It runs on an operating system written in a code language that you cannot see, and you can interact with the machine through a graphic user interface. The language creates the visuals so that you can operate the system without needing to know code. Similarly, the web browser does this for the online languages that take hypertext and hypermedia (text and media that can be conformed to the user's screen) and mark them up to a visual representation. The browser takes the code of HTML and makes it visual.

Figure 3.2
*Do not turn off—
Tim Berners-Lee
computer.*

Source: Wikimedia
Commons

The browser is one of the few devices that properly reads HTML and makes it usable and interactive and it makes the World Wide Web work. Berners-Lee made the first browser on that very computer that ran the web, and it was called the Nexus browser. The downside was that the Nexus browser was pretty clunky and required technical knowledge of online media to navigate it. At age 22, the tech-savvy Marc Andreesen dreamed of improving the experience of the web and co-authored the first usable web browser, called Mosaic. He later co-founded Netscape, the earliest mainstream usable browser. However, because the browser works inside an operating system, Netscape had to get along with the companies that supported its software. Netscape's steepest competition was Microsoft, the largest operating system company in the world at the time. Microsoft retaliated by creating its own browser in 1994, Internet Explorer, and packaged it with the operating system. The competition Netscape faced nearly shut it down.

Now, you have a choice of browsers, such as Chrome, Firefox, Internet Explorer, Safari, Opera, and several more, depending on how technically interested you are. Each of them does virtually the same processing of HTML code to create images and text that are easily readable.

HOW DO WEBPAGES APPEAR ON MY COMPUTER?

Internet Protocol

When you type in a web address, it seems as if the website appears nearly instantly, especially if you've been there before. It works just like dragging and dropping files from your USB drive to a computer. Let's start at the top—the web address itself. The web address is called a uniform resource locator, or URL. (No one ever says "uniform resource locator" out loud; it would be heard as "earl.") The URL is also called a domain name, or a mask, because it masks the actual address of the URL—the Internet Protocol (IP) address. The Internet Protocol address is the location of the files that hold the website you want to visit. Every node and port and drive (and your phone) has a unique IP address that tells the Internet where data are located. For example, ask a site such as Ask Google what your IP is, and it will let you know. At the time of writing, Google's IP address was http://173.194.121.48/. Thankfully, we use domain names so that we don't have to write the IP address each time to visit a site.

Domain Names

That leads us to wonder where domain names come from. When the web was first born, domains were chaotic and unorganized, in dozens of languages. In 1998, a non-profit organization created the Internet Corporation for Assigned Names and Numbers, also known as ICANN. This company organized and standardized the system so that users who made websites could potentially rent any domain and extension available. For example, you can have a domain name with .com for commercial, but a separate domain with .org for organization. Although ICANN distributes and organizes the domain names, it doesn't police the content on any given site. This means that you really can put whatever content you'd like on your page, regardless of extension.

To understand the ICANN system better, think of it in terms of your phone number. Did you ever consider who owns your number? You own your number, as long as you continue to pay your phone bill, and, if you stop, they'll take that number away from you and reassign it. It's the same for domain names—very few sites actually *own* their domain name. ICANN allows resellers such as GoDaddy or Namecheap to rent the domain names, to decentralize the system and allow competition on pricing. Domains are fairly affordable to rent, and you should have your name. As a personal brand, it is important to own your name, so that you can connect it to the URLs of your social media and make it easy for people to find your website. It's also important to put on your résumé or your business cards.

Hypertext Transfer

Now that you've typed in the web address and clicked enter, an interesting and phenomenal technological feat occurs—the transfer of the hypertext from the host hard drive to your browser. To pull information across the Internet, we have to request the data from another drive. The term pull is very important, because we are nearly always pulling the data across the web by request; the web rarely pushes data to you (the exception is apps on your device). We make a request to the host hard drive by typing in the domain web address; it sees the IP address and uses the hypertext transfer protocol, or http, to start the process. See, those little letters at the beginning of the domain mean something.

When the hypertext transfer protocol is activated, it sends the request to the computer that is holding the data of the website, usually housed in something called a root directory. (You can call a directory a folder.) That directory is probably on a hard drive in a server farm somewhere on the Earth. When you host a website, it means you are renting hard-drive space on a drive somewhere in a stable environment. Web-server farms are usually housed in a large, cooled room underground, far from geographic fault lines. Just as your computer gets heated up when you are using it, so do thousands of hard drives running simultaneously.

Figure 3.3

Server farm.

Source: Wikimedia Commons

When the request reaches the root directory, it asks for the files to be transferred to your computer's browser and, in order to speed that process up, separates the files into packets of data that reassemble in your computer. The files, the pictures, and the website style all travel for possibly thousands of miles in less than 1 second, to get to you so you can enjoy your cat pictures. Once the website reaches your browser, it actually downloads the site onto your computer in something called a cache, a small folder on your machine that keeps the website's visual information in case you revisit the site. Because hypertext is a code language, the files are normally pretty small and reside on your machine for weeks or months to assist in speedier web-page loading.

Why Your IP Address Matters

When you visit a site, and the code downloads to your computer's cache, it doesn't just make the website return load faster. It also allows a very small bit of code to live on your computer with it. These tiny little files are called cookies or tracking pixels.

Cookies have been around since the beginning of the web and are designed to expedite your web experience by preloading usernames or passwords and some interactive elements that you may have customized. As social media have become more prevalent, cookies have been used to track users as they surf the web.

Let's say you visit Macys.com and you search for toasters; Macy's will drop a cookie on your computer that remembers your search and the resulting page. There is a convenience next time you visit Macys.com, because the search bar automatically fills in "toasters" after you type the letter "t." Meanwhile, when you visit certain social media sites or search engines such as Facebook and Google, they retrieve that cookie and then sell your data back to Macy's. The goal is to show you advertisements about toasters on the side of Google search results and near your Facebook timeline. That cookie is a remnant of your search history. The more you use the web and keep your cookies, the more specific the advertisements become.

But, let's say you'd rather not be tracked by cookies and you have disabled cookies while you are browsing. Websites have figured that out as well and have incorporated tracking pixels. They are 1×1 images (usually .gifs) that stay on your computer as a file and allow the supplying company to see where you are traveling. As you accumulate multiple pixels, a service can see your history and make your advertising experience better.

To repeat our warning from the Introduction: If you do not pay for it, you are the product.

Web Languages

Hypertext markup language (HTML) may be one of dozens of web languages, but it is the language that makes up the World Wide Web. It's the language we recommend you learn in order to better understand how to create a nice website. HTML is a master language that allows the user to see websites as images and text without the code. For information to be laid out properly on a site, HTML is assisted by CSSs. If you want your site to react to the mouse on the screen or move images automatically, Javascript and jQuery assist HTML. If the site is built with a database or is far too large for the entire site to be sent by packets, sometimes the website's files stay on the host computer while you browse them, and the language for this is called PHP.

Digital media started in a very simple language that eventually evolved into all of our visual languages. Binary language is the original digital media language, as it allowed for the processing of a lot of information, compressed into simple data. In binary, there are only two pieces to process: a 1 or a 0. It's either on or off; true or false; yes or no; in or out. This original language actually dates back to Gottfried Leibniz, in 1679, originally in the context of quantifying religious information. In the hundreds of years since, binary has been used in analog form in several variations, from Braille language to Morse code. Computer scientists in the early 1970s realized that binary could be utilized as a batch processing system to universalize computer data and they called this the American Standard Code for Information Interchange, or ASCII.

Figure 3.4
I/O power button.

ASCII to HTML5

Programming languages are always in development. When Tim Berners-Lee invented the World Wide Web, he did so along with hundreds of other like-minded programmers. The web needed a language, and they settled on ASCII, which is based on the English alphabet and a base-10 numerical scale (0–9). ASCII's main purpose was to convert information into small bits of information that can be reassembled efficiently on different computers. It allows hypertext to be flexible, while still keeping content consistent. For example, two users may have different font choices when visiting the same site. One may have the settings set to a large type size and Verdana font, and the other may have it set to small and Trebuchet. Either way, ASCII delivers the content and displays it, regardless of user preferences.

Just like other programming protocols, ASCII has to be small in size, and it was built on a 7-bit platform. Bits are the smallest part of a programming construct, being either a 1 or a 0. If you put 8 bits together, you get a byte. (Your IP address, for example, is 32 bits if encoded as binary, or only 4 bytes.) A 7-bit programming language makes the web speak in its own unique method.

In 2007, a more universal, 8-bit model, called Universal Character Set Transformation Format, or UTF-8, replaced ASCII. As HTML moves to HTML5, it more closely resembles a classic programming language, and therefore the 8-bit model works much more efficiently in our present.

What binary taught Tim Berners-Lee was that computer languages work best with tags and binary-style switches, and, following the model of programming, HTML followed suit. Using tags enclosed in brackets, HTML is able to communicate a visual output to a browser. For example, to speak in HTML, you would enclose the words in brackets, like this (see Figure 3.5):

<p>HTML is a visual language that displays text and images through browser interpretation. It displays markups like <strong>bold</strong> or <em>italics</em> through the tags that turn on and off.</p>

The tags for each different language use a binary-like system. For HTML, a bracket system such as <tag> turns on the effect, and </tag> turns off the effect. In different languages, different brackets may be used. CSS uses curly brackets,

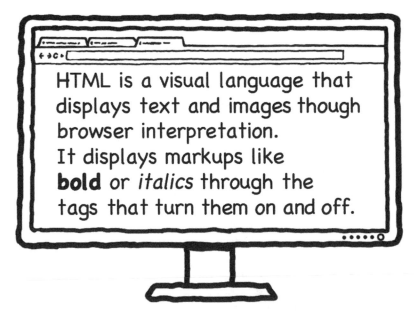

Figure 3.5
Monitor with text: HTML is a visual language that displays text and images through browser interpretation. It displays markups like **bold** *or italics through the tags that turn on and off.*

{ }, to identify style, and we will delve far deeper into code concepts in the following sections. We feel that your understanding of code will make you a savvier participant in the online environment.

DATA WE SEE AND DATA WE DON'T

Inside the visual languages of HTML, CSS, Javascript, and dozens more, there are parts of the code that remain invisible to the viewer on the web browser or screen. This is called metadata. Quite possibly the most important part of categorizing and quantifying digital media, metadata represents all technical data and contains additional code information. Every time you create digital media, metadata is inherently involved. If you start a Microsoft Word document, the metadata includes information about the computer it was created on, the owner of the machine (if you've registered your machine), the date of creation, how many words and characters have been used, and how much space the information occupies.

Metadata helps us categorize the media we create as well. When we write a webpage, we can add lines of metadata in the header of the file that the user cannot see. The goal is to have your media communicate with other technologies and organizational systems. You can see metadata occasionally, when you post a link on Facebook or other social media, and the description of the site automatically appears in the box beneath the link. If the website's creator doesn't include metadata, the site automatically uses the web content to fill the description. We highly recommend you add metadata descriptions and keywords to your sites and we will go into this in more depth in our section on "Understanding Hypertext and a Lesson on Web Code."

FILES ON THE WEB

As well as visual web code, files are transferred across the Internet into your browser and shown as images, sound, video, or interactive experiences. Files are usually included as linked objects that are also stored in subdirectories of a site's root folder. Directories such as "Images" or "Videos" are kept inside the root directory to create a more organized system for the web designer, but, in truth, the web browser doesn't really care where files are kept. As long as a file is requested properly, it can be stored anywhere.

But what are files on the web? As digital media don't have a physical counterpart, files are accumulations of various amounts of code. We often take files for granted, because they nearly always function properly. Let's say you want to post one of your Instagram photos on your website for someone to see. Well, you would take the file from your phone, upload it to your website directory, and then link to the image in your HTML code. (The code tag would look something like this: <img src="instagram.jpg">.) Have you ever considered how the digital photograph actually works?

You now know that data is broken up into packets and travels across the web to be reassembled. This obviously cannot happen with physical media. If you tear up a photo you printed out and try to reassemble it as it was, it would be impossible. Digital media, whether in the form of images, video, sound, or text, are just lines of code. Your Instagram photo appears after you have pressed the shutter button on your camera phone, and the shutter behind your lens allows light to become digitized by the complementary metal-oxide semiconductor (CMOS) chip inside the camera. The CMOS chip converts the light waves into quantifiable electrons, and a digital file builds instantaneously. The file that is created inside your phone is called an exchangeable image file, or EXIF data. The EXIF contains all the technical digital information about the image, from the pixels to the location to the lines of code that recognize your face. You will understand far more about the data located inside the files after reading the section on "Data, the Cloud and Digital Files" in this chapter.

DATA TRAVELING AROUND THE WORLD: THE PHYSICAL PROPERTIES OF THE WEB

The Internet before the World Wide Web was built on centralized systems of many computers and user nodes that interacted with one another. Several major companies, scientific institutions, and universities worked together to create a large, interactive, connected digital environment. The downside was that it had difficulty expanding, because the original architecture of the web was built around huge, centralized computer systems. The World Wide Web helped bring the idea that each computer, connected through a transmission control protocol, or TCP, connected to an IP, can act as part of the connective web and increase the size, volume, and speed of the web. Every user connected to the World Wide Web is connected using a TCP/IP device, commonly called a modem. You either get the modem from your Internet service provider or you purchase one for home or business use. To connect your machines to the modem, you also most likely have a router that connects your computer to the modem with an Ethernet cable or by wireless signal, known as Wi-Fi.

Data Movement Thought Experiment
Let's say you write an HTML webpage on your host server hard drive (which is located in Utah), and your domain is rented from GoDaddy, and your page

includes three images, two videos, and an audio file. The three images are coded as links on your page from three different sources—one from London, one from Tokyo, and one from California. Your embedded videos are taken from YouTube and Vimeo, and your sound file is located on a server in Lima, Peru. You are using a browser in New York, in a library, using a Wi-Fi signal.

When you type in the domain name and hit enter, the domain reads the IP address to redirect the user to your host directory. That means your browser initially goes to GoDaddy in Phoenix, Arizona, and then redirects through your domain nameservers (DNSs) to find your IP address, which contains your root directory, in Salt Lake City, Utah. The browser then reads the code on your webpage, seeking to load all of the content you included.

As it goes down the code from top to bottom, it locates the image in London by sending a request to the hard drive overseas. It turns the request into an additional electrical or light signal, which travels across physical wires and then under the ocean through one of the hundreds of submarine cables that carry data through fiber-optic cables (tiny glass wires) to retrieve the file. The image file is broken into packets and sent back to your browser in New York. The same applies to the images from Tokyo and California.

The videos are embedded: This means that your site has simply created a "hole" where the video will appear. Inside the embed code provided by the hosts at YouTube and Vimeo is the line of code that requests the specific videos to be played. The YouTube video is served up from one of the many Google server farms on the West Coast of the United States, and Vimeo's video most likely comes from somewhere on the East Coast. The two videos will appear at nearly the same time.

Figure 3.6
Undersea cable-laying ship—Cable Innovator.
Source: Wikimedia Commons

Lastly, you sourced a sound file from South America, and, just as for the images, the request travels down wires, but the return to your browser in New York could possibly make a faster route through undersea cables.

Within a second or two, your browser displays the text, loads the CSS style so that the formatting is correct, displays the pictures, and loads the videos and the audio for interactive use. The last part converts the signals, which have traveled across thousands of miles and through dozens of wires, into a radio signal that is broadcast through the air, to be retrieved by your specific IP address on your computer, to be displayed to you.

And, amazingly, despite all this data travel, many people consider our World Wide Web to be slow.

DATA IN MANY FORMS

As you progress through this chapter, we want you to keep in mind that web literacy comes from a general understanding of the platforms you use and how you read the information and subsequently become empowered to participate and create new and digital media. In our hypermedia present, data can be an overused terminology that describes any type of digital media. Although this is true, data takes many forms, from code to statistics, to algorithms, to an aggregate of databases. We do our best to consider the many pitfalls in the misinterpretation of data use.

We recognize that "data" is a plural word, as datum is the singular, and we acknowledge this is a contentious issue in journalism and writing. When we refer to data, we may use either the singular or the plural, depending on the context of the information. Many outlets, from the *Wall Street Journal* to *The Guardian*, consider the term data to change between singular and plural, depending on what data qualifies.[2]

You most likely hear the term "big data" used quite often, as researchers and analysts attempt to interpret the massive amount of information created by users on a daily basis. In your efforts to be a savvy user of the web, we encourage you to think of data in the creation process and become responsible for how you share your data. While you read the following sections, we hope you keep the fact that the material you create online can be quantified in the back of your mind.

A savvy user of the web knows why and how to create new and digital media.

UNDERSTANDING HYPERTEXT AND A LESSON ON WEB CODE

The World Wide Web as we know it today is completely interactive, continually expanding, and progressively becoming more technical to operate from a code perspective. In its current iteration, the web has become so advanced that CMSs such as WordPress and Wix allow users to employ the platforms to create websites without concerning themselves with the code. As far as we see it, this is both good and bad.

It's good because it allows unprecedented access to creating online content to more people every day. It's bad because fewer people will be literate in the basic functions of the web, which could lead them to be taken advantage of by advertisers or service providers.

This section acts as a primer for you to understand the basic construct and operation of the hypertext languages and the code that operate the webpages and CMSs we all enjoy. This section is in no way comprehensive, as there are dozens, if not hundreds, of books and websites on the topic of learning to be literate and specialized in web code. Our intention, in this process, is to offer you some insight into the various ways the web is presented to you and how you can become a better, media-literate, participating creative.

WHY IS IT IMPORTANT TO UNDERSTAND WEB CODE?

This question is nearly the impetus for the writing of this book. When people hear the word "code," they immediately recoil and sigh at the notion of writing strings of letters to make pictures. We find that most users are interested in code, but are highly intimidated. Marc Prensky, the author of the paper "Digital Natives, Digital Immigrants" (2001), explains that today's youth culture is born digital and speaking "natively digital."[3] Prensky later corrected his essay when he realized that he may have called the digital generation too soon, as the youth today will be even more native, as they grow up with touch-screen devices. What Prensky has stayed consistent with, at every speaking event and paper he writes, is that the next language to be literate in is code.

There are different code languages everywhere you look—and we aren't even making a reference to *The Matrix*. When you watch television, it is encoded to fit on your screen. When you look at an app on your phone, it is coded in a specific language. Video games are coded in an interactive code. When you visit webpages, they are coded in web code. We will attempt an overview of some of the languages that you interact with most often on your computer.

This book does not delve deep into programming languages such as Python or Ruby on Rails, but we highly recommend you learn these codes as well, because they create the backbone of the visual codes that make up websites and apps. Languages such as Python and Ruby on Rails simplify the C (all-purpose programming) language and allow users to learn and approach core code knowledge. They are object languages that we suggest you learn if you find yourself really interested in the web languages we'll explain here. The web code languages we'll talk about in this book will help you gain an understanding of, and literacy in, the creative features of website design.

Where to Learn Programming Languages

- Learn Python at python.org (http://python.org), codeacademy.com (http://codeacademy.com), or learnpython.org (http://learnpython.org).
- Learn Ruby on Rails at rubyonrails.org (http://rubyonrails.org) or railstutorial.org (http://railstutorial.org).

"IT LOOKS LIKE AN ALIEN LANGUAGE!"

The first time we right click and hit view source on a website, our students and colleagues believe we've shown them text from Mars. In other words, it can feel so foreign that it may not even be from this planet. In this section, we'll engineer several websites so that you can see what the code does on-screen and how you interact with it. We'll then show you how to install your own site or write one from scratch, to present your work online.

As you know, the web is written in HTML, and the design of websites uses languages such as CSS and jQuery. There are two ways your browser sees a

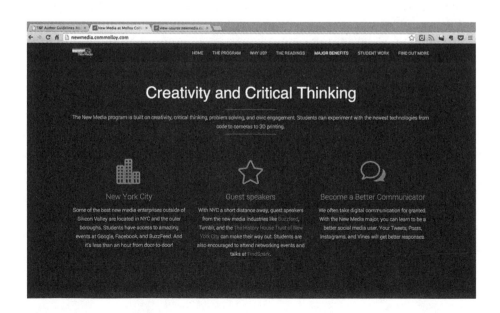

Figure 3.7
Website as visual.

Figure 3.8
The site in Figure 3.7 as source code.

website: client-side code or server-side code. The reason the web is so fast is because your browser actually does most of the heavy lifting when displaying websites. When you click on a website link or type in the URL and hit enter, only the code and the link to the images are sent to your browser. Previously, you may have thought that all the files and images and colors are sent, but that isn't the case. Not only would the downloading of an entire website slow the web down, but it would eat through data surprisingly quickly. All that is sent are the lines of code—which make up very small file sizes.

The code is sent across the web, and your browser reads the code and displays the site. The code contains the elements of the site such as the construct, the shape, the references to the color, and, most importantly, the body content. All the larger files remain on the server of the host, and the browser links directly to them to view them. This is called client-side code, the client being you, the user.

When the site opens, the browser reads the site from top to bottom, reading and loading all the languages as it goes. At the top of the code, the browser sees <!DOCTYPE html> and prepares to display the document. As the browser reads down the code, it loads the <head>, which contains the <title> and all the design elements, metadata, description, and keywords, and preloads any necessary animation scripts such as jQuery. After the </head> is done, it loads the <body>, which primarily contains the <p>content</p> and the images and embedded material. After the </body> is done, the site knows it has finished loading when it reaches the "off button," </html>.

Conceptualize this: Your browser is the website image; before reaching your browser, the website lives as code and files.

Server-side code is similar, but it leaves the majority of the files on the server and loads the site at the host. Your browser acts like a window to the website you are visiting, thereby speeding up your access to the content. This is the case with database web languages such as PHP, a hypertext preprocessing language. PHP is the language that WordPress uses and for a very good reason: quick customizability.

This Still Looks Alien

We know, but you'll get there. Let's break down some of the simpler languages first, before we get to WordPress, which is a preloaded script that you can install. Let's start from the host. When you purchase a domain name, you'll need to host your content and files. There are hundreds of places out there to host your site, such as Midphase.com, Lithium.com, Hostgator.com, Bluehost.com, among thousands. Some hosts offer a unique static IP address, and some use shared IP addresses that save you money. You should rent a host based on how much data you wish to store, how many people will visit your site, and if you'd like security installed in case you will be using your site to sell a product.

When you get your hosting up, you'll need to set your domain name to point at the host by setting the DNS settings. This tells the domain to point to your directory. Your directory really only needs to contain one single file for your website to work: index.html.

The index.html file is your website. You should also have a folder called images, which, obviously, contains all the images on your site. It is really all you need to run a simple site. When you write in HTML, it defaults to the Internet's default style of Times New Roman black text, blue hyperlinks, and purple visited links, sticking to the upper-left corner of the browser. To create layout, you need to incorporate some style. Style can be added directly to the HTML page to redefine elements of your code. You can add style to your page to increase the graphic options. To add style, you let the site know, in the head of the site, all the terms you'd like to redefine. For example, if you'd like the text to be blue, you would redefine the <p> tag.

If you are modifying the <p> tag in the head of your webpage in the <style type="text/css"> section, it would look like this:

```
p {color:blue;}
```

If you are styling the <p> tag on a tag-by-tag basic (which is far more time consuming), it would look like this:

```
<p style="font-color: blue">
```

From then on, any time the <p> tag was used, it would show up as blue. You can redefine any tag on your site by adding style. You can even redefine the <body> tag, which would do a blanket change of everything in the body of the site. But style can do so much more than that. You can create layout, float information, change the margins, and create interactive elements. However, there's a problem with style. It works really well if you only have one webpage, but what if you have dozens? Then you need to copy and paste all of your style onto each page to keep it consistent. That would work fine, until you need to make a small change such as a font size—you'll have to change each and every page!

Or, you can create a CSS. CSS is a design language that redefines website elements and allows the user to have full creative control. The style sheet is created as one page, and then, on each of your webpages, you just have to tell it to find the style sheet in order to use its customization. In the head of your pages, you would include the line of code: <link rel="stylesheet" type="text/css" href="mystyle.css">.

This link leads the page to the style sheet that loads all the style for the site all at once. CSS is written in a slightly different language, but looks very similar to the HTML style. It uses different brackets and a specific grammar.

It looks like this:

```
thingtodefine {whatparttodefine: newdefinition;}
p {color: blue;}
```

You can also add several customizations to the object you are redefining.

```
p {color: blue; font-size: 12px; font-family: sans-serif;}
```

From then on, all things tagged <p> would be in 12-point font and sans serif, such as Arial or Helvetica, and blue.

Code Literacy

You can learn HTML and CSS fairly quickly, but you do not have to keep the entire language in your head. You can use W3C Schools online (http://w3cschools.com) to refer to specific code.

We especially recommend you use CodeAcademy.com (http://codeacademy.com) to take the HTML and CSS introductory lesson to learn the basics. HTML and CSS are open source, which means that anyone has access to the code, and that means you can simply search for your answers in a search engine to increase your skill set.

Each browser also comes with a developer tool to assist you in reverse engineering a website. If you click tools or view developer tools in your browser, it will open a new pane that displays the code of the website. In most developer tools, you are able to alter the code, and the changes will show up on screen. We believe this is a good way to understand how each site works. It is usually activated by pressing alt + control/command + I, but check your browser's help menu if you are uncertain.

COLOR AND FURTHER CUSTOMIZATIONS

In our examples, we have been using the actual names of colors to customize our tags. You have access to more than 16 million colors to use on the web. To use color on your site, you have to refer to its specific hexadecimal color code. You may have seen these codes before, written like this: #141FC4—this is a royal blue. Hexadecimal color is a 24-bit color scheme using the primary colors as its base (each color is 8 bits). The darkness to lightness of the color ranges from 0 to F, or 16 increments. The first two digits correspond to red, the second two correspond to blue, and the third two correspond to green. So, if the hexadecimal number reads #00FF00, the color would be green. A lighter green would be #009900. All white is #FFFFFF, and all black is #000000.

There are only a little more than a dozen web-safe fonts to use. When a font shows up on your browser, it is because your computer already contains the font and displays it. The font itself is not carried from the host to your browser. The three families of fonts are serif fonts, such as Times New Roman; sans-serif fonts, such as Arial; and monospace fonts, such as Courier New.

Today, the web uses HTML5 and CSS3, which means you can integrate "web-kits" that allow for more fonts and color.

Open Source

The term open source means that the user has access to the development code. Traditionally, developers who wrote programming languages would eschew sharing proprietary code in order to create competition and profit. In our current new and digital media environment, there is a push for universal access to code using a free license to the design. Coders and developers write their code in hopes of open collaboration—people who are loosely connected, with a common goal to improve products. As you'll learn later in the book, what you create falls under copyright as intellectual property; in the case of open source, coders give their material away for free.

When you rent hosting, you are given a cPanel (control panel) so that you can operate your website. The cPanel allows you to add directories and files, set up mail, build databases, install software and security, and keep track of visits. The cPanel was written under the aegis of the Apache Software Foundation, which provides software products for the public good.[4] All the parts of your cPanel are open source, and, if you build a high-level under-standing of code and programming, you can make the cPanel better.

The cPanel also provides a software installer that can install GNU General Public License software.[5] The most-used GNU software on the web for website design is WordPress. The General Public License (GPL) was implemented at the start of the World Wide Web in 1989, and, since then, the web has benefitted from collaborative web improvement.

Figure 3.9
GNU GPL.

THE CPANEL AND INSTALLING WORDPRESS

A good web developer is an organized web developer. When you design your site, you should have a structure that you can remember in your head. The index.html file should be in your main directory and your style.css page. To create a set of clean URLs, you'll need to create a new folder for each additional webpage and, in each folder, create an index.html file. This way, your URL structure shows the names of the folders, rather than the files.

    https://github.com/h5bp/html5-boilerplate

versus

    https://github.com/h5bp/html5-boilerplate.html

We recommend you become literate in the web languages of HTML and CSS, as this will greatly enhance your chances of being hired in a creative function, in no matter what industry you choose.

Regardless of how much you'd like to learn about web languages, one thing we insist you do is create your own website. If you need a site online and would like a pre-built website, you should install WordPress using the Softaculous software installer inside your cPanel. Open Softaculous, choose the directory you'd like to load your WordPress, add the site name and subtitle, and your credentials, and hit install. WordPress unpacks in your directory with all the file organization in place. As it runs on PHP, you'll notice the index pages are still there, but they end in the extension .php.

WordPress is a CMS that uses your Apache installer to load the site into your directory all at once. WordPress is the most widely used website creator, praised for its ease of use and customizability. It installs as a PHP script that includes the visual side for visitors and the administration side to add content. WordPress runs on themes that include all the design elements for layout and presentation. You can re-theme your site whenever you like, and we encourage you to try out various themes until you find one that suits your specific style.

WORDPRESS BASICS

WordPress was originally designed as a blogging platform but offers users the capability of creating either a webpage or a blog, or a combination of both. We'll go over the first few steps to customize your WordPress so you can get a site up and running.

To sign into your WordPress, you just have to add /wp-admin to the end of your URL. Once logged in, you will be at your dashboard, the main site of the CMS. WordPress comes pre-installed with a page, a post, and a comment. (You can delete these.) You should create a home page by clicking Pages > Add New and give it a title such as Home or Welcome. You should create one blog post, with an image, to get the hang of the design capabilities. Before we go any further, you should re-theme your site.

Themes

WordPress comes preloaded with the theme of the year. You should change it to something you like. Go to Appearance > Themes and locate a new one. You can go directly to the source of WordPress themes at wordpress.org/themes. When you install a theme, it comes with all of its design elements and runs your site out of the theme folder nestled deep in your cPanel directory. Nearly every theme comes with documentation (the manual) on how to operate the theme properly.

Lorem ipsum

When you use a pre-installed theme or webpage, it will very often come with Latin text in place of real text. This is called *lorem ipsum*. *Lorem ipsum* is used as a space holder to mimic actual text on a site. It's often placed in every location text will be, from metadata to keywords to body content. Make sure, before you begin advertising your site, you have removed all the *lorem ipsum*.

Permalinks

Because WordPress is PHP-based, the URLs will have a PHP structure. Posts and pages will be presented as part of the database. It will look something like this: http://newanddigital.com/?page_id=13. Those PHP URLs do not allow good search results by Google, so you should change the URLs to words. Go to Settings > Permalinks and change the links to "Post name." It should then look like this: http://newanddigital.com/book

Landing Page

When people reach your site, an introductory page that lets the visitor know who you are and what your site is about should welcome them. Go to Settings > Reading and change the settings so that Front page displays a static page and set it to your Welcome page. In that same place, you would set your blog to be displayed on a specific page.

Comments

WordPress leaves comments active on every page and post you create. The nature of the web is to inspire conversation, and, as WordPress is open source, commenting is encouraged. If you'd like to turn off the settings, you can turn them off right away by going to Settings > Discussion and unclicking all the default article settings that allow visitors to comment on your new posts and pages. You can also turn them off on a page and post basis by clicking Screen options at the top of the page you are editing, turning on the viewer for comments and discussion, scrolling down, and turning off the comments and pingbacks.

Media Management

Use the media library to load all your images and files. You can access the media library on each page or by using the library. This is where you'll keep photos, videos, and MP3s.

WORDPRESS ATTRIBUTES

The WordPress CMS is an extremely versatile system, and we recommend you take your time picking a theme and customizing the style. Visit your site on multiple browsers and portable devices, to make sure your site is compatible with various screens.

HTML5

HTML5 is the current iteration of the main web language. HTML5 is the first update of the language since 1997 and adds new tags and compatibility across multiple devices. This version includes new syntax that makes websites more responsive. Using video and audio is far easier with tags such as <video> and <audio>, and it now includes scalable vector graphics. Previous to this version, only text and ASCII graphics were scalable; now, designers can add images and new fonts that scale.

What we find really exciting about HTML5 is that it integrates JavaScript languages seamlessly into the code. You can utilize jQuery, the code that helps animate sliders, buttons, gradients, and scrolls (to name a few), inside HTML5's code. The hope in the future is that jQuery and HTML5 will be both a "back-end" programming language, like Python, as well as the "frontend" design of the website.

jQuery

jQuery is an open-source JavaScript language used by thousands of websites. It's a fairly new language, written to help users add extra features to their site with ease. As an object language, it's somewhat similar to Python and other programming languages. What's nice about jQuery is that you do not have to write it—it's already been written. You just have to use the functions that best suit your need.

Figure 3.10
Query.
Source: Fair Use Creative Commons

For example, if you want a button to grow or shrink when your mouse hovers over it, you would locate just the reference to that specific effect. In your header, beneath your link to your external CSS sheet, you would simply write the line of code: <script src="http://code.jquery.com/jquery-1.11.1.min.js"></script>. (Note: This link is constantly updated, every time the developers update the code.)

If you wanted to create a site that works offline, you can download jQuery at jquery.com. The .min.js file contains the hundreds of pages of code with the spaces and lines removed, which it keeps the file size small and compressed. As it is an open-source code, you can learn to write jQuery using dozens of sites and online courses, and we highly recommend you do so.

Additional Benefits of HTML5

Writing sites in HTML5 allows for a much higher level of flexibility across platforms. You can write floating objects into your site to create sections that appear to move separately from your site itself when seen on different screens. These pieces of code are called divs, and they can each have their own style. This even relates to how many widgets and plug-ins work along with your WordPress site.

As a code language that incorporates object-based programming, HTML5 can integrate application programming interfaces. It seamlessly allows social media sites to integrate feeds into your site or allows you to control aspects of your browser. For example, the Chrome browser is written in HTML5 and allows for projects called Chrome Experiments, which allow coders to manipulate the way the browser operates.

There have been hundreds of Chrome Experiments, and you can see them at chromeexperiments.com (http://chromeexperiments.com). There are HTML5 experiments that range from games to design to sound to interactive music videos. Our favorite project is The Arcade Fire's "The Wilderness Downtown" music video. The music video integrates moving video, graphics, Google Maps, interactive writing features, and browser movement hacks (www.thewilderness downtown.com/).

BECOMING LITERATE

Use these sites to learn more—they will enhance your skill set, make you more creative, and greatly improve your web experience:

- Code Academy (http://codeacademy.com)
- Code.org (http://code.org)
- Udemy (http://udemy.com)
- W3C Schools (http://w3cschools.com)
- Code Schools (http://codeschools.com)

See also the *Head First (Brain Friendly)* HTML guides by O'Reilly Media.

Learning these languages empowers you to read and write and create and manage and lead!

DATA, THE CLOUD, AND DIGITAL FILES

In under a minute, you can take a picture on your camera phone, post it online, and have thousands of people download it. Every time you click the shutter on your camera phone, you are creating a media file nearly instantaneously. We take for granted the amazing number of technical processes that occur in that instant and the moments that follow, from acquisition through upload to download. This section will focus on the technical side of files, sharing, and the web.

CITIZEN JOURNALISM AND THE SHARING PUBLIC

On a chilly New York City Thursday afternoon in January, a ferry full of people traversing the Hudson saw quite possibly the most frightening thing anyone could witness: a plane crashing. Captain Chesley "Sully" Sullenberger, of US Airways Flight 1549, was landing his plane on the Hudson just 6 minutes after takeoff, because the plane had hit a flock of birds. One of the ferry passengers, named Janis Krums, had the foresight to take a picture of the plane now floating in the water, extending its rafts, and uploaded the image to Twitter using a service called Twitpic. While journalists were just learning about the crash, Krums had already shown thousands of people around the world that there were survivors and the plane was intact.

Aside from the ultimately incredible cultural shift that occurred within the field of journalism, what the world was introduced to was the extraordinary capability of technology and sharing media. According to Pew, 54 percent of adult users post a photo or a video that they created to the web.[6] We have become accustomed to sharing, because it works really well and requires little-to-no effort from the user. But how does it work? How is the process so effective? Why should we think about it?

As savvy users of the web, we should be aware of what makes it work. It's important, because the technology of shareable media is most likely to be used in every industry, and your grasp of the vernacular and technique will empower you to create quality content in a world of oversaturation. The audience prefers higher-quality content and will more likely share nicer material. The term citizen journalist is used pretty freely today to mean anyone with a smartphone, and a high-quality camera (which comes with a smartphone) can report information and inform an audience. This means the traditional tools of the trade are now accessible by anyone. This is a significant shift, because the tools of a serious trade such as journalism are technology based. We know this because we can say "citizen journalist," but we cannot say "citizen surgeon."

How Does it Work?

The lens on your smartphone is an active camera. It means that the image is processed in real time on the phone. Your phone's screen acts as the viewfinder, showing you the computer processing the light in real time. As you are probably aware, a camera works by converting light, through a lens, into a range of quantitative depth, either by emulsion on film or by quantifying it through electronic data. In terms of digital photography, the image element after the lens exposes the chip to light, allowing each pixel to create a value of both color and light. The instant you press the shutter key, it records the data of each and every pixel and creates a file of all the information. In much the way that HTML cannot be read without a browser, an image needs a container.

An image captured by your phone is an EXIF. In order to be stored efficiently, it has to be compressed, and the most common compression is JPEG. The JPEG is an advanced technique of image compression that is significantly "lossless" and stores much of the original EXIF data in its file. Your smartphone didn't just capture the value of light on a digital image chip: It captured your camera settings, such as the iris setting, the shutter speed, the time of day, the type of phone you have, and, most interestingly, your GPS location. JPEG keeps this data in an effort to be shared.

The compression that we will talk about is necessary to create shareable media. The web is still limited by broadband speed and data costs. Digital compression is the act of removing redundant data that are not visible to the human eye or audible to the human ear. There is a fair amount of image data that you cannot see, and compression removes and repackages it. Compression where you cannot tell if the image or sound has changed is called lossless compression. If it seems as if there are some quality differences, that is called lossy compression. The file types you use most often attempt to preserve the high quality of the original, while simultaneously reducing the file size.

JPEG and MPEG

Have you ever wondered how file types get their names? Regardless of the fact we post one figurehead on technologies, such as Thomas Edison or Mark Zuckerberg, they do not work alone. Advanced technologies are created by groups of experts who have an extreme depth to their knowledge and a willingness to help the technology progress, as we move forward into the future.

The JPEG is short for the Joint Photographic Experts Group, and MPEG is short for the Moving Picture Experts Group. The teams created the compression algorithm, as well as efficient container files, in order to expedite the files' uploading and playing processes. They are groups of engineers who work along with the International Organization for Standardization. The upside of these containers and the teams who build them is a consistent format that almost anyone can use; the small drawback is that there is limited competition in the world of file structure and open-source progress.

The file types you most likely see consistently are .jpg, .png, .mpg, .mov, .avi, .gif, and .mp4. These are our commonest shareable file types, and that is because, in each case, they are digital data that have been compressed and placed in their container. It's important to know this, because each file type has a function and a reason for use.

Pictures

JPEGs, TIFFs, and PNGs are image format containers. Each contains image data in various ways. As opposed to the RAW format, which comprises exactly the chip data, the JPEG, the TIFF, and the PNG are all files that have been affected by algorithmic quantizing. A RAW file can be huge, because it accounts for all the data from the chip, and each and every pixel is accounted for. Whereas a RAW image file may be about 40 megabytes, the same image compressed as a JPEG would be 3 or 4 megabytes. The reason the JPEG is commonest is because it uses an advanced algorithm called a discrete cosine transform that discards "extra" data and duplicates simple data. It's not a perfect algorithm, and occasionally online images look blocky.[7]

TIFF and PNG are raster graphic image formats (meaning that they are made with pixels) that also compress image data in different ways. TIFF was created by Adobe in the early 1990s, and PNG is an advance of the GIF format. Both of these allow for something called an "alpha" channel. The TIFF and PNG contain an additional 8 bits of information for the sake of a transparency channel. This allows the graphics to be used on top of other images. The extra bits act as a faux layer to support the invisibility.

The GIF

The GIF is one of the earliest file types of the web. In its earliest days, the GIF was invented as a raster-based graphic, like its TIFF and PNG successors. It was designed to compress an image to allow for faster loading speeds. The added benefit of the GIF was the fact that the image could be animated and endlessly looped.

The GIF is lightweight, requires no plug-ins, and is compatible with all devices. In the days of the early web, the only comparable data type was the Adobe Flash file, but the GIF doesn't require plug-ins to operate and takes up minimal processing power. Utilized in early online web communities such as Tripod and Geocities, and made popular through image forums such as 4chan and ytmnd, the GIF boils down video to the most essential moments and loops them infinitely, and they play automatically.

The Tumblr community latched onto the GIF because of the vast number of niche interests and communities that can benefit from a looping animation—from tutorials, to explainers, to fandom, to art, to humor. The repetition is the reason why GIFs are so popular online. Users make GIFs of screen grabs from films, caption television shows, create moving memes, and even make GIFs on apps such as Phhhoto and Cinemagram. The reaction GIF has solidified itself in our online culture, and there have even been several museum shows to explain how the reaction GIF is now part of our online language.[8]

Sound

The commonest and most recognizable file type for sound is the MP3. What's amazing about the MP3 is that it doesn't exist as an audio format! The MP3 is actually part of the MPEG family, and it is one of the most lossy compressions that exist. The MP3 gets its name from being a MPEG-1 (or MPEG-2) Audio Layer 3. (MPEG-3 is an unused HDTV format.) This audio format was the commonest digital audio format of the early web, as the compression allowed users to download complete songs fairly quickly. The audio quality varied according to the bit rate used in the compression. The higher the bit rates per second, the higher the quality (as in 128 kilobits per second, or 192 kbps). Audio compression introduced new ways to compress files using bit rates. You can compress audio using a constant bit rate (CBR) or a variable bit rate (VBR). In CBR compression, you pick the bit rate, and the audio is compressed using that quality, regardless of what occurs in the file. If a piece of audio or music changes wildly in the track, with additional bass or tempo variations, quality will sometimes be lost. The VBR compression allows the compression software to adapt and vary, based on the changes in the file. VBR compression usually results in larger file sizes than CBR compression.

Musicians and sound artists require higher-quality audio, and the audio format that is the highest quality is the MPEG-4. The MP4 file type is for audio and video and, when it is used for audio, the file extension is sometimes seen as .m4a.

Video

Video files are the most complex file formats, requiring heavy processing power to compress the many images without losing too much quality. Video contains images in succession, linked sound, graphics, and metadata combined. Originally, video was compressed using a streaming CBR method as it was digitized from analog sources onto a storage system such as a hard drive.

The downside of this was a high loss of video information, as well as something called video artifacting. When video was primarily interlaced for television broadcasts, the interlaced fields would complicate the digitizing process. In our present, the vast majority of video is progressive, or image sequenced. When video is captured, the succession of video and audio is captured onto a storage device such as an SD card. As soon as the record button stops the recording, the video file is created, and the compression process has already occurred. In order for video to fit onto anything, it needs to be compressed. Each camera and company has its own compression algorithm and file type, using various bit rates (for color depth) and resolutions.

A lot of data and math is required to understand how big a file size of video may be. You would have to consider the resolution (per frame), which is acquired by multiplying the height and the width of the pixels, the bit rate of the video, and how long the clip is. This information matters, because sometimes you will be told a camera offers high-quality video, but it contains a low bit rate, thereby reducing its quality. If you had a Vine video, at 600 {mult} 600 resolution, that lasted 6 seconds, you would find 360,000 pixels per frame of video. Multiply that by 30 frames per second, and you have 64.8 million pixels to compress. And if you imagine that as a low-quality Vine, imagine high-definition or 4K video streams and how their file sizes even manage to move around the web.

The iPhone video camera captures at 1080p HD, which is the same as video you watch on your big television screen. How does it fit all that video onto your phone? The bit rate is low, at only 17 mbps, in comparison with the 50 mbps of standard television. This allows for faster capture and smaller sizes. The file container from an iPhone is a .mov, which is QuickTime's (Apple) native format. If you create video on a PC, often it will be a .avi. Neither .avi nor .mov are universal, and they both require plug-ins and software to operate on various machines. The web is attempting a universal video standard for HTML5, using MPEG-4 compression and leaving the files with an .mp4 extension.

CODECS

A codec is actually a software device that allows for data to be <u>c</u>ompressed and <u>dec</u>ompressed for viewing and use. There are hundreds of codecs for hundreds of uses, from web standards to broadcast settings to streaming configurations. When you are chosing a codec, the most important part of the choice would concern utility. If you happen to be editing a film to be seen on a large screen, you would want access to the highest-quality codec available—something like ProRes 422. If you are shooting for a YouTube video, you can use a highly efficient, lossless codec such as H.264 to create high-quality, small-file-size videos.

The Algorithm and EXIF Data

The EXIF data used in photographs can also be used for image data analysis. Facebook uses EXIF data to process and recognize your face in order to assist with the photo tagging process. It may sound creepy, but your face is like a digital thumbprint that has been quantized the minute you uploaded your first photo. Facebook used the image data to measure the distance between your eyes and your nose and mouth, and now, every time you or your friends upload an image to Facebook, it already knows who should be tagged.[9] Digital data form a very powerful tool that can be used for the good of people, but also could someday be used to sell you products in real life, if a store was equipped with facial-recognition cameras.

THE CLOUD

During the earliest days of machine computing, a man named Gordon Moore observed that transistor technology was increasing exponentially in both storage and physical size. He posited that computer speed and storage would double every 2 years. Moore's Law, as it is known, was not only highly accurate, but continues to work, from our present into our future. Where Moore considered the doubling would be exponential every 2 years, it also compressed time itself exponentially, from 2 years, to 1 year, to months, weeks, days, minutes, and so on. In our data-heavy present, we are creating more than 2.5 exabytes (2.5 billion gigabytes) of data on a daily basis.[10] We call this "big data."

Data are made up of every bit of digital information that you have access to, utilize, create, and share. Our personal hard drives are limited in capacity, and so we are now utilizing the cloud far more often. The cloud is slang for cloud computing, a method of using computers tied together via the Internet, rather than through a local area network. As cloud computing has become streamlined, with high broadband speeds and very low risk of crash and server downtime, we have started to store our data in servers far from our personal computer.

This has allowed superior sharing efficiency and remote-access ability. Many businesses, such as IBM and Google, are reliant on the cloud to maintain daily operations. Access to data in the cloud is an incredible boon to network operations, and, without it, social media would not function well.

Big Data

In *Everything is Miscellaneous*,[11] David Weinberger explains about the overwhelming amount of data that is available online: "In a store, it's easy to tell the labels from the goods they label, and in a library the books and their metadata are kept in separate rooms. But it's not so clear online." The analogy proposed is that, on the web, everything is searchable by all of its data. For his example, he uses Shakespeare. If you only remember a line from a Shakespeare play, you can type it into Google, and Google will return, not just the surrounding text, but the play in its entirety, all its editions, all the performances, the playbills, the characters, and the actors. Each and every word ever digitized constitutes the data of any given object.

The web is a huge archive of all material, converted to digital media, and it is up to the users to parse the information. It's important for you, as a web user, to consider why data is made available and what you do to use it. For example, you can read data that is available to you on nearly everything. If you wanted to know how often a word is used in texts, you can use Google's Ngram viewer[12] (*n* equals sample; gram means word). Google has archived enough available text to show you how prevalently terms, phrases, and words have been used since the year 1800. If you were to search the 2-gram phrase "new media" in the viewer, you would see a steady incline of the term since 1920, with a dip in the 1970s. This trend analysis can assist with research and applications to enhance your collective knowledge on a given subject. You can also use wildcards to show what words are used most often. For example, a search for "digital *" results in the most-used combinations where the word "digital" precedes another word. The top usage has been "digital computers," but, in the recent past, that has been surpassed by "digital data" and "digital signal."

Data is also available to you in ways that you may not realize. When we share web media on social media platforms, we usually copy and paste a link into the share area. Sometimes, the link is very large, spanning hundreds of characters. Each link refers to a file on a hard drive somewhere, and that means it is sometimes buried deep in a database or directory structure. To make links

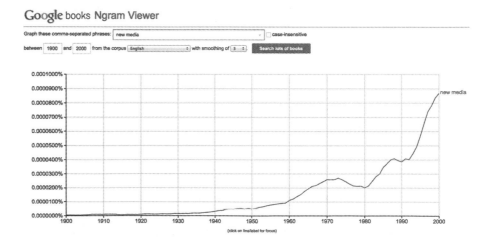

Figure 3.11

Ngram viewer 1: "new media."

Source: https://books.google. com/ngrams

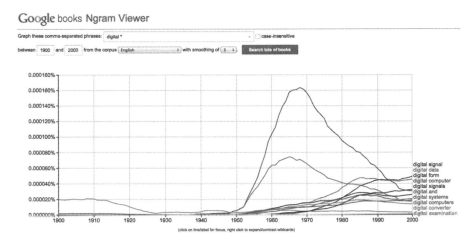

Figure 3.12

*Ngram viewer 2: "digital *."*

Source: https://books.google. com/ngrams

more efficient, URL shorteners can be used, such as TinyURL, Bit.ly, and Owl.ly. These are sites that have purchased the shortest domain name and extension available, and they place your link in their own folder to redirect to your original link. If you had a long link from the Ngram results and you wanted it shortened, you could paste the link in Bit.ly, and it would create a customizable link, such as bit.ly/ngramdigital. The bit link created a 19-character link out of a 471-character link. However, that is only half the story. On any shortened URL, you can gain access to the link's statistics. Big data isn't just about storing data: It's about analyzing it. By adding a plus symbol (+) to the end of any shortened URL, you can see how many people have clicked on that link.

Reading big data is big business. Since the beginning of online digital media, people have profited from data analysis. You do not have to be a statistics professional to read big data either: You just have to have a creative mind. Every time you visit a site and it downloads a cookie or a pixel onto your computer or you click a shortened URL, you are being tracked. As a result, users such as yourself can get a better feel for how well you are participating in the online environment. It's like a huge, mechanical, peer-review system. Most users never take advantage of being able to read their analytics, because numbers sometimes seem overwhelming, but you should take advantage of the technology available to you.

How Long Do Data Exist?

Our digital present and the ever-expanding world of storage show us that anything that is made digital can last forever. Even apps such as Snapchat, which delete media soon after they are shared, are vulnerable to someone taking a screenshot of the image and keeping it. Once it is on the web, it is stored somewhere in the cloud. But the thing about data is that the volume keeps growing. This means that, the more data added, the bigger the cloud; the bigger the cloud, the less significant any single file is. You will learn later in the book how to keep data showing up in search engines, because, although something may be around forever, it doesn't mean it is easily accessible forever.

It is possible to lose your own personal data very easily, and this is why many users have turned to the cloud for storage. If you delete something on your computer, it disappears for good—or so we think. In truth, when you delete something, it actually is not deleted right away. Your computer doesn't delete files; it re-allocates the space for rewriting over the media. In theory, if you accidently delete something, you can retrieve it. It's usually a costly experience, but it's possible to bring it back.

Where Can I Store My Files?

The cloud has an abundance of "free storage" where you can store your digital files. Sites such as Picasa and Flickr host photos and videos, and Dropbox, Bitcasa, and Google Drive can host files. Each offer different services and rights concerning how your content is stored and for how long, and how the files are maintained. Dropbox and Flickr offer their users an allotted number of gigabytes to store their material for free, and they also offer a premium service that allows users to pay for more storage. Why do they have two options? Doesn't storage *always* cost money? The answer is yes—storage always costs money. The reason Dropbox and Flickr offer free storage is because the average user will never come close to their upload limit, and the companies can still count the uploader as a user. If you are given 10 gigabytes for free from Dropbox, you may only upload 1 gigabyte over a few months, but Dropbox can still count you as one of their dedicated users. As we remind you, nothing is free.

Can I Track Data?

There are many free or low-cost data-tracking options online. One even comes with your cPanel when you host a site called Webalyzer. The most popular analyzer is Google Analytics. Google Analytics offers free tracking of your website, with accurate reporting of site visits using Google's software and technology. You have to register your site with Google, and it will generate a short bit of JavaScript for you to paste into the bottom of your code on your site. (It's on the bottom because, as you will remember, the site loads from top to bottom and will register a visit only after the page has fully loaded.) You can use the Google Analytics dashboard to track your visits and set goals. You can track nearly everything you upload online, and we recommend you do so.

How Can I Read Data?

When we look at data, we are looking at a combination of numerical information. The data alone are sometimes too large to read as raw information. We rely on data analyzers to parse the information. Very often, the data are presented in reports, for the audience to read. Although raw data don't lie, the report author or reporter often introduces bias into how they are presented. You, as a savvy web user, should never take data reports as is and should always consider where the information comes from.

How to detect data manipulation?

If data are presented as a study, look at the sample size (that's usually the "n") of the data acquired. If it's a small amount, take into consideration that it may not represent the general population.

Check the demographic of the information and see if the data were gathered from a location with similar types of information with low diversity. This often means the data were "gamed" to look a certain way.

Look for missing or questionable data. If something seems obviously to be missing, it may have been either never researched or removed.

It's possible there may be "false equivalents" in the data—correlation does not mean causation. For example, there was once a study that said, "One minute of video is equal to 1.8 million words," without explaining how this data was configured.[13] This is an amazing piece of data that would make any digital media meeting far better if you were pitching digital video as your promotion plan. Gary Paul debunked this data set by doing simple math: If a "picture is worth 1,000 words," and there are 30 pictures every second, and there are 60 seconds in 1 minute, this results in 1.8 million words. This is data that was manipulated, and you should be aware that this happens all the time.

THE INTERNET OF THINGS

We end this chapter with physical objects. To be a savvy user of new and digital media, you should be aware that the Internet is expanding outward and into machines connected to the cloud. Every time you use a device that requires an app on your phone or computer to operate it, you are using the web and the Internet on a physical object. The Nike Fuelband, the Nest Thermostat, and your Xbox One are all objects that require an app or the Internet in order to operate. As we use the web and the cloud, we have found convenience in our devices that can be tracked on a dashboard interface. The Fuelband doesn't have an advanced screen or interface, and Nike's app that accompanies it is actually the screen for the device. The Nest is really one of the best examples, because it is a thermostat you can control from work or on the go. Nest was purchased by Google, so that it could blend it into its architecture and utilize the technologies.

The web is still a browser-based experience, but many technologies are now using the browser as their screen. Rather than incorporate dated LED technology, why not connect the device via Wi-Fi or Bluetooth and use a display that is already available. The web offers endless options to customize, view, and optimize the experience of the physical object. The fact that this physical object requires the Web in order to operate means that, the savvier you become at using the web, the more likely you are to interact with future technology.

NOTES

1   EMC Digital Universe (2014). "Executive Summary: Data growth, business opportunities, and the IT imperatives." Retrieved from www.emc.com/leadership/digital-universe/2014iview/executive-summary.htm (accessed May 4, 2015).

2   Rogers, S. (2012). "Data Are or Data Is?" Retrieved from www.theguardian.com/news/datablog/2010/jul/16/data-plural-singular (accessed May 4, 2015).

3   Presnsky, M. (2001). "Digital Natives, Digital Immigrants." Retrieved from www.marcprensky.com/writing/Prensky%20-%20Digital%20Natives,%20Digital%20Immigrants%20-%20Part1.pdf (accessed May 4, 2015).

4   Apache.org main page (www.apache.org/).

5   GNU Operating System (www.gnu.org/copyleft/gpl.html).

6   Duggan, M. (2013). "Photo and Video Sharing Grow Online." Retrieved from www.pewinternet.org/2013/10/28/photo-and-video-sharing-grow-online/ (accessed May 4, 2015).

7   Caplan, P. (2013). "What Is a JPEG? The invisible object you see everyday." Retrieved from www.theatlantic.com/technology/archive/2013/09/what-is-a-jpeg-the-invisible-object-you-see-every-day/279954/ (accessed May 4, 2015).

8   The Museum of the Moving Image (2014). "The Reaction GIF: Moving image as gesture." March 12—May 15. Retrieved from www.movingimage.us/exhibitions/2014/03/12/detail/the-reaction-gif-moving-image-as-gesture/ (accessed May 4, 2015).

9   Warzel, C. (2014). "This Is What Facebook Sees When it Scans Your Face." Retrieved from www.buzzfeed.com/charliewarzel/this-is-what-facebook-sees-when-it-scans-your-face (accessed May 4, 2015).

10   Wall, M. (2014). "Big Data: Are you ready for blast-off?" Retrieved from www.bbc.com/news/business-26383058 (accessed May 4, 2015).

11   Weinberger, D. (2008). *Everything Is Miscellaneous: The power of the new digital disorder*. New York: Holt Paperbacks.

12 Michel, J.-B., Shen, Y.K., Aiden, A.P., Veres, A., Gray, M.K., The Google Books Team, Pickett, J.P., Hoiberg, D., Clancy, D., Norvig, P., Orwant, J, Pinker, S., Nowak, M.A., and Aiden, E.L. (2010). "Quantitative Analysis of Culture Using Millions of Digitized Books." *Science*. Vol. 331 No. 6014, pp. 179–182. Retrieved from www.sciencemag.org/content/early/2010/12/15/science.1199644 (accessed May 4, 2015).

13 Paul, G. (2013). 1 minute of video is worth 1.8 million words: Misinformation or hyperbole? Retrieved from http://gary-paul.com/ (accessed May 11, 2015).

CHAPTER 4

Memes and Visual Online Languages

During the second 2012 presidential debate at Hofstra University, many engaged citizens were tuned in and watching how Governor Mitt Romney was faring against incumbent candidate President Barack Obama. Veronica DeSouza was one of the viewers of the debate and was especially proud because the event was taking place at her alma mater. Recently unemployed, Veronica took to social media to promote her personal brand and she decided to live tweet the debate to her followers. About an hour into the debate, moderator Candy Crowley asked Governor Romney about pay equity for women: Romney responded with a comment about qualified women candidates and then said his now infamous quote: "I went to a number of women's groups and said: 'Can you help us find folks?' And they brought us whole binders full of women."

Veronica reacted by going immediately to Tumblr to register the URL bindersfullofwomen.tumblr.com. She made a crude Photoshopped image of a set of women in an open binder and posted it on her Tumblr.[1] Within the first hour, Veronica's blog attracted 8,000 new followers and had over 1,800

Figure 4.1
Binders full of women, by Veronica DeSouza.

submissions by the next day.[2] The meme was born, and several Twitter accounts appeared, as did a Facebook page, and even a political action campaign got in on the meme.[3] Two weeks later, Veronica was employed at Digg, and her meme lives on as one of the memorable moments of the 2012 presidential campaign.

WHAT'S A MEME?

When we asked a group of students what they thought a meme was, the majority responded with their favorite image macro—Bad Luck Brian, Most Interesting Man, Success Kid. What many didn't realize is that they had used the term "meme" to describe just one small example of memes. This chapter will focus on a different type of media literacy and the theory of memes in visual culture that derive from a new and digital environment. Memes have been around for as long as there have been humans. It is derived from the Ancient Greek term *mimeme*, which means "imitated thing," and Richard Dawkins updated the term in 1976 in his book *The Selfish Gene*. Dawkins's adaptation of the word "meme" is designed to be similar to "gene," because a meme is defined as "an idea, behavior, or style that spreads from person to person within a culture"[4] and has a path of evolution and change.

Dawkins recognized that, in an age of visual culture, culture could be transmitted rapidly from person to person and mind to mind. The meme is the genetics of the "abstract kingdom" of the mind, and strands of that kingdom are ideas.[5] The idea itself is a meme and can most easily be described as something abstract shared between a group of people who understand the idea and cause the idea to replicate, thereby causing it to evolve and mutate. Have you ever had an inside joke between a group of friends? That's kind of like a meme. You can refer to the joke, and several people around you may understand the meaning, but those outside the idea are left without the information. The idea can morph into various forms of new and digital material, such as image macros, videos, GIFs, or messages on social media.

Dawkins continues to explain, in *The Selfish Gene*, that a meme has three properties that ensure its spread across the web and into culture: longevity, fecundity, and copy fidelity.[6] In other words, it has to last long enough to merge into our thoughts, outside its original context; it needs to be replicated in a given amount of time; and it requires the audience to collectively agree on its accuracy and fidelity to the original. Although memes are created online and exist in a microenvironment, they have a macro effect on the way people think, behave, and act socially.[7] Memes, like ideas, do not appear in a vacuum: They are part of a cultural process of interpretation, dissemination, revision, and agreement.

Memes compete for attention and they live by being referred to and continually used. After a meme has run its course, it may fall out of style or relegate itself to an older reference, no longer needed in popular culture. Take, for example, the term "jump the shark." The term has come to mean the moment a television series takes a twist or new story path, alienating enough of the audience to cause a drop in viewership. In our streaming media present, the term is rarely used, as the audience is looking for more niche material (more on this in Chapter 6). The term "jump the shark" originated in the television series *Happy Days* in 1977, when The Fonz, dressed in his leather jacket, literally jumped the shark during a water-ski jump, in the episode "Hollywood: Part 3." From that point forward, it was difficult to take the show seriously, and, simultaneously, the phrase "jump the shark" was coined. With its lack of use in today's vernacular, the term is no longer widely employed or understood by a large group of people.

Memes have evolved and changed and mutated throughout all of history. The meme can travel without visual culture, as it can be transported with mimicry and imitation, but, in this chapter, we will focus on memes and language derived from a new and digital media visual culture. Images and visual media are stronger at delivering messages in a meme-like manner. As Susan Sontag explains in *Regarding the Pain of Others* (2003), visuals have a more highly significant effect on an audience, because the visuals create a "synthesis" that connects the image to the actual event through reproduced representation.[8] Memes such as "Binders Full of Women" have significant beginnings and endings (the debate through the presidential election), and some continue for years as part of the way the web's community members communicate (doge, lolcats). Memes fight for survival in the hypermedia landscape of the web and are rarely mourned when they slowly move out of current popular culture. Our intention is to inform you of the various different types of meme used in the online space and the origins to some of the most popular visual memes.

We will focus on the proper meme grammar and linguistics of memes and how these rules are established and enforced. As a user of the web, your ability to read and create memes will make you an asset to the digital media environment and, as in Veronica's case, can lead to a career possibility. Your ability to understand the web better will make you a better participant and a highly engaged user capable of creating original media.

Know Your Meme

Memes have been researched academically since Richard Dawkins's *The Selfish Gene* (1976). KnowYourMeme.com (http://knowyourmeme.com) is one online source, above all others (including Wikipedia), that researches memes and online culture. You should frequent the site quite often if you are interested in memes and their function. The site was created in 2008 and later became part of the Cheezburger meme network. As with most Internet databases, you are encouraged to submit information and "Internet phenomena" to the site to add to the research.[9]

I CAN HAZ MEMES?

We're not sure what the fascination with cats is either, but, contrary to popular belief, using cats in visual culture didn't start when the World Wide Web began. In the earliest days of photography, people dressed cats and photographed them. In 1905, photographer Harry Whittier Frees photographed cats for post-cards with witty and cute captions underneath them. Even earlier, Thomas Edison had several cats box each other on film in 1894.[10] The fascination with cats obviously predates visual media (see Ancient Egypt) and it directly pervaded our modern media environment.

In 2006, a community member of the 4chan message boards posted a picture of a chubby grey cat smiling (yelling?) as an image macro, with the words "I CAN HAZ CHEEZBURGER?" written across it in white Impact font with a black border (stroke). It began, not only a style of image macro involving cats, but also a meme language known as "lol speak" or "kitty pidgin," and all it requires is a user to Photoshop some poor grammar and misspellings onto a picture of a cat. The thought process is that the text is actually coming from the inner monologue of a cat—and cats can't spell or write well. Lev Grossman covered the meme in 2007 and explained that the meme became a "running gag that

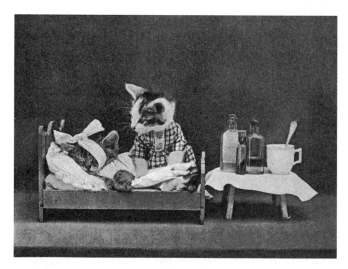

Figure 4.2
Harry Whittier Frees cat dinner postcard—1905.

Figure 4.3

A lolcat having an issue with focus.

Source: Wikimedia Commons—GNU

won't stop running, but instead reproduces and mutates in the petri dish of the Net's collective imagination."[11]

To participate in this meme requires an understanding of the linguistic nature of the meme itself. Not only do you have to imagine the cat speaking, but you also have to make the text apply appropriately to the image. If a cat is jumping, you can add the text INVISIBLE BIKE to add humor. Grossman also explains that it's easier to show lolcats than explain it, so it's in your best interest to simply Google lolcats in the image search. The search will return thousands of images with lolcats, and you will see a variety of image macros that have been made in this meme.

VISUAL LANGUAGE

We'll start with image macros, because they are possibly the easiest entry point to our discussion on memes. An image macro is simply an image (usually agreed upon by the web community) with additional text added for humorous effect. Memes are part of the visual language, which means that explaining them in text will not offer a clean interpretation. The language of meme requires the viewer to participate in the understanding of the meme for it to continue to be used. The image macro was originally used on message boards and forums, where the image could be seen, altered, and customized to explain an emotion or a feeling.

Image macros condense long responses into a singular file that displays a mood or feeling regarding a response. For example, there's a picture of a cat pushing away from someone's hands trying to pet it, and the text simply says: "DO NOT WANT!" That image macro can then be used as a response to someone's post, instead of text explaining a reason to not want something. Sound familiar? It should: You do the same thing with emojis and emoticons.

Emoticons and Emojis

One of the biggest downsides of digital culture is transmission loss of meaning and depth in text in short messages. For example, when you text someone, it is nearly impossible to express sarcasm without saying that your statement is meant to be sarcastic or ironic. Mood and meaning are lost without assistance. As we speak in the first person on text and on Twitter, we lack the narrator's assistance in providing additional meaning. Today, we show our mood and meaning by using emoticons and emojis, small iconographic cartoon faces and icons that assist in our messages. As Scott McCloud says in *Understanding Comics* (1993): "We don't just observe the cartoon, we become it."[12]

Use of the emoticon began in 1982 at Carnegie Mellon University, to help distinguish funny posts on message boards from serious posts.[13] To post funny information, you can use :-), and, for serious information, use :-(. In our present, software and operating systems convert our emoticons to "smileys" and more iconographic imagery. The emoji has a Japanese origin, meaning picture character, and they are created using ASCII code. Unlike emoticons, which can be created by using colons, semicolons, parentheses, letters, and brackets, the emoji is created with code to be translated by the operating system. This offers far more images and meanings than simple emoticons, and their growing variety has created meme-like qualities of imitation in real life and online.

Image Macros

The image macro isn't just constrained to lolcats, and you can come across any number of image memes online, from Bad Luck Brian, who exemplifies a young man with the worst possible luck ever, to Condescending Willy Wonka, who is mean spirited and sarcastic. In the nature of memes, not everyone will know all the memes, but some will understand the ones they like—like an inside joke, or a "selfish gene."

What's nice about memes and image macros is that any user can participate in the creation process. When lolcats appeared in the mid 2000s, they were a participatory, inside joke. Aaron Rutkoff wrote in the *Wall Street Journal* (2007) that lolcats are appealing because they are simultaneously obscure and accessible. Lolcats didn't just start the image macro trend: They changed the language on the visual web. Technologist and entrepreneur Anil Dash explained to Rutkoff that, "an in-joke used to be constrained by geography and who you knew socially," but lolcats are a "very large in-joke" that blurs the lines between the geeks and the passive users.[14]

There's nearly an image macro for every reason, and, if there isn't, it will soon be there. Image macros take very little skill to create—you can use Photoshop and Impact font or you can use a meme generator online. The difficulty of image macro memes is the proper grammar. You can't just write anything on an image macro. In most cases, the image macro is built like a haiku in format: text/image/text. The text at the top is the set-up, and the image relates to the text punch line at the bottom. For example, if you'd like to ponder something irreverently philosophical, you can use the "Philosoraptor" image macro to ask the question. Philosoraptor is one of the "advice animals" image macros, which range from "Advice Dog" to "Courage Wolf." Philosoraptor allows the user to ask a question such as, "If the opposite of pro is con/Is the opposite of progress congress?" or "Why do people say the sky's the limit/When there are footprints on the moon?"

The skill in image macros lies in the appropriate pace and delivery of the joke. They have a grammar that behaves like a comedian's punch-line set-up but requires the image to support the joke. Therefore, if you are using

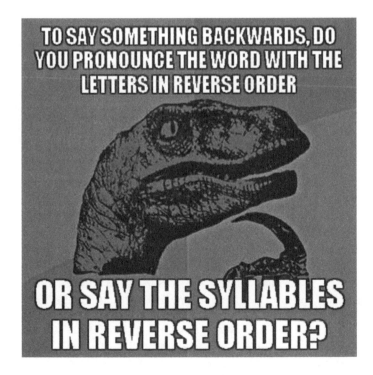

Figure 4.4

Philosoraptor considering pronunciation.

Source: Creative Commons

"Success Kid," you have to make sure your message is related to success, such as, "Plugged in USB in the dark/Went in on the first try." The word success is never said, because the image of the young boy fist-pumping complements the message. There is a grammar to each and every image macro meme that requires the user to study the technique before posting. If you happen to do it wrong, you will most definitely find out your mistake right away, from web commenters or trolling users.

Trolls and Memes

We feel it is extremely important to mention that the source of many memes is 4chan.org. Although you have learned that the site is a forum for the group Anonymous and is also known as a "meme factory," it also creates a vast number of inappropriate memes and encourages troll memes. Many memes we do not encourage are from the sites "rage comics" and "troll faces," as they are often used in combination with mean and derogatory posts on the web. Be careful when using troll memes or any imagery that attempts to subjugate an online group of people. In other words: Create and participate and play nicely. The one group that will absolutely let you know you have used a meme inappropriately is the trolls.

THE LANGUAGE

Humans are born with language capability as a part of their survival and communication. Web and social technologies have their own specific languages as a result of their limitations and creative misuse. Text messages, or the Short Message Service (SMS) feature, on your mobile device may be new to the technology, but short-form language dates back to the telegraph, when users had to pay by the character. The same applies to text messaging that limits the character count to 160 characters. This caused the impetus to shorten text to allow for more information to be contained in any given message.

The shortened language of "txtspk" is condensed wording. The language is a community-agreed-upon short form that abbreviates and creates terminology for speaking. Everyone knows LOL for "laugh out loud" and BRB for "be right back", but there are hundreds of other acronyms and condensed words.[15] JK denotes "just kidding," NAGI is "not a good idea," and NSFW means "not safe for work"; if it gets bad enough, there's even NSFL—"not safe for life"! Many users are accustomed to using this language nearly instinctually, because it's become part of the common style of communication.

How to Make an Image Macro

If you are using Photoshop, you can often find a meme template online that is usually higher in resolution and comes with the blank areas for text. Use the font Impact with a 2–3-pixel black stroke and write in your text on the image, in the haiku style of text, image, and text. There are also several meme generators online that will create the meme for you but will leave their watermark on the image. Some choices online are memegenerator.net and quickmeme.com

Lolspeak

One of the earliest image macros appeared when a user uploaded a picture of a wide-eyed owl with one simple line of text "O RLY?" and it joined the language and growth of the meme language of lolcats. Lolcat language was designed to be coming directly from the cat's mind. In lolspeak, the language could be used on any image or meme.[16] If you find similar faces to the shocked owl's, you can place the "O RLY?" text on it, and it will work. Then, it entered common vernacular when people started using lolspeak in common language. Instead of saying "Hello," you could mimic the cat and say "Oh Hai!", and it wouldn't confuse the user if they were aware of the original meme. Eventually, lolspeak was used so often that it didn't require knowledge of the original meme and could be used on text messages and emails during normal friendly conversation.

Lolspeak is its own language and is separate from earlier geek languages or hacker slang such as L337 ("leet" or elite) speak. Lolspeak is a community-organized language and, through the act of the meme, it has created its own remixable products. The most extensive of these is the Lolcat Bible, a collaborative wiki organized by Martin Grondin in 2007 that translated the Old and New Testaments into lolspeak. Using lolcat characters in place of biblical figures, the web community created one of the strangest alterations of the English language ever produced. Lolspeak even has academic discourse, and, according to a paper by Lauren Gawne and Jill Vaughan (2012):

> LOLspeak reflects the asynchronous style used in the local discourse context of LOL-based Internet sites. The original image macros and the LOLcat Bible are both non-dyadic communicative styles—along with the asynchronous nature, this meant that people had time to compose their utterances.[17]

The Lolcats Bible[18]

Genesis 1

Boreded Ceiling Cat makinkgz Urf n stuffs

1 Oh hai. In teh beginnin Ceiling Cat maded teh skiez An da Urfs, but he did not eated dem.

2 Da Urfs no had shapez An haded dark face, An Ceiling Cat rode invisible bike over teh waterz.

3 At start, no has lyte. An Ceiling Cat sayz, i can haz lite? An lite wuz.4 An Ceiling Cat sawed teh lite, to seez stuffs, An splitted teh lite from dark but taht wuz ok cuz kittehs can see in teh dark An not tripz over nethin.5 An Ceiling Cat sayed light Day An dark no Day. It were FURST!!!1

6 An Ceiling Cat sayed, im in ur waterz makin a ceiling. But he no yet make a ur. An he maded a hole in teh Ceiling.7 An Ceiling Cat doed teh skiez with waterz down An waterz up. It happen.8 An Ceiling Cat sayed, i can has teh firmmint wich iz funny bibel naim 4 ceiling, so wuz teh twoth day.

9 An Ceiling Cat gotted all teh waterz in ur base, An Ceiling Cat hadz dry placez cuz kittehs DO NOT WANT get wet.10 An Ceiling Cat called no waterz urth and waters oshun. Iz good.

11 An Ceiling Cat sayed, DO WANT grass! so tehr wuz seedz An stufs, An fruitzors An vegbatels. An a Corm. It happen.12 An Ceiling Cat sawed that weedz ish good, so, letz there be weedz.13An so teh threeth day jazzhands.

14 An Ceiling Cat sayed, i can has lightz in the skiez for splittin day An no day.15 It happen, lights everwear, like christmass, srsly.16 An Ceiling Cat doeth two grate lightz, teh most big for day, teh other for no day.17 An Ceiling Cat screw tehm on skiez, with big nails An stuff, to lite teh Urfs.18 An tehy rulez day An night. Ceiling Cat sawed. Iz good.19 An so teh furth day w00t.

20 An Ceiling Cat sayed, waterz bring me phishes, An burds, so kittehs can eat dem. But Ceiling Cat no eated dem.21 An Ceiling Cat maed big fishies An see monstrs, which wuz like big cows, except they no mood, An other stuffs dat mooves, An Ceiling Cat sawed iz good.22 An Ceiling Cat sed O hai, make bebehs kthx. An dont worry i wont watch u secksy, i not that kynd uf kitteh.23An so teh...fith day. Ceiling Cat taek a wile 2 cawnt.

24 An Ceiling Cat sayed, i can has MOAR living stuff, mooes, An creepie tings, An otehr aminals. It happen so tehre.25 An Ceiling Cat doed moar living stuff, mooes, An creepies, An otehr animuls, An did not eated tehm.

26 An Ceiling Cat sayed, letz us do peeps like uz, becuz we ish teh qte, An let min p0wnz0r becuz tehy has can openers.

27 So Ceiling Cat createded teh peeps taht waz like him, can has can openers he maed tehm, min An womin wuz maeded, but he did not eated tehm.

28 An Ceiling Cat sed them O hai maek bebehs kthx, An p0wn tch watorz, no waterz An teh firmmint, An evry stufs.

29 An Ceiling Cat sayed, Beholdt, the Urfs, I has it, An I has not eated it.30 For evry createded stufs tehre are the fuudz, to the burdies, teh creepiez, An teh mooes, so tehre. It happen. Iz good.

31 An Ceiling Cat sayed, Beholdt, teh good enouf for releaze as version 0.8a. kthxbai.

(Made available and used with the GNU Free Documentation License)

Doge and Doge Speak

In an age of memes and digital communities, languages have lifespans. In February 2010, a Japanese kindergarten teacher named Atsuko Sato posted pictures of her new dog, a Shiba Inu named Kabosu, online.[19] In one of the pictures, Kabosu was giving a side glare, and the picture ended up on a subreddit to be shared with the other users, under the term "doge." In December 2012, the picture ended up in another subreddit called /r/DogsI WannaHug, and someone posted it with a different type of inner monologue speak, using an entirely new convention. Rather than Impact font, the new font was Comic Sans, written in several places in multiple fluorescent colors.

The doge meme changes the language of lolspeak and lolcats into a new, original form of internal monologue talk.[20] Whereas the cats spoke in poorly written full sentences, doge (and dogs) speaks in a happy and surprised, short, broken English. The image of the Shiba Inu dog, superimposed with the Comic Sans text saying things such as, "Wow," "So scare," "What r you doing?", "Concern," "Keep ur hands away from me," comes from an odd Tumblr called Shiba Confessions.[21] In terms of how to use the language, you have to identify the content of the image and then separate out the words and qualify them with "so," "such," "many," "much," and "very" added. The doge meme

Figure 4.5
*Doge meme
(not the original).*

Source: Creative
Commons

went in two immediate directions—one involved adding text to dog images, and the other involved adding doge speak to any image, from sports to food to politics.[22]

Linguist Gretchen McCulloch explained, in 2014, that the doge speak can be broken down into "doge phrases," such as "such fall," "many happy," and "much feels," and "doge words," such as "wow," "amaze," and "excite."[23] McCulloch says that any sentence could be converted to doge speak. Using her example, we can convert our previous sentence to this: "Much McCulloch" "So sentence" "very conversion" "Wow." With a little practice, you can do it as well. When Reddit users were put to the task, they translated Romeo and Juliet to doge speak.

What light. So breaks. Such east. Very sun. Wow, Juliet.
What Romeo. Such why. Very rose. Still rose.
Very balcony. Such climb.
Much love. So Propose. Wow, marriage.
Very Tybalt. Much stab. What do?
Such exile. Very Mantua. Much sad.
So, priest? Much sleeping. Wow, tomb.
Such poison. What dagger. Very dead. Wow, end.[24]

The Doge Meme Expands

As the time of writing, there was still an "Easter egg" (a secret left in a digital environment) on YouTube that converted YouTube to Comic Sans if you typed "doge meme" in the search bar. The doge meme spread in a very odd way across the web and into real life. A new digital currency was produced to satirize the bitcoin, called Dogecoin, and it is used as an alternative digital currency. The parody currency gained a large community following on Reddit and fundraised the money necessary to sponsor a Nascar car. The Dogecoin car raced at Talladega Speedway twice in 2014, driven by Josh Wise.[25]

THE MEME ENVIRONMENT

The Dogecoin car is a phenomenal example of how online memes and odd Internet vernacular can be noticed in a physical environment. Ideas online manifest in a visual style and permeate, replicate, and proliferate culture so well that they often become part of our daily use. Making silly images of cats talking becomes the image macro and a way to speak to your friends in a silly manner. By the time you are reading this book, there could be a completely new meme that dominates the web.

Over the course of the rest of this chapter, we will give you some additional historical context of memes that have occurred and how they appeared. We will show you how some memes shape our discussions about culture and bring societal issues to a visual present. This chapter will help you understand how to identify visual trends and become literate in web visual grammar and it will encourage you to participate in meme creation.

THE VISUAL MEME ON THE WEB AND IN REAL LIFE

Online tools and web access do not cause memes to occur: They require creativity and an engaged web audience. The users of the web create memes, and the activity of creating a meme is a community agreement that must survive a battle for attention. The "networked individualism" that makes up communities online also helps generate content that has value to unique users and the web community at large. Being web savvy means being literate in the tools such as Photoshop or meme generators, as well as understanding the grammar and the language. When users participate in memes and shared ideas, they are being individuals together.

In this section we are going to talk about memes as trends and experiences in physical space, before we discuss the solely web-based memes. We feel that explaining some of the fads or trends that have seeped into visual culture outside the web provide a glimpse at how to become a better participant. We will talk about fad memes such as "planking," "owling," and even "Tebowing," and we will discuss hashtag memes that were transformed by the audience online. Some of the earliest trends on the web were clearly a result of access and technology, and the more recent memes are similar, but far more community oriented.

As we continue to reiterate, we in no way provide comprehensive coverage of these web cultures, but please use our supplied examples to provide a context for exploring the new and digital media environment. We strongly suggest you follow up anything we have mentioned and continue to explore the memes online, and we recommend you visit KnowYourMeme.com, the largest known database of memes online. You will find current and old trends and you can contribute to their research. We also recommend you participate in Reddit or Imgur forums to keep up with visual trends.

TECHNOLOGY AND ACCESS TRENDS

Limor Shifman, author of *Memes in Digital Culture* (2014), defines the Internet meme as, "(a) a group of digital items sharing common characteristics of content, form, and/or stance, which (b) were created with awareness of each other, and (c) were circulated, imitated, and/or transformed via the Internet by many users."[26]

Previous to Reddit, Twitter, 4chan, and other communities that could create memes at a rapid pace, artists and creative individuals participated in meme-like activities. The web created a hypermedia environment of creation, but that did not prevent ideas from occurring and appearing simultaneously. In 2006, two separate, but extraordinarily similar, photo projects were posted online. Both Ahree Lee and Noah Kalina uploaded multi-year photo projects known as photo-a-day projects. Although neither Ahree Lee nor Noah Kalina had any idea that the other was creating their project, the results were eerily similar. The two put a fair amount of dedication and perseverance into their projects, and, when they posted them online in 2006, thousands of similar posts were created. In this way, the trend of the photo-a-day was not created by the web, but by the ease of use of web cameras, editing software, and later, web distribution.

Photo trends are often seen as a result of the web, but were very often present in culture previously. Take, for example, the work of the photographer Nicholas Nixon, who photographed his wife and her three sisters every single year since 1975.[27] What we see as a contemporary media trend, because it happened to appear on AtomFilms and YouTube, was actually part of our visual culture far earlier. The idea became circulated and imitated and transformed with more users having access. The photo-a-day meme continues to be popular into our present, and you will often find articles posted about people still participating and taking photos every day or week for many years.[28]

TROPES AND CLASSIC MEMES UPDATED

Before the advent of screen-based media, visual culture existed in the form of performance and live entertainment. Around the turn of the last century (we mean the late 1800s), when Edison was experimenting with his cats boxing on film, vaudeville reigned as the popular entertainment medium. Vaudeville was a live art form mixing burlesque dancing, comedy, dance, and music meant to entertain a live audience. When performers went on just a bit too long, something known as "The Vaudeville Hook" would come out of the side of the curtain and pull the performer offstage, to extended laughter. Soon, the hook became a part of the show and was anticipated as an addition to the performances. The hook was parodied in Disney films, early black-and-white-era silent films, and early television shows. We still see "The Hook" on major entertainment award shows such as *The Academy Awards* or *The Emmys*, in the form of music playing when someone goes on for too long.

Of course, in our Internet age, savvy web users have updated the meme in the digital space. In 1984, a man named Charlie Schmidt recorded his cat Fatso, dressed in a t-shirt, playing a short piano track with its human-operated paws. In 2007, Schmidt uploaded the video to YouTube with the name "Cool Cat," and it sat quietly on the web until the video was used as a resurrection of the vaudeville hook.[29] The "Keyboard Cat" video went viral and brought along with it the meme of the century-old entertainment trope. As you'll learn in the next chapter, accident videos and fails made up the majority of early virals. Comedian and MyDamnChannel.com manager Brad O'Farrell remixed a video of a man rolling down an escalator, with the Keyboard Cat "playing him off." From there, the video was circulated so widely it became viral and it was remixed (imitated and transformed) with hundreds of other "fail" videos.

Capitalizing on the meme, Charlie Schmidt created PlayHimOffKeyboard Cat.com and invited users to contribute to the meme.[30] The meme gained popularity fairly quickly, adding an additional layer to viral videos by adding the meme to them. Virals, by comparison with memes, are singular in experience and do not often become memes. Memes offer themselves to the aforementioned attributes that Limor Shifman describes. This meme included fails from a Fox News commenter passing out on-screen to an awkward marriage proposal, all ending with the quirky Keyboard Cat theme playing them off the screen.[31] In order to keep the meme going, a generator called "Auto Keyboard Cat" was created to help users participate in the everlasting trope.[32]

PRANKS AS MEMES

The bait-and-switch is one of the oldest frauds ever carried out by human beings. The premise is simple: You advertise or explain one thing and, when the buyer or viewer shows up, you give them something else, usually of lesser value. This act is as timeless as gullibility, so, of course, the Internet would make this theme into a meme. In the case of the web, there is a famous version of this meme that has permeated all facets of common culture, and it's called "The Rick Roll." Born from 4chan, the act is simple and easy to execute on the web. You boast about something worth looking at, supply the hyperlink, and it leads to Rick Astley's "Never Gonna Give You Up" (1987) music video.

Pranks are timeless, and this meme offers common content in form and stance, created with the awareness of the meme. In order to use this prank meme, you have to be aware that it is possible. The joy of participating in a "Rick Roll" comes from knowing the person who clicks on the link will end up with the same video. Any time a highly anticipated movie is coming out, inevitably someone will boast that they have a "leaked" version of the trailer

Figure 4.6

Rick Roll on a bulletin board.

Source: Creative Commons

or some clip. You will unwittingly click on it and be brought to Rick Astley's video. Again.

It was used on everything from WikiLeaks to April Fools' jokes to Astley himself jumping out of a parade float at the Macy's Thanksgiving Day Parade. It's a meme that can be used any time, and the more savvily you use it, the more entertaining it is to the web audience.

MEMES IN REAL LIFE

As Rick Astley showed during the 2008 Macy's Thanksgiving Day Parade, memes are entertaining the more they appear in our popular culture. The Rick Roll meme began online and spread to our physical space and, although at times it appears annoying, it still creates a humorous result. Sometimes, a strange act placed online becomes a meme in the digital space through the participation of the real audience. As a meme becomes popular, it attracts the attention of those who would like to play along. Take, for example, the odd physical meme called "Planking." Not to be mistaken for the ab exercise, planking was originally called "The Lying Down Game" and was created in Australia.[33] The act, like many memes, is a simple one: Lie face down, with stiffened arms and legs (like a board), in random places, have a picture taken of the act, and post it online with the hashtag #planking.

Planking is technically a "photo fad," but, as it exists because of the web and community support and replicates and evolves, it acts as a meme. Its circulation from Australia around the world was a result of the visual culture of participation. Its transformation and imitation allowed "plankers" to try the act in strange places, in order to transform and raise the bar for fellow participants. The act of participation in a meme that occurs in the physical space sometimes has unforeseen consequences. In 2011, a young Australian man named Acton Beale died when attempting planking on a seven-story-high balcony railing.[34] This unfortunate accident also caused the meme to enter our cultural understanding of memes and caused it to become even more popular. Odds are, when you search #planking on a social media platform, you will still find people participating in the meme.

Physical memes transformed into variations of the original planking in the style of "owling" or "Tebowing." Owling is basically squatting in the strangest places in an attempt to imitate an owl doing owl things. The web community created the meme because "planking is so last week," and this gives a true example of how memes compete for attention. The "Tebowing" meme is simple mimicry of quarterback Tim Tebow's act of kneeling and praying after he scores a touchdown. It became highly imitated and used in the same way as the other physical fad memes where people had to do the act, photograph it, and share the image.

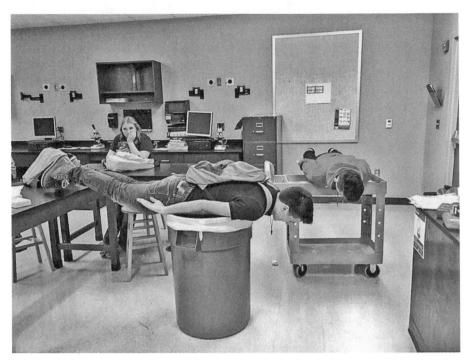

John Wick @Zack_Mroue · Oct 31
Me & @robertbenners #planking 📷 pic.twitter.com/yBmGLAHUfO
↩   ♺ 2   ★ 6   •••

Figure 4.7
John Wick and Robert Benners planking in class.

Memes With Meaning

When a meme enters our common cultural experience, it can be recognized by the masses. When doge made its way to a Nascar race car, it may have caused confusion among some viewers, but the cultural recognition was a fair payoff. Aside from the unfortunate death of Acton Beale, the planking meme made its way into common culture through various means. As the meme trend grew in popularity, the rap artist Xzibit tweeted: "Planking was a way to transport slaves on ships during the slave trade, its [sic] not funny. Educate yourselves."[35] Thus, many users who had never heard of planking or participated in the act were aware of its complications. The creators of the meme had to clear up their intentions by expressing that the meme comes from acting like a wooden board and they didn't mean any relation to the way humans were horribly mistreated.[36]

Planking was even used as a method of protest in the Philippines, after a huge transport strike as a result of high gas prices. Filipino citizens planked in the middle of a large roundabout to protest the hikes and disrupt traffic. The protest resulted in a Quezon City representative filing a bill called the "Anti-Planking Act of 2011."[37] As you can imagine, this didn't have the desired effect the representative thought it would have, and Twitter and the web community tweeted in support of the planking protestors.

Hashtag Memes

Unintended consequences occur far too often when corporations and less savvy web users attempt to create memes. As you are learning in the process of reading this book, you cannot fake authenticity. To disseminate the planking or owling memes, you can share them on social media using the hashtag, so they become part of the larger aggregate of new media content. During the 2014 Sochi Winter Olympics, McDonald's took to the web to promote a hashtag campaign to support our athletes abroad and it used the #CheersToSochi hashtag to do so. What McDonald's failed to consider was the imitation process of web uses. LGBTQ activists purchased the .org version of the same domain name and usurped the hashtag to attack Russia's homophobic rules.[38]

This happens quite often in a digital world of replication and meme transfer. Two interesting "backfires" are #myNYPD and #CosbyMeme. The New York Police Department thought it was activating an online audience when it tweeted a photo of happy NYPD officers with the caption, "Do you have a photo w/a member of the NYPD? Tweet us & tag it #myNYPD. It may be featured on our Facebook." As you would guess, many web users added photos—of police brutality, beatings, and takedowns during protests, from the Occupy Movement to traffic stops. The meme was immediately trending for all the wrong reasons, and thousands of users participated.[39] The strangest backfire is when a Bill Cosby representative added a photo of Cosby to a meme generator hosted at BillCosby.com and asked people to create image macro memes of him. The web audience participated wildly by subverting and creating image macros that commented on his rape allegations that stemmed from a 2006 court case. Many of the response memes were very explicit and NSFW.

When corporations or users who may not be as savvy as you try to jump into the online space without considering the audience, the web's users may subvert the message and cause the company to backtrack. It not only takes time to understand the environment of the savvy web, it requires you to talk to your friends before attempting a hashtag campaign. Try to talk to various people in different social circles about what your goals are before you execute the digital promotion using the hashtag. Very often, someone may help you find a possible downside before you post.

THE MEMES OF THE ONLINE WORLD

In the pre-web traditional media environment, traditional gatekeepers maintained their hold on media distribution and blocked the average user from creating and participating in visual experiments. In our hypermedia environment, all you need is a small amount of technological competence and you can distribute your creativity while simultaneously participating with like-minded "networked individuals."

In this section, we'll focus on several popular memes you are most likely aware of and explain how they started, what impact the memes had on our common culture, and how some of the images inspired the business of using memes to raise awareness of news events. From "Disaster Girl" to "Sad Keanu" and "Strutting Leo" to "Pepper Spraying Cop" and "Binders Full of Women," memes empower users to become savvy users and participate in creative endeavors and civic awareness.

REMIX MEMES

The planking meme showed a version of meme circulation known as mimicry, which is different than the remix meme. The remix meme usually requires the user to be aware of the meme's various remixes, as well as having some technological skills. A remix meme is not as easy to do as an image macro meme, because, in order to participate, you'll definitely have to use Photoshop or an online photo manipulation tool. It means taking part of an image and cutting it onto another layer, with each iteration and imitation trying to outdo the previous attempt in creativity and wit.

According to Limor Shifman, there are two types of remix meme: the juxtaposition image meme and the frozen-motion remix meme.[40] The juxtaposition meme takes a facial expression or an act out context and inserts it into an image that deserves the punch line. In video form, this would be the "Play Him Off Keyboard Cat" meme, and there are several variations of this meme that appear nearly every time an expression appears in an image by accident. Shifman explains that juxtapositions call for mimetic responses because the photos are taken out of context, and their reappropriation to other contexts feels almost natural. In the frozen-motion meme photo, a photo of someone mid-motion is taken out awkwardly and placed in and on weird, out-of-context information.

"Disaster Girl"

Dave Roth didn't mean to inspire a juxtaposition meme when he photographed his daughter Zoe in front of a burning house in 2004. Roth later submitted the photo to a *JPG Magazine* photo contest about capturing emotion. The magazine thought the picture was great and shared it on several web platforms. The photo called for a caption for Zoe's look, and, from there on, Zoe became the caption, as users added her image to accident and tragedy photos such as the *Costa Concordia* cruise-ship disaster, the *Hindenburg*, and Windows Vista Business Edition. If it seems like a disaster, you can use the "Disaster Girl" image.

"McKayla Is Not Impressed"

McKayla Maroney is one of the most talented gymnasts on Earth, and she wasn't too happy to win the silver medal at the 2012 Summer Olympic Games in London, UK. Bryan Snyder of Reuters photographed her on the podium making a scowling expression. The "McKayla Is Not Impressed" meme comes

Figure 4.8
McKayla and Barack are not impressed.

Source: Wikimedia Commons

from a previous meme called "Spock Is Not Impressed," where a folded-armed Spock from *Star Trek* stands in juxtaposed meme images. McKayla's image has been used as an image macro with unimpressed text such as, "You don't serve coke? Pepsi is fine," and added to scenes of extraordinary greatness where she's unimpressed, such as the Sistine Chapel, the Egyptian pyramids, double rainbows, and, of course, next to Tim Tebow praying. When McKayla was invited to the White House, she met with President Obama and even made the scowl along with the President.

"Bubbles Girl"

The frozen-motion meme of a little girl running with bubbles in her hand is still a bit of a mystery, including who took the photo, who the young girl may be, and why she's running. What we do know is that this image appeared on 4chan in 2009 as a new meme among dated memes. (Dated means older by several months to a year in comparison.) The little girl is seemingly running, and so she is a juxtaposed frozen-motion image showing intent of running away—from *Jurassic Park* dinosaurs, bulls, lolcats, and police.

"Sad Keanu" and "Strutting Leo"

The prevalence of photographers capturing celebrities means that, without a doubt, there will be awkward images available to manipulate. Keanu Reeves sitting on a park bench, eating a sandwich: That is all a member of the paparazzi needed to send to the tabloids and simultaneously gave the Internet a meme to be remixed. Ron Asordorian, working for Splash News, took a photo of Keanu in 2010. Keanu is most likely just lost in thought, but it looks as though he's a bit sad, and, from then on, "Sad Keanu" has been juxtaposed in thousands of images, of both happy and sad events. It's such a mimetic trend that the Internet community nominated June 15 "Cheer Up Keanu Day," when users send positive content on behalf of the actor in order to make his day happy.

Conversely, there is a frozen-motion image of Leonardo DiCaprio strutting on the set of *Inception*. His jubilant, cheerful walk has been added as a frozen-motion image, as the "Strutting Leo" happily walks away from tragedy, through random film scenes, and even on water. There's also a frozen-motion "Prancing Cera" meme, made after director Edgar Wright uploaded a photo of Michael Cera from the set of *Scott Pilgrim vs. The World*. "Prancing Cera" has been added to the oddest photos and locations you can imagine.

Memes as a Business

Although memes are creative, expressive, viral, and artistic, there are times when this cultural movement is turned into a profit by corporations. Images and likenesses can be copyrighted, and people can request ownership of the images and become representatives of the characters and subjects of memes. As images gain popularity and enter the visual culture off the web, products and brands may use the recognizable image for product endorsement. The Grumpy Cat meme phenomenon went viral owing to the photograph Bryan Bundesen took of his sister's cat Tardar Sauce's naturally frowning face. Bundersen posted the picture on Reddit, and it became a viral hit. This caught the eye of the opportunistic agent Ben Lashes (real name: Benjamin Clark), who represents and manages Internet cats such as Nyan Cat and Keyboard Cat. Lashes contacts owners when memes become viral to see how they can make a profit and continue the momentum of the new sensation. Grumpy Cat has taken advantage of the new-found fame, as Broken Road Productions has worked on a Lifetime Television film called *Grumpy Cat's Worst Christmas Ever* and a book titled, *Grumpy Cat: A Grumpy Book: Disgruntled tips and activities designed to put a frown on your face*, and there is also a beverage.[41]

What is important about the Grumpy Cat sensation is that memes can become a commercial success. Corporations copyright images, and agents make a profit from the viral success when it translates into physical products such as toys, television appearances, and t-shirts. The original images of Grumpy Cat, doge, and many others are copyright, and you cannot use them on a commercial project without permission.[42]

MEMES AND SOCIOCULTURAL SIGNIFICANCE

When a meme becomes recognizable enough to be referenced in form and shape without the original media accompanying the meaning, the meme is truly embedded in our consciousness. Some images are so significant in our visual history that the framing and structure of the image contain the meaning. For example, on the 24th anniversary of the Chinese Communist Party crackdown on protestors in Tiananmen Square, the Chinese government blocked any reference to the protest on social media and search engines. The "Great Firewall" of China blocked any mention of the protests, from the words "today" and "remember," to the date and photos. Savvy web activists challenged the censorship by using the iconic "Tank Man" image as a meme. The users replaced the tanks with large rubber ducks (like the one docked in a Hong Kong harbor), and the activist image made its way around Weibo, China's version of Twitter, and helped other users try to imitate and circulate further memes.[43]

Figure 4.9

Iconic Tank Man photograph, by Jeff Widener/Associated Press, remixed with ducks.

Source: Wikimedia Commons

In the United States, meme sharing sometimes helps citizens see an alternative view to the way politics and culture work. Like Veronica DeSouza's "Binders Full of Women" Mitt Romney meme, images can bring awareness to issues that we should be discussing. A similar meme was the "Pepper Spraying Cop" meme from 2011. At a protest in UC Davis, where students were holding a sit-in protest on campus as part of the Occupy Movement, a police officer pepper-sprayed several students at close range in a seemingly casual manner. The video went viral and brought to light issues of police militarization, protest movements, and Internet reactions. Internet users created a cut-out of the cop and encouraged users to participate in the meme where you juxtapose the cop with any image—the more inappropriate the better.[44] Some notable examples of victims of the pepper spray include the Founding Fathers, Mt. Rushmore, and the Declaration of Independence. This highly political meme is still referenced when situations of unrest and protest occur in the United States.

MEMES ARE CULTURE

We end this chapter by reminding you that memes empower all users with access to image manipulation software, giving them the ability to participate. If you recognize any image that is quickly circulating, being imitated and transformed, you are watching a meme in real time. Some memes enter our common culture in the form of slang or language, such as the terms "bae" (before anyone else), selfie, or fail, and some enter our mind as something culturally relevant and unforgettable.

We want to remind you to be aware that, in our image-based culture, you should never assume immediately that something is true because there is photographic evidence. The side effect of access and the technological approach is that users become far savvier and competent at using the tools that can manipulate and trick other users. This happens politically and globally, to create messages such as when Iran's propaganda team Photoshopped an extra launched missile into an image in 2008, and the Internet had a field day, adding more missiles, Jar Jar Binks, cats, and Wile E. Coyote's Acme boxes.[45] Make sure you check the source of the meme before you believe it to be true. Many people try to trick less savvy social media participants during times of stress and duress, such as adding sharks to water during hurricane floods. The photo manipulation is easily done and shares extremely quickly. If an image seems too good/crazy to be true, you are most likely correct. Use Snopes.com to verify or just simply Google the image using the image search tool at google.com/imghp, to reverse search images to their source.

NOTES

1 The original "Binders Full of Women" post. Retrieved from http://bindersfullof women.tumblr.com/post/33747457705/binders-full-of-women (accessed May 5, 2015).

2 Kwoh, L. (2012). "'Binders Full of Women' May Help One Woman Get a Job." Retrieved from http://blogs.wsj.com/atwork/2012/10/17/romney-binders-full-of-women-sparks-fame-for-laid-off-blogger/ (accessed May 5, 2015).

3 Franke-Ruta, G. (2012). "Binders Full of Women: A meme that means something." Retrieved from www.theatlantic.com/politics/archive/2012/10/binders-full-of-women-a-meme-that-means-something/263740/ (accessed May 5, 2015).

4 *Merriam-Webster Dictionary*. Retrieved from www.merriam-webster.com/dictionary/meme (accessed May 5, 2015).

5 Gleick, J. (2011). "What Defines a Meme?" Retrieved from www.smithsonian mag.com/arts-culture/what-defines-a-meme-1904778/?no-ist (accessed May 5, 2015).

6 Dawkins, R. (1976). *The Selfish Gene*. Oxford, UK: Oxford University Press.

7 Shifman, L. (2014). *Memes in Digital Culture*. Boston, MA: MIT Press.

8 Sontag, S. (2003) *Regarding the Pain of Others*. New York: Farrar, Straus & Giroux.

9 Know Your Meme. About page. Retrieved from http://knowyourmeme.com/about (accessed May 5, 2015).

10 Edison, T. (1894) "Boxin Cats." Seamus McGoon, YouTube. Retrieved from www.youtube.com/watch?v=k52pLvVmmkU (accessed May 5, 2015).

11   Grossman, L. (2007). "Creating a Cute Cat Frenzy: Talking cats have taken over the web. But are great online fads like this one a dying breed?" Retrieved from http://content.time.com/time/magazine/article/0,9171,1642897,00.html (accessed May 5, 2015).

12   McCloud, S. (1993). *Understanding Comics: The invisible art*. New York: William Marrow Paperbacks, p. 36.

13   Houston, K. (2013). "Smile! A history of emoticons." Retrieved from http://online. wsj.com/articles/SB10001424052702304213904579093661814158946 (accessed May 5, 2015).

14   Rutkoff, A. (2007). "With 'LOLcats' Internet Fad, Anyone Can Get in on the Joke." Retrieved from http://online.wsj.com/news/articles/SB118798557326508182 ?mg=reno64-wsj&url=http%3A%2F%2Fonline.wsj.com%2Farticle%2FSB1187 98557326508182.html (accessed May 5, 2015).

15   Citizen, J. (2012). "92 Teen Text Terms Decoded for Confused Parents." Retrieved from http://techland.time.com/2012/05/03/92-teen-text-terms-decoded-for-confused-parents/ (accessed May 5, 2015).

16   Beale, S. (2007). "Roll Your Own LOL, Not Just For Cats Anymore." Retrieved from http://laughingsquid.com/roll-your-own-lol-not-just-for-cats-anymore/ (accessed May 5, 2015).

17   Gawne, L. and Vaughn, J. (2012). "I Can Haz Language Play: The construction of language and identity in Lolspeak." Retrieved from https://digitalcollections. anu.edu.au/bitstream/1885/9398/5/Gawne_ICanHaz2012.pdf (accessed May 5, 2015).

18   The Lolcat Bible. Wiki page. Retrieved from www.lolcatbible.com/index.php ?title=Genesis_1 (accessed May 5, 2015).

19   Know Your Meme: Doge. Retrieved from http://knowyourmeme.com/memes/doge (accessed May 5, 2015).

20   Broderick, R. (2013). "Everything You Wanted to Know About Doge but Were Afraid to Ask." Retrieved from www.buzzfeed.com/ryanhatesthis/everything-youve-ever-wanted-to-know-but-have-been-too-scare (accessed May 5, 2015).

21   Shiba Confessions Tumblr. Retrieved from http://shibaconfessions.tumblr.com/ (accessed May 5, 2015).

22   Chen, A. (2013). "Doge Is Actually a Good Internet Meme. Wow." Retrieved from http://gawker.com/doge-is-an-actually-good-internet-meme-wow-1460448782 (accessed May 5, 2015).

23   McCulloch, G. (2014). "A Linguist Explains the Grammar of Doge. Wow." Retrieved from http://the-toast.net/2014/02/06/linguist-explains-grammar-doge-wow/ (accessed May 5, 2015).

24   Source of Doge Romeo and Juliet. Tumblr. Retrieved from http://daysofstorm. tumblr.com/post/68101267671/new-vogue-ravyn-chibi-koun (accessed May 5, 2015).

25   Payne, M. (2014). "NASCAR Driver Josh Wise Will Drive the Dogecoin Car Again Thank to Two New Fundraisers." Retrieved from www.washingtonpost.com/ blogs/early-lead/wp/2014/05/28/nascar-driver-josh-wise-will-drive-the-dogecoin-car-again-thanks-to-two-new-fundraisers/ (accessed May 5, 2015).

26 Shifman, L. (2014). *Memes in Digital Culture*. Boston, MA: MIT Press.

27 National Gallery of Art: Nicholas Nixon. Retrieved from www.nga.gov/exhibitions/ nixoninfo.shtm (accessed May 5, 2015).

28 Stone, A.R. (2014). "Dad Filmed His Daughter for 15 Seconds Each Week Since Birth to Age 14: The result will leave you breathless." Retrieved from http://aplus.com/a/father-filmed-his-daughter-once-a-week-for-14-years (accessed May 5, 2015).

29 Know Your Meme: Keyboard Cat. Retrieved from http://knowyourmeme.com/ memes/keyboard-cat (accessed May 5, 2015).

30 Play Him Off Keyboard Cat main site. Retrieved from http://playhimoffkeyboard cat.com/ (accessed May 5, 2015).

31 Coyle, J. (2009). "'Keyboard Cat' Spreads on Web, TV." Retrieved from http:// usatoday30.usatoday.com/tech/hotsites/2009-05-22-keyboard-cat_N.htm (accessed May 5, 2015).

32 Lowensohn, J. (2009). "Weekend Webware: DIY keyboard cat videos." Retrieved from www.cnet.com/news/weekend-webware-diy-keyboard-cat-videos/ (accessed May 5, 2015).

33 Eddy, M. (2011). "The 65 Best Planking Pictures From Around the World." Retrieved from www.themarysue.com/best-planking-pictures/ (accessed May 5, 2015).

34 Milian, M. (2011). "'Planking' Death Puts Spotlight on Bizarre Web Craze." Retrieved from www.cnn.com/2011/TECH/web/05/18/planking.internet.craze/ (accessed May 5, 2015).

35 Xzibit. Twitter status, July 6, 2011. Retrieved from https://twitter.com/xzibit/ status/88795039257468928 (accessed May 5, 2015).

36 Hughes, S. (2011). "Is 'Planking' Connected to the Slave Trade?" Retrieved from www.washingtonpost.com/blogs/blogpost/post/is-planking-connected-to-the-slave-trade/2011/07/08/gIQAz1aj3H_blog.html (accessed May 5, 2015).

37 Flock, E. (2011). "Anti-Planking Act Proposed in Philippines After People Plank in Manila Streets." Retrieved from www.washingtonpost.com/blogs/blogpost/ post/anti-planking-act-proposed-in-philippines-after-people-plank-in-manila-streets/2011/09/20/gIQAVZl8hK_blog.html (accessed May 5, 2015).

38 Merevick, T. (2014). "LGBT Activists Launch 'Cheers to Sochi' Parody Site After 'Highjacking' McDonalds' Hashtag." Retrieved from www.buzzfeed.com/tony merevick/lgbt-activists-launch-cheers-to-sochi-parody (accessed May 5, 2015).

39 Phillip, A. (2014). "Well, the #MyNYPD Hashtag Sure Backfired Quickly." Retrieved from www.washingtonpost.com/news/post-nation/wp/2014/04/22/well-the-mynypd-hashtag-sure-backfired-quickly/ (accessed May 5, 2015).

40 Shifman, L. (2014). *Memes in Digital Culture*. Boston, MA: MIT Press.

41 Rosman, K. (2013). "Grumpy Cat Has an Agent, and Now a Movie Deal." Retrieved from http://online.wsj.com/articles/SB100014241278873244126045785133527 95950958 (accessed May 5, 2015).

42 Erickson, C. (2012). "Meme Management: Meet the man who reps Internet stars." Retrieved from http://mashable.com/2012/04/17/meme-management/ (accessed May 5, 2015).

43   Romano, A. (2014). "Tiananmen Square Protesters Slip Memes Through China's Web Censors." Retrieved from http://mashable.com/2014/06/04/tiananmen-square-memes/ (accessed May 5, 2015).

44   Chen, A. (2011). "UC Davis Pepper Spray Cop Is Now a Meme." Retrieved from http://gawker.com/5861431/uc-davis-pepper-spray-cop-is-now-a-meme/ (accessed May 5, 2015).

45   Hudson, J. (2012). "Busted: Iran's jarring Photoshopped missle test image." Retrieved from www.thewire.com/global/2012/05/busted-irans-jarring-photoshopped-missile-test-image/51940/ (accessed May 5, 2015).

CHAPTER 5

Viral Videos

If you ask a random group of people if they have ever seen the video "Charlie Bit My Finger," there's a good chance you will get a positive response. That's because the video has nearly 1 billion views, equating to one-seventh of the world's population. It's a fairly simple, minute-long video showing two children named Harry and Charlie on a chair, and Charlie bites Harry's finger. It sounds pretty simple, but, as you've learned from the previous chapter, you cannot explain the video in words and expect to get the same reaction and enjoyment as you can by viewing. You need to see this video and, once you have, you'll feel compelled to share it—as will those who see it after you. Just like coughing on a subway car, videos can travel like a virus.

A viral video is a term used to describe a video that has been consumed and shared in an exponential manner, similar to the way an airborne virus may spread. Someone watches a video online and then shares it with a group of friends, on social media or through email. The recipients then watch and feel compelled to forward it to new viewers. It goes from discovery to group saturation fairly quickly, with a rapid view count increase and then usually a plateau, where the views no longer rise rapidly. Virals continue to be seen for a long time after the initial discovery, but are usually replaced by the next best shareable video.

THE VIRAL VIDEO

The most-viewed viral video in history is Psy's "Gangnam Style" (2012), and odds are it still is when you are reading this book. "Gangnam Style" is the first YouTube video to cross the 1 billion and 2 billion views record, and it goes without saying that Psy, the popular South Korean pop star who produced "Gangnam Style," became a worldwide sensation after his hit was released. The video is based somewhat satirically on a posh region of South Korea called Gangnam. In the video, Psy dances along with children, models, horses, chess players, bus and subway passengers, and on a toilet. The video combines

Figure 5.1
Viral video sharing.

comedy, children, animals, explosions, attractive models, and an addicting electronic dance track with a lot of bass. The video literally contains all the most common content of a viral video.

Over the course of this chapter, we are going to focus on some of the history of viral videos, as well as some sobering reality concerning the viral video industry itself. In the last part of the chapter, we will use several case studies of successful viral campaigns and reverse engineer them to see how viral videos succeed in becoming part of our collective sharing conscious. As we present the case study of the band OK Go, we hope you see how the audience has adapted and changed over the last decade. Understanding how the "KONY 2012" (2012) video became viral will enlighten you as to why we watch viral media. We will also discuss the viral advertising campaigns of Old Spice, as well as the viral masterminds who work for *Jimmy Kimmel Live*.

YouTube is an ever-expanding platform where web video is uploaded and shared, thousands to millions of times per day. In no way can we claim a comprehensive approach to this material. With our carefully selected examples, we aim to help you refer the models and the methods to the hundreds of different videos that occupy the online space. Check out the companion material to follow along and continue to participate in the sharing of viral content.

THE VIRAL VIDEO RECIPE

When you see a video posted on your social media feed, what makes you click play? Then, after viewing it, what makes you want to share the video? The most-shared videos online seem to have some significant common traits in their subject matter. Simply put, if a video contains babies, cute animals, some provocative material, an accident or blooper, some community support, and some mystery, or has a combination of several of these elements, the video could become viral. Sometimes, it also requires someone with a lot of followers to mention the video for it to have a boost in views. Viral videos are usually stand-alone pieces of material, not derived from previous memes, and ordinarily have no beginning or end. They are just pieces of visual material that seem disconnected from the context. According to Carol Vernallis, the aesthetic includes "bold graphic design and well-judged scale."[1] Vernallis explains that the viral video's limited length and its quality help attract the attention that it gains. If the video doesn't fit into a certain quality standard, people may not share the video as often.

Why We Watch

There are hundreds of thousands of viral videos about babies, aside from "Charlie Bit My Finger—Again!" (2007). The ones that seem to rise to the top are videos that can be remembered and described to other people outside the web's environment. The simplest, most shared of these are "Baby Laughing Hysterically at Ripping Paper (Original)" (2011), "Kung Fu Baby" (2006), and "Talking Twin Babies—Part 2 official video" (2011). In all four of these examples, we get babies who are still unable to form full sentences, biting, laughing, making expressions, and babbling. It's really all that babies primarily do (and not much else!). Yet, when posted online, these specific examples shine much more than the hundreds of thousands of other baby videos.

These specific examples are perfectly timed for sustaining a view and the desire to share. From the look of the thumbnail, to the timing of the content, these baby videos stand out among all the millions of videos. Watching them gives you a sense of the uncanny behavior that some infants demonstrate—but all contained in a compact, shareable video. In the video "Charlie Bit My Finger—Again!", we see perfectly timed action. In the first few seconds, we see Charlie bite Harry's finger and, by the seventh second, we hear "Charlie bit me!" For the next 45 or so seconds, we see Harry put his fingers in peril once again for the sake of humor, and Charlie bites him again. ("And it really hurts!")

Beyond the fact that babies are instant Internet gold, these videos also do something that reinforces the viral quality of the content: They play to our attention span. With the incomprehensible amount of video content, our attention spans appreciate content that is less than 5 minutes, according to a ComScore study.[2] Additionally, the video should grab the viewer's attention in 8 seconds[3] and it should be able to be seen clearly on a small screen.[4] Babies are cute and attention-grabbing, but the video must fall into our human viewing habits and desires as well.

Speaking of small screens, a fair amount of success in the viral realm is based on the possibility of being clicked on. Whether the video is shared in an email, on a Facebook feed, or from the YouTube search, the thumbnail plays into someone's decision to click the video. Vernallis further explains, "YouTube clips tend to feature simplistic and evocative representations of the body and shape—either as face, body part, or body whole."[5] Although no formal study has been completed to identify what thumbnails are clicked most, Ryan Broderick at BuzzFeed found that any thumbnail with a human face or body part is more likely to be clicked on if no context is provided.[6]

Unpredictability

Children are likely to go viral for a similar reason that animals are: They are unpredictable. In most accident virals, such as "fail" videos, you can nearly predict the outcome at the onset of the video. (A wobbly skateboarder aimed toward a jump will most likely crash and lose some teeth.) When you put a camera on a child or an animal, you are not guaranteed a fixed and predicable story. For example, "Zombie Kid Likes Turtles" (2007) and "'Apparently' This Kid Is Awesome, Steals the Show During Interview" (2104) show the unpredictability of children. In the first video, "Zombie Kid" Jonathan is at a state fair when a reporter comes up to him and asks him about his face paint. His smiling answer: "I like turtles!" What makes the video even funnier is the unprepared confusion of the reporter, who seems utterly bewildered. Compare Jonathan the zombie to Noah Ritter at another state fair, who must have recently learned the word "apparently." The reporter asks Noah how he liked the ride, and he replies, "It was great! And apparently I've never been on live television before!" He goes on to steal the next minute of video from the overjoyed (and unprepared) reporter.

In both examples, we see the reporter wildly unprepared and caught candidly off guard for the subject's response. This is one of the reasons to watch and share viral videos as well—they break down our expectations. We have become accustomed to reporters' being poised and professional, so, when they react awkwardly (and you mix in an adorable child), you have yourself a viral hit.

Animal viral videos are even more likely to be expected to be unpredictable. We have no idea what animals are thinking, and, when they do weird things, especially out of context, we have a desire to watch and share. "The Sneezing

Baby Panda" (2006) is pretty self-explanatory, but, even when you see it, you sense the unpredictability. The moment seems so calm, as a mother panda chews her food, and her baby sleeps—only to unexpectedly sneeze and frighten the mom. It's jolting, unpredictable, and adorable. "Battle at Kruger" (2007), one of the most-shared viral videos of animals, is known for being one of the best "eyewitness" videos posted online.[7] The video shows a dramatic fight between lions, buffalo, and crocodiles at Kruger National Park in Africa. This video is perfect for viral unpredictability, as well as the sheer odds of ever witnessing such an event. From "Thriller Cats" to strange animal encounters to dogs afraid of cats, the more cute and unpredictable the video, the more likely the view count will increase rapidly.

Shareability

After a video is watched online, the only way that it can actually become a viral video is if it is shared repeatedly. You can see that unpredictability, brevity, aesthetics, and comedy seem to do quite well with sharing, but there is one more ingredient that needs to be included: emotional impact. We have to feel for the subjects in the video in some way. As with memes, virals work by a similar method and have to relate to us in one way or another. In order for us to share the video, we have to be reasonably sure the receiver will enjoy the video as well. Just because we enjoy a viral, it does not mean everyone will. However, when you look at the list of the top virals 5 years into YouTube's existence (the 2010 *Time* magazine list), the list contains pretty shareable content.[8] From "Charlie Bit My Finger" to "Kittens, Inspired by Kittens" (2008) even to "Daft Hands" (2007), the videos appeal to a mass audience, which is necessary for a massive amount of views. From the millions of videos uploaded, there are only several hundred that amass enough rapid views to be considered viral.

In order to claim a viral status, viral videos must be similar to memes, attaching to our collective conscious. You have to somehow feel that, if you don't share it, you may actually be doing someone a disservice by leaving them out of the loop. As virals and memes work primarily as visuals, the viral video requires mass insider knowledge so that it can be brought up in public. Like the example of the construction workers at the beginning of the book, we don't want to feel left out of the shared experience. The viral video is a compact, shareable clip that sticks around and makes you feel for it every time you add a view.

There are thousands of videos online considered to be "viral," and, as we mentioned, there is no way to create a thorough account of them. For all we know, a new "Gangnam Style" could come out tomorrow and we would have no way of catching up so rapidly.

Figure 5.2
Winnebago man.

INTERNET PEOPLE AND THE HISTORY OF THE VIRAL VIDEO

Back in the days of VHS videotape, broadcast engineers and dub (copy) room workers would clip out the bloopers from a broadcast and create a reel of the funniest moments. Long after the original material was forgotten, the blooper reels were still copied and shared and handed on from person to person. One such video that had circulated on videotape for years before it ever came close to web distribution was the outtakes of an industrial Winnebago sales video featuring a salesman named Jack Rebney. Rebney, a burned out, embittered newsman from the West Coast, was dubbed "The Angriest Man in the World" after the curse-word-laden outtakes of his video made their way online. For more than 20 years, the video went "viral" in real life, shared and seen over and over by collectors of odd video media. When YouTube opened its upload doors, one of the many owners of the tape uploaded the clip. Millions of views later, Rebney is immortalized as "Winnebago Man" and is featured in the 2009 documentary by the same name.[9]

THE SHORT HISTORY OF THE VIRAL VIDEO

Back in 1989, *America's Funniest Home Videos* appeared on ABC Television. The show encouraged anyone with a video camera to submit their funny, homemade (amateur) video to compete for award money and vacations. The personal camcorder had only first appeared in the early 1980s, and, by the end of the decade, people had amassed hundreds of thousands of hours of inane footage. Occasionally, something cute, unexpected, shocking, or unusual was captured on camera and yearned to be shared. The broadcast model of *America's Funniest Home Videos* helped encourage video-camera owners to submit their content so it could be shown, but the term "viral video" had not yet been coined. When the browser was invented, email became commonplace, and video files became shareable, the first rapidly shared videos began to appear in people's inboxes.

In 1995, Matt Stone and Trey Parker's short clip called "The Spirit of Christmas" started getting distributed around the web. The short was made while Stone and Parker were in college and it became the precursor to *South Park*. Its odd, clunky format and its story of several dirty-mouthed eighth graders watching Jesus fight Frosty the Snowman and Santa made the clip shareable to the masses. It was so amateur in style that many people shared it without knowing its origin.

The "viral" in viral media comes from a year 2000 marketing idea by Seth Godin. Godin explained his secrets of new success: the "Ideavirus."[10] In the article, the term "virus" is used more than 40 times to describe something like a meme, but more persistent over a short period of time. The idea was to turn a single online experience into something massively widespread. Godin never says "meme," because he knows that memes are reproducible and remixable—he means viral, something that is remembered for its originality.

INTERNET PEOPLE—THE ORIGINALS

"The Evolution of Dance" (2006) is a 6-minute video featuring motivational performer Judson Laipply running through a veritable history of dance moves, from Elvis to André 3000. For years, Laipply's video remained one of the most-viewed videos on YouTube and now ranks as one of the few non-music videos in the top 100 most-viewed videos ever on YouTube. Viral videos have no set standard or formula, but we'll try to categorize some of the videos by explaining why we watch them.

We Watch Because—It's Weird

One of our favorite viral videos to use as an example is one that we find most viewers enjoy because of its odd mimetic qualities. It pleases us, but we're not sure why. The "Dramatic Chipmunk" (2007) is neither dramatic, nor a chipmunk, but, in 6 seconds, makes almost everyone who watches it laugh. As the prairie dog in its glass case turns, the camera zooms into its little face.

The added dramatic music gives us a suspenseful feeling of anticipation. The short clip is perfectly shareable because it is so obscure. The original full-length video is from a Japanese talk show and is so out of context to a Western audience that the clip makes no sense, as itself or as the original.

Another odd and enjoyable clip, out of context, is "Leeroy Jenkins" (2006), staged inside the video game *World of Warcraft*. In the video, a group of friends appear to be plotting their next line of approach, taking themselves quite seriously, as they calculate numbers down to the statistics of survival and cache of weapons. All seems to be going by plan until Leeroy returns from his kitchen to his headset and controller (not featured in the video) and yells his battle cry: "Ok chums! Let's do this! Leeeeeroyyyyy Jennnnnkiinnnsss!" He storms into the battle prematurely, and what follows is one of the funniest instances of digital character shock on YouTube. For about 1 second, no character moves or talks, until we hear, "Oh my God, he just went in." The battle ends in terrible failure when all the teammates die once again, and, while on headset, we hear Leeroy say, "It's not my fault" (although it is).

The odd sets of circumstances that make up these specific stories are so unique that it would be hard to replicate them any other way. The moments are authentic and original, although out of context of their actual source material. "The Dramatic Chipmunk" is pulled from an obscure Japanese show, and Leeroy Jenkins is pulled from someone's recording of their *World of Warcraft* gameplay. It's almost as if this could be presented as art, because they stand alone so well.

We Watch Because—It's Not Us (But They Are Us)

As *America's Funniest Home Videos* figured out years ago, sometimes we enjoy watching other people get hurt or embarrassed, simply because it isn't us. As we'll explain next chapter, we humans are an awkward bunch, and sometimes it makes it easier for us to see we are not alone. There are so many clips that fall into this category, but some that we should highlight are "Star Wars Kid" (2006), "Numa Numa" (2006), "Scarlet Takes a Tumble" (2008), "Boom Goes the Dynamite" (2005), "Miss Teen USA 2007," Chris Crocker's "Leave Britney Alone!" (2007), and Tay Zonday's "Chocolate Rain" (2007).

These videos are all viral videos with millions of views and they are all very different in style and delivery. The one thing they have in common is that all the people in the video are embarrassing themselves in some way. That is not to say that they were embarrassed *during* the taping of the video. It's only as we watch it that we feel empathy for their behavior. The "Star Wars Kid" is a great example, because the poor kid, Ghyslain Raza, never meant for the tape to be seen. It was posted online by his so-called friends and then viewed millions of times. It's been remixed and referenced hundreds of other times.

We feel a weird sense of comedy and laughter, but also a bit of cringeworthy enjoyment that we are fortunate enough not to be Raza.

The cringe feelings of the other videos carry them to their millions of views as well, and we can share together a moment of someone else's misfortune. In nearly all of these examples, the Internet people have had their moment in the sun to explain themselves or own up to their oddness: some on the show *Tosh.0* and some on other web outlets. Raza, who originally distanced himself from the embarrassing video, now uses his notoriety to fight cyberbullying.

The YouTube Top 100

YouTube's Top 100 most-viewed videos are over 90 percent music videos. Just because it is heavily viewed doesn't mean that it is a viral video. As channels such as MTV and VH1 shift away from showing music videos, the web is the primary outlet for viewing music video content. Additionally, many viewers use YouTube playlists to play music for listening, rather than videos for watching. This increases the view count, without anyone actually watching the video. This is how many videos stay on the top 100 lists.

YouTube uses the Vevo music player to show music videos, and this still counts as part of the YouTube list.

We Watch Because—They Want Us to

Sometimes, people on the Internet do stupid things that get shared wildly. We can best sum up this response with a YouTube comment from umlungu360 in their response to NovaSeraAngel's comment on the "Leeroy Jenkins" video that people do the stupidest things to get famous: "This is the Internet. If you don't like the fact that people find fame by doing stupid things then you might want to eat your modem."

In the earliest days of YouTube and before, the advent of the web camera and digital video compression empowered users to express themselves in unique ways. From Andy Milonakis to ZeFrank to Liam Sullivan's "Shoes," the weird stuff people create can sometimes go insanely viral. Andy Milonakis, the forever young-looking prankster, made a pretty stupid music video in late 2002 called "The Superbowl Is Gay" and rants how everything is "gay," like cologne, DVD players, DVDs, and cats. Milonakis uses "gay" the way an immature grade-schooler would, in that it means "lame." The *Washington Post* reported on Milonakis in 2005 when they found the video in a pre-YouTube world.[11] Andy posted the video on a site called AngryNakedPat.com, where it gained millions of views. His bold attempt at crude humor and his childish looks and behavior attracted the attention of Jimmy Kimmel, and Milonakis was hired to do some of MTV's *Jackass*-style stunts.

The all-empowering camera is equal access for all, but, for those bold enough to use it, no matter how weirdly, there could be some viral fame. Some are one-off experiences such as Liam Sullivan's "Shoes" (2007) and the "Back Dorm Boys Lip-sync of I Want it That Way" by the Backstreet Boys (2006). Although these users made additional videos, they are best known for their hits.

Some users have long used the web camera to create long-lasting viral content and happen to know the recipe well enough to produce viral content consistently. The online performance artist Ze Frank is the type of personality who understands the online audience well enough to make content that the audience loves to share. Ze Frank's work ranges from video art projects to vlogs to a faux-documentary series called *True Facts* (2013–). Ze Frank got in early on the web video platforms—in 2001, he made a digital video Christmas card that went viral on his personal site. Since winning a Webby award in 2002, he has continued to create obscure and creative videos online. He isn't just being Ze Frank on the screen: He purposely plays up some of the oddities of the web, overpronounces words, and treats his video productions as if they are live and unpredictable. Ze Frank is aware of the viral recipe and uses it in all of his work.

Saturday Night Live Becomes Viral at Age 31

As a cultural television institution, *Saturday Night Live* (*SNL*) ranks as one of the most respected productions in history. In its 31st year, executive producer and show creator Lorne Michaels knew he had to alter the show to appeal to a new generation of content viewers, and so he hired a sketch-writing trio known as the Lonely Island, made up of comedians Jorma Taccone, Akiva Schaffer, and Andy Samberg. On Saturday, December 17, 2005, *SNL* aired their first digital short, "Lazy Sunday," and by the next morning it was already a viral sensation. "Lazy Sunday" consists of Andy Samberg and Chris Parnell rapping as they spend their day walking around New York's West Village.

The catchy rap verse in the sketch sounds like it's about drug culture, when Samberg and Parnell rap, "It's the Chronic-What-cles of Narnia!" The nerd rap disguised as gangster rap was exactly what *SNL* needed to enter the online world. Director Paul Thomas Anderson was even impressed and said, "It's something the likes of which we haven't seen on *SNL* anytime recently."[12] Over the course of the next decade, the Lonely Island made bunches of viral hits for SNL, such as "D> in a Box" (2009), "I'm on a Boat (ft. T-Pain)" (2009), and "Like a Boss" (2012). The last is a consistently used meme in pop culture.

The Lonely Island was a fixture of *SNL* until the end of the 38th season, when the team went independent to produce films together.

We have to appreciate and respect these viral videos, because they are the blood and veins of the web. These videos are so much part of our collective Internet unconscious that, even if you only recognize one of the afore-mentioned videos, you understand how it works in terms of the online environment. Weezer appreciated the Internet's characters so much that its music video for "Pork and Beans" (2009)[13] features a fair number of Internet celebrities. Viral videos are usually accidental, and your normal, awkward behavior could be the next multi-million-view video that everyone talks about.

WHAT MAKES A VIDEO GO VIRAL?

Bear cubs. Bear cubs in a dumpster. A man named Bear losing his mind over a double rainbow in the sky. Some videos have hundreds of views; some have millions. In 2014, Bear Vasquez's first-person video of his reaction to seeing a double rainbow in Yosemite had more than 40 million plays. How does an obscure video appear out of the ether and make its way into the viral mindset? Kevin Allocca, YouTube's trends manager, explained at his TED Talk that Bear "just simply wanted to share a rainbow" in early 2010. It wasn't until more than a year later that it went viral. This is because the video was mentioned on Jimmy Kimmel's Twitter account.[14]

Allocca explains there are three characteristics of the viral video that cause a spontaneous and rapid growth in views and cultural experience: tastemakers, creative participating communities, and complete unexpectedness. As mentioned, a video may have unpredictability, but that doesn't automatically make it go viral. In our chapter on memes, we recognized that community support for an idea can help boost it, but, in this section of the chapter, we'll focus on the tastemaker effect—the results of influencers in media with large audiences mentioning a video, therefore causing the video to go viral.

Is it possible intentionally to create a viral video? We think so, and this section will focus on four case studies of viral success stories. We'll call them professional viral videos, because they were produced in order to create an amazing shareable effect. In these examples, we hope you draw your own conclusions about how we, the audience, are willing participants who continue to increase the view count, even though we know the secret to their virality.

The videography of the band OK Go, from its 2003 music video "Get Over it" through its 2014 video for "I Won't Let You Down," displays how OK Go's aesthetic and production values honor the desires of the online video audience. The "KONY 2012" video has had more than 100 million views and was made by the nonprofit Invisible Children; it is nearly 30 minutes long, a length that is almost unheard of for viral videos. "KONY 2012" has been the fodder for academics for many years, but we offer a cultural look at why you enjoyed it so much and why you can actually watch it again.

The corporate viral video advertising campaign of 2012–2014 for Old Spice with the Old Spice Guy uses advertising techniques to create viral experiences that are, without a doubt, some of the most successful corporate models to be used for brand awareness. From avant-garde commercials, to social media blitz campaigns, to trolling websites, the Old Spice campaign continues to break new ground in viral technique. With that in mind, we'll discuss Jimmy Kimmel's "Twerking Fail" video. The video is a perfect simulacrum of the world of viral content, and we will talk about how it was done in detail. Many YouTube users have attempted fake virals, and some have succeeded to an extent, but Jimmy Kimmel's team used some of the best ethnographic research on viral content ever produced. From the room, to the quality, to the style, a lot of thought goes into the faux authenticity of a fake viral. You can't fake real—but you may get away with it for a while.

"GET OVER IT"

From the early 1990s through the early 2000s, music video production was a competition. From Madonna to Michael Jackson to Backstreet Boys, music video costs were in the millions, as they competed for the attention of the album- and ticket-buying audience. By the early part of the twenty-first century, it was expected that a large part of a band's budget would be for music video production. Music videos sold the image of the band, and the record company would get a solid return on its investment if a band sold out a concert as a result. Even independent labels were expected to create big-budget videos. In 2001, the indie band OK Go signed with Capitol Records and it released its first album in 2002.

Capitol gave OK Go nearly half a million dollars to produce its music video for the single "Get Over it." The music video was highly produced, with hundreds of edits and visual tricks. It competed in the same visual space as all the top 20 Billboard bands, and the video paid off. The band toured for more than a year and half on its newfound fame. Damian Kulash, the lead singer of OK Go, had an idea to keep the audience excited at the concerts: a choreographed dance to end all their encore performances. Damian's sister, Trish Sie, is a choreographer and she helped the band create a niche performance. They danced to the song "A Millions Ways."

In 2005, the world of visual media shifted drastically. (We go much more in depth in the following chapter.) Music was becoming digital, and distributors were turning toward digital rights management (DRM) to manage their downloads. Damian took a stance against this tactic, saying that the audience didn't want to be regulated, and that fans wouldn't opt for "strings attached" music if they can find the file for free.[15] His point of view attracted the attention of the audience of music lovers who enjoyed the web for its freedom. Although OK Go wasn't the most popular mainstream band, its desire to go against the system made its members folk heroes of the web.

Oh No

OK Go's next album came out at just the right (or wrong) moment, near the onset of YouTube and web video distribution. Damian's own stance on DRM came back to bite him when his record company agreed that the audience would rather find free material than pay. The aptly named album *Oh No* came out to average reviews and became buried in the mix of other college radio music. Damian asked his sister to help them make a cheap, low-budget, entertaining music video. Capitol gave the band almost nothing in the form of budget for this new album's videos. The band put together the music video for "A Million Ways" for about $15 (about $484,985 cheaper than the last video).[16]

The video shows a static camera shot set up in a backyard. The band's members, dressed in their performance clothes and shoes, stand awkwardly as the previous track on the CD ends. A simple title card appears on screen: "OK GO in the backyard dancing." Then it happens, a three-and-a-half-minute choreographed experience of the band doing one of the oddest dances performed by any band. Somewhere between synchronized swimming and performance art, the band sways, dips, and shuffles around the screen until the track ends. And the camera never moves, and the video never cuts. The

Figure 5.3
OK Go "A Million Ways."

aesthetic is like the early web video itself, of static camera shots of vloggers and odd awkward moments and raw video. Damian, the band, and Trish Sie understood the web's viewers and presented directly to them.

The band uploaded the video on a standalone website called 1000000 ways.com, and it was getting 250,000 views per week—more than the album's sales in total. Damian and the band knew this was the right move to connect to the audience on their level, but Capitol didn't agree. Damian explained at The Open Video Conference in 2010 that one of the Capitol Records executives told the band that, if this news "gets out, you're sunk!" And the video was pulled from the web.

Open Minds

This moment in viral history is something to be noted. Even in the earliest days of the video-sharing sites, virality could be achieved by understanding the style the audience appreciated. In many ways, that style is instinctual. OK Go had been doing its silly dance for "A Million Ways" since the late 1990s, when they had just formed in Chicago. The real, in-person audience loved it, so why wouldn't the online audience? And, in fact, the online audience really enjoyed the style, as it was real and authentic and awkward and a bit absurd— just like *everything else* online!

The next single, "Here it Goes Again," needed a video. Damian immediately called his sister. He wanted something similar, but bigger and better. The next video cost nearly $10,000, of which $8,000 was spent on treadmills. Again, a static camera was used, in what is clearly a dance studio, with a tarp draped over the large mirror behind them. The band once again does a choreographed dance, this time assisted by the well-rehearsed, smooth motor movement of two rows of four treadmills, all operating simultaneously, and the video is again performed in one take. The label had no idea what to do with it, because it didn't fit in the MTV space or any conventional music video style; Capitol posted it on StupidVideos.com. The band took matters into its own hands and posted it on YouTube a few weeks later. It immediately went viral, scoring between 600,000 and 800,000 views per day and over 2 million views by the end of the week. The indie band OK Go was asked to perform at the Video Music Awards (on treadmills) and featured in *USA Today* talking about new techniques. In a twist of pure, corporate irony, Capitol Records' executive vice president, Ted Mico said, "We learned there's no substitute for an open mind."[17]

Henry Jenkins considers "Here it Goes Again" to be a perfect fit for YouTube. He told *USA Today*, in 2006, that the video is "a visual spectacle that you want to show to someone else."[18] Jenkins explains that true authenticity is hard to pull off. Damian agreed and felt that the web gives the band a direct connection with the fans. And this is really what it's all about—connecting to the fans and the audience. If you can master that, you have the potential for sharing content rapidly. The media are already viral; it just takes the right moment to fulfill their path.

Over the last decade, OK Go has produced more than three-dozen music videos, and all have fit directly into the current trend of similar video aesthetics. The band even decided to make a video for every track on the album *Of the Blue Colour of the Sky* (2008). The aesthetic varies per track, but all fit into a YouTube environment. The song "WTF" is filmed in front of a green screen and takes advantage of digital artifacts and video trails. "End Love" is a single-take video, shot in a park over the course of 4 days, using new camera timelapse technology. (Yes—4 days! Uncut!) "White Knuckles" features dog tricks and IKEA containers, all choreographed to make a visually stimulating dance (dogs and dancing—viral recipe).

Independence and Support

The most impressive videos from that album mark the band's split from EMI/Capitol Records. The band decided to become independent and start its own record company, called Paracadute.[19] Although being independent has its benefits of keeping more profits, it also has the downside of lack of funding. The video for "All Is Not Lost" was combined with a Google Experiment, like The Arcade Fire's "The Wilderness Downtown" project we talked about in Chapter 3. But what solidified OK Go as a viral powerhouse was the video for "This Too Shall Pass." While on tour, the band recorded a one-take version of this video with the Notre Dame marching band, with live audio from the marching band. It was a throwback to the band's origin—simple, rough, low-res, and uncut. Soon after it released this version of the video, it released the Rube Goldberg machine version of the video—an intense, single-take, huge-machine, timed experience.

The Rube Goldberg machine version of "This Too Shall Pass" changed the way we understand video funding and execution. It cost several hundred thousand dollars to make and required 89 takes and three "full machine takes" to record and dozens of staff members to create. And it required knowledge of how to fund it. Taking a tip from "Where the Hell Is Matt" (2008), the band realized it could ask a company to sponsor the video. "Where the Hell Is Matt" is a video about Matt Harding in an around-the-world experiment to document people dancing in all regions on Earth, from Saigon to New Guinea to Seattle. Matt was seen on the web, and Matt Lauer invited him on the *Today* show. The *Today* show acted as the tastemaker, encouraging others to see the video. When Matt got the attention he needed, he matched up with Stride Gum to sponsor his video. With 50 million views, Stride Gum's investment paid off.

OK Go was offered support from State Farm for the production of the huge "This Too Shall Pass" video, and now the video is one of the best-known productions from the band. It has mastered the idea of branded content without losing authenticity. In a music video called "Needing/Getting," the band made a music video using live audio and the Chevy Cruze car. Thirty seconds from the video were extracted and used as a commercial during the 2012 Super Bowl. This authentic approach to branded content is not easy. You have to build your audience first, and then gain monetary support. You cannot start with money in mind.

OK Go's album *Hungry Ghosts* (2014) was supported by its fans using a crowd-funding platform called PledgeMusic, and the band promises to continue to break ground with original and creative videos. The video for "The Writing's on the Wall" (2014) features a single-take, *trompe l'oeil* visual effect that required a large, choreographed crew and impeccable timing and framing. The video "I Won't Let You Down" (2014) represents the capabilities of video production in the viral age. The band dances on high-tech scooters, while hundreds of umbrella-wielding backup dancers open and close in a synchronized art display—while being recorded by a drone that eventually flies above the clouds.

Figure 5.4
OK Go "I Won't Let You Down" (2014) music video.

"I Won't Let You Down" is sponsored by Honda, who supplied the scooters, but no one will care about the brand—they'll watch the video over and over and share it because it displays the coolest possible evolution of web video available. OK Go, as a band, goes to great lengths to balance its corporate sponsorship and dedication to its fans. In order to focus on its artistic work, without exploiting its audience, the band maintains consistent communication with its fans in the digital space and remains as transparent as possible. OK Go's videos, in order from 2003 to the present, display not only the current technical prowess of video production, but also a keen attention to what the audience wants to see. As you've read, viral videos usually happen by accident, and views are driven by tastemakers, unpredictability, and community support. OK Go has become a tastemaker with vast community support, and it is always coming up with new and unexpected projects. And we'll continue watching and sharing.

Virals Out of Context

OK Go's "Needing/Getting" used the Chevy Cruze compact car in the video, and then Chevy used the first 30 seconds of the video as one of its 2012 Super Bowl commercials. To air the commercial during the Super Bowl cost Chevy several million dollars, much more than it paid OK Go to produce the video. It paid off for both Chevy and the band.

This method of viral appropriation doesn't always succeed as well. Take, for example, the honey badger Pistachio commercial. The viral video "The Crazy Nastyass Honey Badger (Original Narration by Randall)" (2011) is a viral sensation as a quirky remix of a *National Geographic* special about the angry little badgers, produced in 2007. The "Nastyass Honey Badger" remix is along the lines of other *National Geographic*-style remixes, with voice dubs over the animals on screen—this one happened to go more viral than most because of the narration. The video became a meme and has been referenced widely. On September 30, 2011, Pistachio aired a commercial during *Dancing With the Stars* featuring the Randall narration and a similar script to the viral video.

If you were to have seen the commercial on *Dancing With the Stars* that night, along with 13 million other people, you might have been confused, if you didn't know the origin video. If you aren't web savvy, you may not actually understand many of the references Pistachio's commercials make in reference to viral videos. It didn't hurt Pistachio one bit, but it does help as a great example of how memes require time to enter our common consciousness and to be seen by a mass audience.

"KONY 2012"—THE 30-MINUTE VIRAL VIDEO

There's no set rule for how long a viral video should be to become viral, and there's also no set, standard recipe, but, when a 30-minute video gets 43 million views in 2 days, you should be interested in how that happened. On March

5, 2012, the "KONY 2012" video went live on YouTube, and, by the end of the first night, every single box that the organization Invisible Children made for the campaign to stop the Lord's Resistance Army (LRA) warlord Joseph Kony had sold out. The video was made by Invisible Children, an organization whose goal it was to bring Joseph Kony to justice, and it did a far better job on the video production than it originally thought. Jason Russell, the CEO and protagonist of the video, assumed that virality meant getting maybe between 500,000 and a million views in a year and would be successful. They had 120 million in 5 days.[20]

How could this happen? Well, according to Kevin Allocca's breakdown of how videos go viral, it contains all the necessary elements: tastemakers in the form of stars such as Angelina Jolie backing the project;[21] the unexpectedness of the contents of the film—many people had never heard of Kony or the conflict in Africa; and it had a large community of supporters, including the US Congress. But still, at 30 minutes, there must be something else as part of the success. And there definitely is. We are going to break down the film into its major elements, to explain how, sometimes, virality isn't determined by videos shared on the Internet, but by the collective conscious of viewers in the form of tropes.

The Experiment

In the video "Kony 2012," we aren't introduced to the enemy of the film until nearly 9 minutes into the production. The first few minutes are vital to grabbing the attention of the audience. For the opening sequence, a calm Jason Russell sets the mood for the next few minutes by explaining that more people are on Facebook now than the world's total population 200 years ago. In framing the story, the video shows positive viral videos in a montage, such as "Thumbs Up for Rock and Roll" (2011) and "29 Years Old and Hearing Myself for the 1st Time!" (2011). By adding these positive images and a deep piano track, Russell sets the mood for something *we want to watch*. He then explains how to watch the video: "The game has new rules. The next twenty-seven minutes are an experiment. But in order for it to work, you have to pay attention." As you'll find out more next chapter, if you want the web audience to do something, you just have to ask them. In the case of "Kony 2012," it's an experiment: What do you have to lose?

In any good story, there are storytelling elements that are pretty standard in order to carry us through the plot. It has to have a beginning, middle, and an end, character development, rising action and falling action, and exposition. At the onset of this video, the audience has no idea who Jason Russell is, and so the first object of this video is to help the audience get over their collective doubt of the protagonist, our hero Jason Russell. The first few minutes give a backstory to Russell (family man, caring father, activist) and then introduce a supporting character, Jacob, a victim of the LRA abuses in Uganda. The images used in this first part are both supportive of, and positive for, Jason, and equally horrifying when it comes to Jacob and the other refugees sleeping in a camp (5:36).

Jacob's story is heartbreaking. The emotional impact of his testimony is an incredible and authentic sadness that we, as an audience, wish never happened to him. Eight-and-half minutes in, Jason Russell explains that 2012 is the year we can catch Kony, our antagonist, "and change the course of human history." And Kony is then introduced, with an expiration date at the end of 2012. To get the full sense of how to understand who Joseph Kony is, we are introduced to the next supporting actor, Gavin Russell, Jason's son.

Gavin's part is simple: He is *us*, the viewer. While we are not aware of the issues beyond what we've been told thus far, Jason asks the boy who the bad guys are, and we are given an insight to how the project was written. Jason asks Gavin if he knows what his dad does for a living, and Gavin answers that he "stops the bad guys" who happen to be "Star Wars people." Gavin goes directly to the biggest, baddest bad guys he knows, and they happen to be Darth Vader and the Stormtroopers. This analogy makes sense, as you will see in a bit. Gavin is shown images of Joseph Kony and Jacob, and then Jason explains to his son the horrors of what Kony does. At 10:17 into the film, the boy is dismayed by the news and does a subtle shake of his head. He's hurt, and so are we. We are now invested—*we will* watch the rest of the film!

Make Him Famous

Over the course of the next 10 minutes, the exposition of the film explains all the efforts Invisible Children is making to stop Kony, and the progress it has made. The film asks the viewers to pressure famous people (tastemakers) such as Rihanna and Justin Bieber to support the cause. The goal is set in place: Make him famous—as famous as other terrible humans, such as Hitler and Osama bin Laden. The video shows rallies and protests, and, just when the audience feels nearly empowered, it employs Shepard Fairey, the viral-esque street art remixer.

Fairey is best known for his Obey street signs and his Obama "Hope" poster, which many believe helped Obama in his polls.[22] His skill set is remixing other work to be visually stimulating. He says, "I'm not a corporation or own a news station, I just don't have any say. But see what I've done and I think it's empowered a lot of people to realize that one individual can make an impact."

In the 25th minute (25:23), the deep bass "I Can't Stop" by Flux Pavilion plays, and we are in! Let's light a flare, run around, and catch Kony!

But instead—we shared the video and believed we did our part.

The Magic of Storytelling—Peeling away the structure

At the Northeast Media Literacy Conference in 2012, the "KONY 2012" phenomenon dominated the conversation of more than half the panels, as it probably did at any media literacy function. The video felt like an anomaly, as it debuted on YouTube to a viral boost so rapid that it beat the previous record holder, "Susan Boyle's First Audition" (2009). It wasn't a hard stretch to make a very similar comparison between the "KONY 2012" video and the Susan Boyle video, because, perhaps, they are the same video.

In traditional storytelling, the elements are nearly universal to any good story. As mentioned previously, the elements exist to keep the viewers' attention and to move the plot along. But, if you strip out all the elements, what do you have? A protagonist we don't know and we must learn to trust. An antagonist that, through elements involved in the story, we learn to hate. Supporting characters help us trust the protagonist and support the plot. And a quality exposition leads to a climax that creates an emotional impact to remember our hero and support the cause.

In the first few seconds of the Susan Boyle video, we get a close-up of her face and we, the audience, immediately judge her, before the actual game show judges of *Britain's Got Talent* even see her. Susan walks out onto the stage and faces her enemies: Simon Cowell, Piers Morgan, and Amanda Holden. You can see from their faces that Susan is already at a disadvantage and she'll have to fight to survive. In this video, the supporting characters are very literal: The judges are judges, the supporting characters are the emcees, and the audience (like Gavin Russell) is actually, well, an audience. And they all play their parts perfectly. Simon asks Susan what she wants to be, and she replies: "Like Elaine Paige!" This is met with rolling eyes and our collective agreement that this'll be tough. Then she sings, "I Dreamed a Dream" from *Les Miserables*, and the battle begins. Our jaws drop, because she sings it beautifully, and, over the next 4 minutes, we're treated to a story plot that takes James Cameron 3 hours to complete in his movies.

And that's where it starts to make sense: Simon Cowell is the "Star Wars People," because the bad guys are always the "Star Wars People." *Star Wars: The Empire strikes back* is the same plot as "KONY 2012" and "Susan Boyle's First Audition," and the same as *Avatar* and *Titanic*. It is the one story that is so consistently found in popular films, and it's called the *monomyth*, or the hero's journey. Joseph Campbell borrowed the term from James Joyce's *Finnegan's Wake* to describe the story that we seem to share most often.[23] It is a storytelling trope that describes easy-to-carry storylines, from some of the oldest stories we've ever heard to the most sci-fi plotlines we know. When people are asked what *Avatar* is about, some of the responses are "*Pocahontas* (in space)" or "*Dances With Wolves* (in Space)," and that's because those films

Figure 5.5
The hero's journey.

Source: Wikimedia
Commons

are *also* the monomyth. It's no wonder that *Avatar* is the highest-grossing film of all time, if "KONY 2012" and "Susan Boyle" are the fastest-growth videos—people love that story.

As a good reader of new and digital media, you should ask questions about why something can go viral. It may fall into Kevin Allocca's recipe of taste-makers, active community, and unpredictability; or it may fall into the shock and awe and cuteness category; or it just may be a story that we like to hear over and over.

Viral Activism

The "KONY 2012" video obviously received a fair amount of criticism of its campaign because it so quickly rose into the cultural commentary. Anything that gains a quick rise, such as a viral video, will attract attention and commentary. In the case of "KONY 2012," the nonprofit Invisible Children was targeted, because, when people looked into how much of the money raised went directly to stopping Joseph Kony, it turned out to be less than people originally believed. Many felt the funds were better spent on supporting aid groups in Africa. (The film alone cost $3.8 million.)[24]

The "KONY 2012" video allows us to have a discussion about "clicktivism" versus actual activism. Clicktivism, also known as armchair activism, is a form of viral sharing that convinces the user that they have made a difference, simply by sharing the content. In reality, that just raises the brand awareness, rather than making a difference. In the summer of 2014, a viral meme appeared called "The ALS Ice Bucket Challenge," which acted as both a fundraiser and a viral activist campaign. The campaign was designed to raise awareness and attract donations for research into amyotrophic lateral sclerosis, also known as Lou Gehrig's Disease, a disease that causes nerve cells to break down and die, with no known cure. The viral campaign, which started in the Boston area in the summer of 2014, was a success.[25] It raised over $100 million for ALS research. Although many criticized the ice bucket challenge for misused funds, as with KONY, in both situations awareness of an issue was raised.

Ultimately, the best campaign is a campaign that causes awareness and funding and support. This is incredibly hard to do, but the video method of virality seems to be the most powerful method.

RESELLING DEODORANT THROUGH VIRALS

The Old Spice brand of deodorant, anti-perspirant, and body spray used to have an image issue. Once used primarily by an older male crowd (see: elderly), it wasn't viewed as an appealing product by young men at all. That all changed when the ad agency Wieden+Kennedy hired former football player turned actor Isaiah Mustafa to play "The Man Your Man Could Smell Like" in 2010. Through a brilliant gamble, savvy writing, and playing on a recent advertising trend of "you" campaigns, Old Spice completely changed its image, and a primarily younger male crowd purchases today.

"You" Campaigns

In 2009, just 3 years after *Time* magazine named "You" person of the year, ad agencies worldwide started thinking about how to attract "you" to their products. "You," here, is defined as the overall you, not the personal you, as in the you of YouTube. Yahoo! rebranded in 2009 to a you-type style with its "It's You" anthem commercial,[26] and the now defunct Flip camera ran a similar campaign. The most effective of these campaigns was the HTC "Quietly Brilliant" advertising campaign, by Deutsch LA Inc. The mobile phone maker HTC has tough competition, with Apple dominating the market, and the campaign exploits "the emotional connection now common between man and phone,"[27] found the rhetoric and civic life course at Penn State. HTC's campaign keeps the pronouns simple and speaks in second person, making you feel as if you need this phone because it *gets* you better than anything else. Rhetorically, it works in an eerily similar way to a fortune cookie, in that it always feels directed to you personally.

"The Man Your Man Could Smell Like"

In the following year, Old Spice utilized the same methods of attracting viewers to its brand. It starts as a standard cologne commercial would, with a shirtless man in a towel. But it's different, because the Old Spice guy isn't talking to men–he's talking to women. It's a completely unpredictable commercial shot in one take (see: OK Go), where the scene around the Old Spice guy rapidly shifts from a shower scene to boat to a beach, on a horse. His rhetoric is that of the fortune cookie, where he holds open a clam filled with "two tickets to that thing you love—look again! The tickets are now diamonds! Anything is possible when your man smells like Old Spice and not a lady."

In 2 weeks, the commercial on YouTube had more than 3 million views, and now, over 50 million. The oddness of the commercial and the frank "you" rhetoric make the video shareable, even if you don't want to purchase Old Spice products. Over the next few years, Old Spice pushed the boundaries of odd campaigns by downplaying the specific details of their product and selling the image of "you." Old Spice stays with the trends of virality over time to sell to the present audience. Hiring Terry Crews, another actor and former football player, Old Spice increased the weirdness of its ads to continue with unpredictability.

"Interneterventions"

In 2013, Old Spice's parent company Procter & Gamble took advantage of the gullibility of social media users by creating a prank viral campaign that looked like odd products that people would click on out of curiosity, such as solid-gold headsets, cologne with protein, and black-leather sheets. The Old Spice "Interneterventions" campaign disguised amusing commercials starring Isaiah Mustafa behind odd websites. In order to attract a younger crowd, the brand aimed directly at guys who may click on competing products.[28] The campaign brings the user to a realistic-looking website, which sounds an alarm, and the commercial begins. At the end, users are encouraged to prank another friend who may be making "embarrassing life mistakes."

If a company that is three-fourths of a century old can change its image using viral campaigns, there's hope for any brand. It just has to be weird and unpredictable and shareable. The weirdness of the campaign put it in meme territory, making it something that makes you feel that you have to see to believe. And, in doing so, Old Spice shaved 50 years off its aftershave audience.

Viral Seeding

The term "broadcasting" takes its name from a piece of farm equipment that cast seeds in a broad throw. In terms of video placement, another term that comes from farming is "seeding." If you need an immense number of views of your video in a short length of time, there are seeding companies that exist to help you increase your play count.

If you want to see how viral videos are ranked, you can check the Viral Video Chart,[29] run by Unruly Media. The chart tracks viral movement of content through a combination of view count, shares, and mentions. Virality isn't just about how many times a video is seen; it is also about how much the video embeds itself in our digital culture. Unruly Media operates the chart because it needs the data to gauge its viral success. "Unruly is the leading programmatic platform for social video advertising," its website states. Social video advertising means that, sometimes, the reason you are stumbling across a viral video is because it was actually planted there—or "seeded" on your feed. For a somewhat pricey fee, you can pay companies such as Unruly Media or the social video agency the Viral Factory to "deliver online engagement through compelling content."[30]

Unruly Media's work has ranged from Cadbury (the parent company of Stride Gum) to the Old Spice campaign. Sometimes, you need to ask yourself how you are coming across that viral commercial—is it by chance, or did a company seed it there to grow into a beautiful cultural flower?

Corporate video seeding is relegated to viral video distribution; it can be used to spread videos for any campaign. The online audience often overlooks the reasons as to why a video is placed on its feed or in its advertising line of sight, unaware that the video was placed there intentionally. The same tools used to make you laugh at a new campaign may also be used to spread a message that may not be in your best interest. Seeding companies are getting better at making video placement look "organic" or placed for natural user reasons, but you should keep a skeptical eye on why a video gains so many views so quickly.

VIRAL HOAXES AND SUCCESSES

We end this chapter with one of the biggest misconceptions about viral videos: that they can be easily made. Very often, we hear students or consultants complain to us that they've been asked to "make something go viral." The term is thrown around widely after several advertising campaigns successfully "went viral," and now others would like to appear savvy and part of the growing trend. Our advice is not to try to go viral, because that isn't always a good thing. Sometimes, videos go viral for the exact opposite reason someone would want. The Missouri East Hills Mall commercial is so poorly made that it went viral. The Reddit community found the ad and posted it as "Terrible Mall Commercial" (2014), and it now has more than 2 million views. The producer of the video set out to make a "viral" video in a serious manner, but director Chris Fleck's best intentions went viral because it was so bad.[31]

It is possible to make a viral video; it requires an extreme attention to detail and authenticity. It also requires timing, trend watching, and placement. On August 25, 2013, Miley Cyrus and Robin Thicke performed together at the MTV Video Music Awards, to a medley of their songs ("We Can't Stop" and "Blurred Lines"), and the performance ended with Miley giving Robin Thicke "an up close and personal private twerk show as the song climaxed."[32] For the next week, the odd, risqué, bottom-bouncing dance dominated the pop-culture news and reporting. On September 3, a little over a week later, the video "Worst Twerk Fail EVER—Girl catches fire!" (2013) was uploaded on YouTube. The video shows a young woman seemingly home alone, creating a web video showing off her twerking skills. She props herself on the door, dancing away, until her roommate comes home, knocking the dancer down onto a coffee table, and she catches fire. The video ends abruptly in the middle of the screaming aftermath. It gained millions of views in a week—and it was fake.

Attention to Detail and Research

Making a viral video requires watching lots of viral videos and studying all aspects of them— from the timing to the camera moves to the reactions of the people involved. If you want to trick people, you have to assume that the viral audience may be cynical and looking for potential flaws. When G4BreakingNews posted "Eagle Picks up a Baby" (2012), so many people watched it that the Montreal's National Animation and Design Center (Centre NAD) had to post a notice assuring people that their babies are safe from being snatched by an eagle.[33] The video has rawness, authenticity, and unpredictable timing that make the viewer want to believe it, but, on multiple views, the CGI is evident. Art students created the effect in computer graphics in their simulation workshop production class at Centre NAD and most likely got a high passing grade.

Jimmy Kimmel understands that late-night television needs the boost of online video to support its viewership, as the late-night audience may not be his target audience. Kimmel consistently makes web videos that go viral, with *America's Funniest Home Videos*-type audience dares such as his "YouTube Challenges," "I Told My Kids I Ate All Their Halloween Candy" (2011), and "I Gave My Kids a Terrible Present" (2012). Kimmel encourages the viewers to tape their kids' reactions to devastating news and send the videos in to *Jimmy Kimmel Live*, where he reedits them into a compilation.

When Jimmy Kimmel wanted to experiment with original viral material, he hired Brad Morrison of Slim Pictures to create a viral sensation. Morrison admits to watching lots of twerking videos and all the details: "who was in them, where they were shot, what was in the background, what the lighting was like, etc."[34] After doing a fair amount of research, Kimmel's staff built a set to mimic a dorm room, because fire wouldn't be permitted on an actual college campus. The details were down to the molding and light switches. Because of copyright, they couldn't use just any track, so they used something from their music library called "Grind Games." They then hired Daphne Avalon, a stuntwoman, to play the role of the doomed twerker. She wore common yoga pants, and Brad Morrison even left her tag out as an added detail. Morrison hired Daphne because he needed someone who wouldn't be recognizable but also was willing to take a fall and catch on fire. Lastly, they shot the viral with a MacBook Pro computer to create full authenticity.

Riding on the wave of the twerking news, the video blew up and gained millions of views, until Jimmy Kimmel announced on his show that he would be inviting poor Caitlin Heller from Kansas City, Missouri, onto his show to talk about her incident. Caitlin/Daphne was Skyped in on her web camera (the offending capture device!), and then, while Caitlin was explaining "her accident," Jimmy appeared next to her at her dorm and then, through the magic of television, revealed Daphne as an actress on live TV. The reveal has more views than the original twerking fail video, because it truly is an unpredictable event. In the "uncut" version of the video, Jimmy shows up to put Caitlin's fire out and turns off the web camera.

Viral Videos With an Asterisk

The effect of a viral video is not only momentary visual enjoyment, but could also potentially be making you complicit in societal issues that require community attention. The video "Star Wars Kid" is a great example of virals we shouldn't watch and share. Ghyslain Raza did not intend for that video to get out to the public. When his classmates placed the video online, the video went viral, and Raza fell victim to immense amounts of cyberbullying. Watching and sharing the video make us complicit in Raza's pain. In the present, Raza is now a lawyer and has utilized the video to bring awareness to cyberbullying.

"Star Wars Kid" isn't the only video we should talk about in this manner. The very viral remix videos such as "The Bed Intruder Song" (2010) by schmoyoho and "Ain't Nobody Got Time for That!" (2012) by parodyfactory1 allow us to have a conversation about exploitation. In both videos, the viral fame comes from the remixer, not the original content, and, in both examples, the video is a remix of an interview of a black American from a seemingly lower socioeconomic region. This type of viral is exploitive, as it popularizes black culture without confronting the issue of how the reporter originally came across the interview and why the news agency allowed the interview to go on air as is. Additionally, in both situations, the subject is a victim of unforeseen and unfortunate circumstances that were out of the interviewees' control, and we, the viewers of the viral video, seem to ignore the potential setback to both Antoine Dodson and Kimberly "Sweet Brown" Wilkins. By watching the videos, we are making light of the issues of attempted rape and property destruction that are harmful to communities.

This type of exploitation for entertainment has always occurred and can be seen even in happy videos such as "29 Years Old and Hearing Myself for the 1st Time!" (2011), which shows the joy in a woman's face as her cochlear implants are turned on. This video tells the viewer to watch the woman objectively and unfortunately sidesteps what it means to truly understand and appreciate deaf culture and the significance of being hearing impaired. Sarah Churman was born deaf, and we celebrate the feat of her hearing for the first time, rather than celebrate her for who she is naturally.

To be a savvy user of the web means to be considerate of larger societal issues and understand the power we, the viewers, have in the act of viewing and sharing. We are capable of increasing awareness for issues that are often ignored and we are equally capable of ignoring issues embedded in the content. Be aware of what you watch and you will be a smarter viewer and online participant.

VIRALITY IS YOU

For videos to go viral, they may need tastemakers such as Jimmy Kimmel; they may need the unpredictability of a single-take, quirky ad campaign; they may need a supportive community willing to drive up views and continue to share new and original music videos; and, sometimes, it just needs the same story retold in a new and interesting way. But the only way a video goes viral is if you watch and share the video, over and over and over and over and over . . .

NOTES

1   Vernallis, C. (2013). *Unruly Media: YouTube, music video, and the new digital cinema*. New York: Oxford University Press.
2   Greenfield, R. (2013, August 8). "The Internet's Attention Span for Video Is Quickly Shrinking." Retrieved from www.thewire.com/technology/2013/08/internets-attention-span-video-quickly-shrinking/68114/ (accessed May 6, 2015).
3   Statistic Brain. (2014). Attention span statistics. Retrieved from www.statisticbrain.com/attention-span-statistics/ (accessed May 6, 2015).

4   Greenfield, R. (2014, September 18). "How Big Does a Screen Need to Be to Watch a Film?" Retrieved from www.thewire.com/technology/2012/09/how-big-does-screen-need-be-watch-film/56971/ (accessed May 6, 2015).

5   Vernallis, C. (2013). *Unruly Media: YouTube, music video, and the new digital cinema.* New York: Oxford University Press.

6   As told to the Molloy College New Media program, October 2013.

7   Carlson, E. (2008, March 24). "YouTube Awards 'Chocolate Rain,' Other Top Videos." Retrieved from http://abcnews.go.com/Technology/story?id=4502057 (accessed May 6, 2015).

8   *Time* (2009, September 9). "YouTube's 50 Best Videos." Retrieved from http://content.time.com/time/specials/packages/completelist/0,29569,1974961,00.html (accessed May 6, 2015).

9   Winnebago man. Retrieved from http://winnebagoman.com/ (accessed May 6, 2015).

10 Godin, S. (2000 August). "Unleash Your Idea Virus." Retrieved from www.fastcompany.com/40104/unleash-your-ideavirus (accessed May 6, 2015).

11 Segal, D. (2005 August 11). "Who's the Comedian?" Retrieved from www.washingtonpost.com/wp-dyn/content/article/2005/08/10/AR2005081002371.html (accessed May 6, 2015).

12 Itzkoff, D. (2005, December 27). "Nerds in the Hood, Stars on the Web." Retrieved from www.nytimes.com/2005/12/27/arts/television/27samb.html?_r=0 (accessed May 6, 2015).

13 Weezer (2009). "Pork and Beans." Retrieved from www.youtube.com/watch?v=PQHPYelqr0E (accessed May 6, 2015).

14 Allocca, K. (2012, February). "Why Videos Go Viral [transcript]." Retrieved from www.ted.com/talks/kevin_allocca_why_videos_go_viral/transcript?language=en (accessed May 6, 2015).

15 Kulash, D. (2005, December 6). "Buy, Play, Trade, Repeat." Retrieved from www.nytimes.com/2005/12/06/opinion/06kulash.html?_r=0/ (accessed May 6, 2015).

16 According to Damian—Presented at the Open Video Conference, October 1, 2010.

17 Maney, K. (2006 November 28). "Blend of Old, New Media Launched OK Go." Retrieved from http://usatoday30.usatoday.com/tech/news/2006-11-27-ok-go_x.htm (accessed May 6, 2015).

18 Ibid.

19 OK Go (2010, March 9). "OK Go Announces New Label." Retrieved from www.youtube.com/watch?v=Mdyb_Ip_R8w (accessed May 6, 2015).

20 Sanders, S. (2014, June 14). "The 'Kony 2012' Effect: Recovering from a viral sensation." Retrieved from www.npr.org/2014/06/14/321853244/the-kony-2012-effect-recovering-from-a-viral-sensation (accessed May 6, 2015).

21 Child, B. (2012, March 12). "Kony 2012: Angelina Jolie calls for Ugandan warlord's arrest." Retrieved from www.theguardian.com/film/2012/mar/12/kony-2012-angelina-jolie?INTCMP=SRCH%20back%20the%20campaign (accessed May 6, 2015).

22 Arnon, B. (2008, November 13). "How the Obama 'Hope' Poster Reached a Tipping Point and Became a Cultural Phenomenon: An interview with the artist Shepard Fairey." Retrieved from www.huffingtonpost.com/ben-arnon/how-the-obama-hope-poster_b_133874.html (accessed May 6, 2015).

23 Campbell, J. (1949). *The Hero With a Thousand Faces.* New York: Pantheon Books.

24 Curran, K. (2012, March 8). "Donating to Kony 2012: Where does the money go?" Retrieved from http://boston.cbslocal.com/2012/03/08/donating-to-kony-2012-where-does-the-money-go/ (accessed May 6, 2015).

25 Reddy, S. (2014, August 14). "How the Ice-Bucket Challenge Got Its Start." Retrieved from http://online.wsj.com/articles/how-the-ice-bucket-challenge-got-its-start-1408049557 (accessed May 6, 2015).

26 Yahoo! (2009, September 28). "Anthem (It's You)." Retrieved from www.youtube.com/watch?v=Z0tukrdXz-Q (accessed May 6, 2015).

27 Randclife (2013, October 10). "HTC 'You' Campaign." Retrieved from https://sites.psu.edu/randclife/2013/10/10/htc-you-campaign/ (accessed May 6, 2015).

28 Thornton, M. (2014, January 22). "This New Old Spice Video Is the Most Hilarious Internet Ad so far This Year." Retrieved from www.buzzfeed.com/maycie/is-this-new-old-spice-video-the-most-hilarious-internet-ad-s#.gr4Q6mJeJ5 (accessed May 6, 2015).

29 Viral Video Chart. Unruly Media. Retrieved from http://viralvideochart.unrulymedia.com/all (accessed May 6, 2015).

30 The Viral Factory. Retrieved from www.theviralfactory.com/#!/agency (accessed May 6, 2015).

31 Carbone, G. (2014, August 19). "The East Hills Mall's Back-to-School Commercial Goes Viral for All the Wrong Reasons [video]." Retrieved from http://news.moviefone.com/2014/08/19/mall-back-to-school-commercial-viral/ (accessed May 6, 2015).

32 Mlynar, P. (2013, August 25). "Miley Cyrus Twerks, Gives Robin Thicke Some Tongue at VMAs." Retrieved from www.mtv.com/news/1713017/miley-cyrus-robin-thicke-vma-twerk/ (accessed May 6, 2015).

33 Centre NAD. Retrieved from http://blogue.centrenad.com/2012/12/19/centre-nad-reassures-montrealers-no-danger-of-being-snatched-by-a-royal-eagle/?lang=en (accessed May 6, 2015).

34 Ferra, A. (2014, October). "Director Brad Morrison Reveals How He and Jimmy Kimmel Made the Best Twerk Fail Video. Ever." Retrieved from www.fastcocreate.com/3017194/director-brad-morrison-reveals-how-he-and-jimmy-kimmel-made-the-best-twerk-fail-video-ever (accessed May 6, 2015).

CHAPTER 6

Multimedia Storytelling

By now, you are becoming pretty savvy at the new and digital media environment. You've explored websites, viral videos, and memes, and you understand how and why users participate. This chapter will expand your knowledge to the most valuable sections of the digital environment: storytelling in the online space.

THE EVER-EVOLVING MULTIMEDIA STORYTELLING ENVIRONMENT

Throughout the history of visual storytelling, television producers have relied on the audience to guide them in the storytelling process. Since the advent of the online media distribution outlets, the audience has fragmented more than any professional could have predicted, and, as we move toward the end of the second decade of the twenty-first century, we aim to give you an understanding of the new and digital environments. The evolution of visual media is a drawn-out process, and only in the last few years has storytelling rapidly changed.

In "New Narrative Programming in the Digital Space," we look into early web series, such as *We Need Girlfriends*, *Chad Vader: Day shift manager*, and *The Guild*, that serve as foundation material and inspiration for thousands of future web series producers. During the 2007 Writers Guild of America strike, the online narrative environment shifted when several famous actors and directors took to the broadband space to produce high-quality content. Comparable with the 1987 writers' strike that spawned *Cops* and the subsequent reality genre, the 2007 strike resulted in unlimited access to the web and was an invitation for independent creatives in a new environment.

Vloggers, or *YouTube personalities*, are storytellers who use themselves as main characters to fulfill the audience's demand for a relatable persona to watch on the screen. In the early days of YouTube, just after the upload craze of copyrighted material, bloopers, stunts, cats, and babies, storytellers appeared.

Early adopters such as Peter Oakley (geriatric1927) and Tyler Oakley (not related) used the YouTube platform to express themselves and tell their personal stories. We will show you how to participate as a vlogger, beginning with several case studies on the early days of YouTube participation. Several of the early adopters, such as Shane Dawson and Tyler Oakley, continue producing content and evolve along with the audience. Their methods and attention to detail help YouTube evolve as well.

The nature of digital media allows content to be downloaded, manipulated, and re-uploaded by any user with access to the right tools. In "The Remix Culture" section, we will cover the online art form and prevalence of remixes and explain several examples of remix culture, from amateur remixes to highly produced remixes such as Kutiman's ThruYou project, Nick Bertke's Pogo, and "Brian Williams Raps Rappers Delight" from *The Tonight Show Starring Jimmy Fallon*. As popular as it is, remixing comes with drawbacks—namely issues concerning copyright and theft or alteration of intellectual property. Expanding on some of the issues discussed in Chapter 2, this section will introduce Lawrence Lessig, Kirby Ferguson, and remix activists such as Elisa Kreisinger.

As a result of the content created by new media participants, the traditional media markets are shifting, and traditional content creators have been forced to come to a rapid understanding of the value of the broadband video experience. Services such as Netflix, which surpassed HBO in subscriber revenue in 2014,[1] are competing with 30-year-old brands to produce television series and independent films made for the streaming audience. In less than a decade, broadband video went from a video depository to becoming one of the sole ways that people receive media. As a result, the growing number of "cord-cutters," (those who have chosen not to have cable) has pressured the cable companies and distributors into thinking differently about the model of how people are watching content and how content should be made.

Fragmented visual media audiences have changed "the business of multimedia storytelling" by identifying where and when they want to watch programming. From web television channels such as My Damn Channel or Funny or Die to high-concept programming such as *Video Game High School*, *Epic Meal Time*, and *Comedians in Cars Getting Coffee*, online multimedia content is chaotic, creative, and fascinating. We will show you how vloggers have transformed themselves into media conglomerates, how YouTube channels have teamed up for profit sharing, how brands have moved to the creative space, and why traditional television has chosen outlets such as Netflix and Amazon.

This is an exciting chapter, with a lot to watch and understand, as we offer a vast survey of material while we simultaneously educate you and inspire you to participate.

The Prehistory of Multimedia Storytelling

Before "Mr. Television" Milton Berle appeared on stage, a quartet of gas-station attendants entertained the audience with a song about how much care the "Merry Texaco-men" put into their work. After their presentation, Milton Berle would walk out in one of his zany outfits to the anticipation of over 45 percent of the American television audience. Back in 1949, programming was considered *branded entertainment*, also known as sponsored content. *The Texaco Star Theater* pulled in the majority share of the audience because there were very few networks (three to be exact—NBC, ABC, and CBS). Those who were fortunate enough to have a television set in their home watched "Uncle Miltie" once a week.

In the 1940s and 1950s, television sales in the United States took off, and television programming became the primary medium for advertising. Shows such as *The Colgate Comedy Hour* or *Kraft Television Theater* dominated the airwaves.[2] The television personality became the viewers' entertainment fix. Lucille Ball and Jackie Gleason redefined comedy, changed the viewer habits to a captive audience, and designed the model of the situation comedy, which is still used today.

For decades, the model of television stayed consistent, changing themes and content, but not format. In the late 1980s, the landscape of television media changed. The Writers Guild of America went on strike in 1987, and a set of producers developed a way to create content in the absence of writers—TV without a script. The show *Cops* was born and ushered in a genre of programming known as non-fiction, or reality television. In 1989, the same year that the World Wide Web was launched, a new program invited viewers to submit their own videos to compete for a prize: *America's Funniest Home Videos.*

The 1990s audience unknowingly shaped the culture of what was to come. In the early 1990s, the reality television niche began to take hold, with MTV's *The Real World* and *Road Rules*. The invention of the web browser in 1994 enabled forward-thinking Internet techies to begin capitalizing on the web's new user base. As a result, the sense of empowerment, participation, and creativity pushed these new media professionals to create content that would openly compete with traditional media. Film, television, newspaper, and book publishing peered at the online environment with a wary eye. There had always been a process to get an idea from conception to viewership in traditional media, but, on the web, the gatekeepers were no longer preventing creative material from reaching the audience.

EARLY DIGITAL STORYTELLING

The web browser allowed any user access to HTML code and nearly unlimited space to make projects. Coders and creators found they could launch a multimedia website within days or weeks—projects that would have taken weeks or months previously. Other technologies of the mid 1990s included the CD-ROM, a now unbelievably small, self-contained file system. CD-ROM technology was valuable to developers, as well as traditional film and television producers, because it could contain interactive video and special features. The best-selling CD-ROMs of the 1990s happened to be the games *Myst* and *Doom*. *Myst* was an open-world game (now a common model in present game franchises such as *Assassin's Creed* and *Grand Theft Auto*) that became a hit. It appealed to a gaming audience, as well as a movie audience, as the story was scripted. In its time, people "talked about *Myst* the same way they talk about *The Sopranos* during its first season: as one of those rare works that irrevocably changed its medium."[3] A game such as *Myst* empowered the user with technical know-how to consider creating and designing as well.

This inspiration struck Scott Zakarin, a commercial director and industrial filmmaker who realized that the digital space allowed creators to experiment for niche audiences and create passion projects. (Zakarin is profiled in the book *Digital Babylon: How the geeks, the suits, and the ponytails tried to bring Hollywood to the Internet*.) The Internet allowed Scott to create his own creative future in this new space, but he knew Hollywood producers and traditional media executives wouldn't jump in right away. Scott was enamored by the idea of the web and "the novelty of being in an electronic cave with a group of strangers."[4] He merged the concept of the "electronic cave," more commonly known as the chat room, with a broadcast TV structure and wrote a television show to be made exclusively for the web, called *The Spot*.

Scott became addicted to the idea that you can create fictional characters in the online space. You can make an account with any name, enter a chat room, and role-play a character. Scott created several characters with "quirky, neurotic personalities—anything to push people's buttons."[5] The experience left him with the idea of a television show that was like *Melrose Place* (a popular 1990s television series) meets *Reality Bites* (a geeky film about Generation X). *The Spot* launched in June of 1995, making it one of the earliest versions of web television. Set as a "cyber serial" show about "real" characters in a Southern California beach house, the show was very popular among some of the web's early adopters. The characters reminded the viewers of themselves in the chat rooms: an odd, quirky, and sophomoric community. The show had live chat sessions, online communities, and forums, with dedicated fans and real-life get-togethers. The show ran until 1997 and changed the online multimedia environment forever.

In 1997, AOL created a new online entertainment network called Entertainment Asylum. The network was an interactive mix of *Entertainment Tonight* and *Access Hollywood* for the web and featured celebrity interviews and special segments.[6] Zakarin was named president of programming at Entertainment Asylum because of his knowledge of the industry and his groundbreaking attempt at web video. Patrick Keene of Jupiter Communications, an Internet analysis company, told the *New York Times* that, "AOL is a real success at building community—about 30 percent of AOL usage is chat—and its marketing strength of about 10 million subscribers."[7]

Jupiter Communications' founder Josh Harris also plays a large role in the history of multimedia storytelling. As the head of a company that analyzed website traffic, he noticed a growing trend of people looking to find original multimedia content online. He and a team of creatives and artists invented a website called Psuedo.com, a web television network offering dozens of niche channels for viewers to choose from. Harris later went on to create a streaming-video Orwellian surveillance experiment in 1999 called "Quiet: We live in public," where 100 artists and volunteers allowed themselves to be watched and streamed 24/7. (The experiment was shut down by the New York Police Department on January 1, 2000. Josh Harris, Psuedo.com, and his experiments are explained in Ondi Timoner's documentary *We Live in Public*.)[8] Harris told Bob Simon of *60 Minutes* that his online television network would eventually compete with channels such as CBS.

Although Harris was eventually proven correct, the dotcom bust occurred in 2000, and thousands of sites, such as Psuedo.com, were the victims of audience evacuation when people left such sites en masse owing to their frustration with the lack of high-speed Internet connections and large files to download. People liked the idea of watching shows such as *The Spot* or visiting Psuedo.com, but didn't like waiting for long load times and enduring buffering issues and low frame rates.

So, what happened to multimedia content creation in the gap between the dotcom bust and the broadband video sites?

THE GAP: 2000–2005

As mentioned in the last chapter, grassroots creators with access to video cameras and low-cost animation software found the Internet to be a boon to short-form creative material. When it came to storytelling and longer-form content, actual video was found to be too immense in size to work properly. Matt Chapman and his college friend Craig Zobel created a Flash-animated online web series called *Homestar Runner* in 2000. Chapman animated the series in Flash and voiced all the characters. Originally conceived as a parody of children's books, *Homestar Runner* took off online as an animation series that spanned nearly a decade.

The series revolved around characters Homestar Runner and Strong Bad, but had dozens of additional characters and story arcs. The animation of the series was not intense or smooth, but the writing and the witty comedy attracted thousands of viewers and dedicated fans. "The designs were simple, poppy, and instantly recognizable," Todd VanDerWerff writes in the A.V. Club feature about *Homestar Runner*. "Couple those appealing visuals with the well-defined characters and sneakily amusing scripts and [Chapman and Zobel] had a recipe for Internet success."[9] The show also understood how to appreciate its audience. The cast of the animated series would accept email from the viewers and answer it on the show.

The site is still up at HomestarRunner.com (www.homestarrunner.com). The sizes of the site's graphics are the average size of screens at the time of *Homestar Runner*'s heydey (2002–2005), and all of the content and episodes are still online. As a side note, the "doge" meme originated on *Homestar Runner* in a puppet show episode in 2005, where Homestar tries to distract Strong Bad from his work and says that Strong Bad is "his dog" but spells it D–O–G–E.

BROADBAND VIDEO HOSTING

Vimeo, Dailymotion, grouper, vSocial, motionbox, metacafe, bolt, blip.tv, Revver, and YouTube. These were the top ten video outlets of 2006, among over 1,000 outlets to upload video.[10] How did YouTube win out as the most popular video upload site of our current era?

In late 2004, many web users had acquired high-speed broadband Internet access via DSL or cable modem, and digital cameras were becoming more commonplace. Although there were hundreds of places to upload video files, what was missing was a repository of searchable and shareable videos. Chad Hurley, Steve Chen, and Jawed Karim had an idea for the video site after Janet Jackson's "wardrobe malfunction" during the 2004 Super Bowl and the devastating tsunami in the Indian Ocean in December 2004. Every time the founders looked for footage of either of these events, they couldn't locate them online. They decided to make their own video site to store various videos. The team registered the domain name youtube.com on February 14, 2005 and uploaded the video "Me at the Zoo" on April 23, 2005. The official launch date was set for November 2005, though users could access it before the launch.

YouTube's ease of use, speed of translating videos to a shareable flash format, and the benefit of shareable metadata, made YouTube the go-to place for video uploads. Around the time that Matt Sloan and Aaron Yonda were uploading the premiere of *Chad Vader: Day shift manager* in July 2006, YouTube boasted 65,000 video uploads per day, and Internet users were consuming more than 100 million videos daily.[11] In October of 2006, the same month that Ragtag Productions uploaded the first episode of *We Need Girlfriends*, Google offered to buy the site for $1.65 billion—the deal was completed a month later.

The lava from the explosive volcanoes of new media that erupted in the mid 1990s started to cool in 2007, and the landmasses of the web took hold just after the 2007 Writers Guild of America strike. In contrast to the strike in 1987, auteurs, creatives, and producers had a plethora of outlets where they could produce new media material online in 2007. When Joss Whedon produced *Dr. Horrible's Sing-a-long Blog*, he inadvertently created a new civilization of creators in the multimedia storytelling environment. As we see from our present day, the new networks online are legitimately competing with traditional environments. The creators found a new ground to live on.

THE NEW LAND OF MULTIMEDIA STORYTELLING

Since 2005, YouTube has evolved, along with the creators and audience participants. At first, a location to simply "Broadcast Yourself," a slogan with a double meaning to say it is both a DIY platform and also encouraging you to broadcast, YouTube became a culture. In 2006, *Time* magazine named "You," as in YouTube, the person of the year.[12] The site started a partner program in 2007 where celebrities and vloggers alike were able to profit share the advertising dollars. YouTube states that thousands of channels make more than six figures a year in profit.[13] The site became a place to grow ideas and share powerful videos, a place to broadcast commentary on societal issues that traditional media would ignore. Multimedia storytelling platforms helped users topple governments in 2011, brought attention to Joseph Kony, and aided Barack Obama to attract attention to the Affordable Care Act. YouTube currently boasts more than 100 hours of content uploaded to the site every minute, and nearly 700,000 years of video are downloaded per month.[14]

Over the next few sections of this chapter, we'll introduce you to the vloggers and early adopters on YouTube, the savvy editors and creators who remix media and turn shareable media into art, and web-series producers bypassing the arduous path of traditional broadcast, and we'll show you how to get involved as a creator. As you've made it to this part of the book, we expect that the previous information you have learned about web literacy, memes, and virals will play a role in how you read and follow this chapter. But, most importantly, don't just read this chapter—create and participate in the multimedia storytelling environment!

NEW NARRATIVE PROGRAMMING IN THE DIGITAL SPACE

In his brown corduroy pants and geek-chic black-rimmed glasses, Steven Tsapelas found comfort in his basement bedroom surrounded by *Arrested Development* posters and Batman lunchboxes. Steven had just finished writing a short film about a Midwest news station he intended to produce in the coming weeks. Steven called his partners in production, the adventurous, explosion-loving friend Angel Acevedo and the quiet, classic-cinema aficionado Brian Amyot, to start the production process and read over the script. It was late 2005, and the media industry was shifting rapidly.

Steven, Angel, and Brian made up the aptly named production company Ragtag Productions. The quick-thinking team had become popular on the 48-hour film festival circuits in New York City after graduating college in 2004. While discussing their new project, the Ragtag bunch reconsidered their short-film approach and instead wrote up an 11-episode television series that would span a feature-length film's running time. The story would be about three guys who recently graduated college and moved out to Queens, New York, in hopes of finding love. They titled the project *We Need Girlfriends*.

What Steven didn't realize at the time was that he, as well as thousands of active creatives across the country, was figuring out the visual desire of the new audience. The new audience is made up of participants rather than passive viewers. The new audience wants a role in the creation process and wants to feel as if what they are watching relates to them. Steven knows the audience, because he was writing content for himself.

The section shifts to the earliest storytellers of our current era, with several case studies on projects and users that showed early signs of success and *longtail* audience achievement. Our case studies will follow some early web series such as Ragtag Productions' *We Need Girlfriends*, Aaron Yonda and Matt Sloan's *Chad Vader: Day shift manager*, and Felicia Day's *The Guild*. We will discuss the common character theme visible in online narrative production as the projects have evolved. From Joss Whedon's *Dr. Horrible's Sing-a-long Blog* to Freddie Wong's *Video Game High School*, the characters of the web have always been different from those of traditional broadcast.

WRITING THE CHARACTER OF THE WEB

The first episode of *We Need Girlfriends* launched on YouTube on October 31, 2006. The production called for 11 episodes to be released at the end of every month at midnight. Although released to very little fanfare, the series went on to grab the attention of Hollywood producers such as Darren Starr (*Sex and the City*) and Greg Daniels (*The Office*). Darren Starr found the awkward sincerity and authenticity of the characters to be compelling to a new media audience. What made *We Need Girlfriends* popular with its audience was that the characters were relatable to the viewers. To those who watched the series, it felt like the characters were familiar friends.

The reason we are to focus on *We Need Girlfriends* as our first case study is because of the characters in the show. We believe there is a lot to learn from the way *We Need Girlfriends* was written in 2006 that will aid the savvy user of the present. The authentic and sincere personalities on web television shows competed with major television network characters in an independent space. Stephanie Rosenbloom of the *New York Times* coined the phrase "The beta male,"[15] because that character is the opposite of the alpha character commonly seen in shows of the time, such as *Entourage* or *Lost*. There were three main characters in *We Need Girlfriends*: Henry, modeled after Steven; Rod, modeled after Angel; and Tom, modeled after Brian. The show takes place in and around Astoria, New York, where the creators lived, and many of the scenes were shot in their own apartment.

The Ragtag crew knew that the new and digital creator has to produce regardless of the limitations. From the beginning of web-series production to present, the savvy creator has always managed to self-produce their content. This is similarly seen in Aaron Yonda and Matt Sloan's savvy production process for the web series *Chad Vader: Day shift manager*. In the series, Chad Vader (obviously based on Darth Vader) is the day-shift manager at the Empire Market. Chad has personality difficulties with his co-workers, employees, and customers. The production team borrowed a Wisconsin supermarket to produce their series. In their desire to tell their story, they had to work out how important it is to find locations that work and take advantage of the opportunities they had available to them. In most cases, the storyteller understands that they have access to their own house and network of friends who may offer their locations to the production. Having a passionate project attitude helps the creative gain access for production. The passion pays off: George Lucas was impressed by the series, and Matt Sloan was chosen to voice Darth Vader in the video game *Star Wars: The force unleashed*.[16]

THE BETA PERSON

Creating the beta male was something a bit uncommon on television in 2006, but today he is a very common character in visual media (here forward called the beta person because, although the characteristics of the awkward authentic beta person are more likely embodied in a male personality, the characteristics are not limited to male characters). The beta person is "You," the person willing to hold a book about becoming a savvier user of the online experience. The beta person is someone you can relate to, in your group of friends, perhaps, or your siblings. Most importantly, the beta person is someone you want to watch and relate to and see how they negotiate their space in their daily lives, whether fictional or real. Learning and growing up in a digital age is not easy, and having examples of similar people to watch makes navigating the environment a bit easier.

In *We Need Girlfriends*, the beta person is part of the anti-Entourage group, "that gentle, endearingly awkward, self-conscious soul for whom love is a battlefield."[17] In most cases, it's a character who doesn't attract a mainstream audience in traditional broadcasting. Advertisers in the traditional markets are looking for characters for the audience to escape to and idolize, not recognize. The general audience is not really attracted to someone who resembles who they already may be. In the case of Henry, Rod, and Tom of *We Need Girlfriends*, the characters are a bit timid and quirky, but secure in their weirdness. The *We Need Girlfriends* characters were not written by a team of television show writers in a writers' room, and their dialogue isn't corrected by dozens of notes. Their performance is bare and awkward. Much like the people who create the product.

In his essay *Awkwardness* (2010), Adam Kotsko explains that we are in an era of awkwardness, especially in visual entertainment. "Awkwardness dominates entertainment to such an extent that it's becoming increasingly difficult to remember laughing at anything other than cringe-inducing scenes of social discomfort," he writes, referring to *The Office, Curb Your Enthusiasm*, and Judd Apatow films.[18] Although the characters on television and film may present a level of beta character, the web personalities that follow exhibit a sincere strangeness only found in the online space. The web beta person is a niche subject, just like that of the vloggers. They don't entertain mass audiences; they fulfill the fans of their specific interest area.

We Need Girlfriends Episode 1

The following is a script from *We Need Girlfriends*, Episode 1. It's important that you read the style in which it is written in order to understand how unique web-series writing is and how it differentiates from traditional television.

We Need Girlfriends

"The pilot"

by

Steven Tsapelas

EXT. APARTMENT BUILDING—DAY

Our three leads, TOM, HENRY, and RODRIGUEZ, unpack boxes from their car. SARAH, Tom's girlfriend, comes out from behind with another box. AN ATTRACTIVE GIRL exits the building.

RODRIGUEZ:

Squirrel.

TOM:

Go ahead and watch the car, guys.
Me and Sarah can bring this load
up.

(to Sarah)

God, they look terrible don't they?

INT. STAIRWAY—DAY

Tom and Sarah bring up the boxes.

TOM:

Can you believe their luck? Both of
their girlfriends just dumping them
right after graduation. Poor guys.

INT. TOM'S NEW ROOM—DAY

The room is empty.

TOM:

This is where the big bed will go.
I ordered a big one, you see, so
you can **stay** over more often.

Tom puts a picture of him and Sarah on the ledge.

TOM:

We're finally doing it, Sarah.
We're living on our own. It's like
everything we've always talked
about.

Sarah suddenly grabs Tom and hugs him.

SARAH:

How are you, Tom?

TOM:

I'm pretty good. Why are you
hugging me so tight?

TOM (cont'd):

(sudden realization)

Oh dear God, no.

CUT TO:

EXT. FRONT PORCH—DAY

Tom has his head buried in his hands. Sarah is halfway down the block. Henry and Rodriguez watch her walk away as if they're losing their own girlfriend. Henry waves. Sarah doesn't wave back.

The opening sequence of the first episode sets up the plot for the entire series. The characters' arc is established right away: They "need girlfriends" for the duration of the plot. It's not just the writing that creates the beta person: The action and personalities complete the image. As you can see, the Ragtag crew consider their characters as actual people. The beta character is someone who is not afraid to lay bare all their quirky personality traits and display themselves as overgrown adolescents.[19] Rod and Henry are presented "as is" and are portrayed immediately in images, as their characters are. Rod unloads a box that says "Rod's porn A–H," and Henry's box is a QVC box labeled "Toys and Wrestling VHS." On traditional television, you would most likely never see a character pairing of this much difference, but, in actual life, friends and roommates are often very diverse. The horrors of a break-up are also on full

Figure 6.1
Rod: "Squirrel."

Figure 6.2
Tom: "Why are you hugging me so tight?"

display, as the actor Patrick Cohen, who plays Tom, shudders at the realization that he too is all alone.

You should watch the entire series of *We Need Girlfriends*, because many current web-series creators credit the show as their inspiration to create in the online space. Pay close attention to the character arcs and the trials the characters endure.

Chad Vader: Day shift manager is an early web series that went quite viral in its early days. Chad Vader is masked, and the audience is unable to see his expressions, but Matt Sloan voices Chad so well that we can feel the awkwardness in the scenario. In the opening sequence, Chad, recognizable as one of the most brutal villains in movie history, walks up behind his employee who is stocking shelves and quotes some of Darth Vader's most violent threats, only to be countered by the stockboy's snarky retorts. The "evilness" of the Vader look is removed in the first minute of the show, when we find he is just as fallible and timid as any manager in real-life retail space. As the series progresses, we learn Chad's personality weaknesses and his struggle with his peers and co-workers, which even a villain's costume cannot hide.

The point in our timeline where the beta character became cemented into the online narrative culture occurs near the Writers Guild of America strike in 2007. The first point is from Felicia Day's *The Guild*, and the second is from Joss Whedon's *Dr. Horrible's Sing-a-long Blog*. *The Guild* launched in July 2007, just 5 months before the Writers Guild of America strike. *The Guild* opens with Felicia Day directly addressing the camera, as she is recording her vlog in diary form. It opens with a candid monologue that sounds typical of a recorded diary. Felicia's Cyd starts her monologue, "So. It's, uh, Friday night. And still

Figure 6.3
Chad Vader.

jobless. Yay. I haven't left the house in a week. My therapist, uh, broke up with me. Oh yeah, there's a gnome warlock in my living room. Sleeping on my couch."[20]

Felicia Day's Cyd Sherman is a gamer in the MMORPG *World of Warcraft.* She captains a team of people working together for a common game goal, also known as a "guild." The series begins when the normally unseen team-mates meet in real life and find they are far different than their online characters. It's possible that MMORPG players may go their entire game experience without knowing what the actual player ever looks like. The act of meeting one of your co-players in real life draws on real fears of social anxiety and potential mishaps. These characters would not likely be cast in traditional media, because they are so specifically niche they exist in a subculture that many people don't know about or may be critical of. *The Guild* lasted for six seasons (2007–2013) and directly inspired *Dr. Horrible's Sing-a-long Blog.*

Dr. Horrible's Sing-a-long Blog was Joss Whedon's creative project during the writers' strike. Joss Whedon, now known for his work on major action films, was then best known for his cult television shows, *Buffy the Vampire Slayer* and *Firefly.* During the strike, Joss, like many other writers, refused to cross the picket line, but, unlike with previous strikes, where unionized writers and directors had no other outlet, by 2007 web video had become a new outlet for creatives—as long as they wrote for the online audience.

Dr. Horrible's Sing-a-long Blog does just that. Made under the table, Whedon's show is a genre-busting comedy–drama–scifi–musical starring Neil Patrick Harris as Dr. Horrible, Nathan Fillion (*Firefly*) as Captain Hammer, and Felicia Day (*The Guild* and eight episodes on *Buffy*) as the love interest, Penny. Dr. Horrible is the main character and antagonist, set on world domination, but unlike movie and television villains, he is just a common, active web vlogger willing to talk to his camera about his issues and insecurities. We sympathize with him because he reminds us of our friends or loved ones, but he doesn't really intimidate us. This is similar to Chad Vader—they play against our intuition to dislike the enemy.

Web series became far more prominent after *Dr. Horrible's Sing-a-long* Blog, because Whedon cast popular actors into the show. The show was made in three episodes, launching over three nights. The characters draw you in because of their familiarity and sincere traits, and the viewers are left devastated at the shocking ending. The ending, especially the last 2 seconds, shows the audience that, if you want to make an authentic ending, you have to use the web.

HOW CAN YOU MAKE A WEB SERIES?

Creators of new media content refuse to fit into the norms presented by a traditional entertainment hegemony and aim for only a small portion of the audience. The creators create for themselves and their friends. When learning to write for new media, you should remember to write beta characters. Do not be afraid to show the characters as they are and would be if you were to meet them in real life. Try your best to write down actual dialogue that you have heard—include all the "uhs" and "ums," because that is how people actually speak. To be authentic on the web, you have to convince the viewer that you know the person you created and you know them so well you gave them the same quirks. In other words—write you.

As we learned previously in the chapter on viral videos, the concept of storytelling is most important. If you understand plot, character arc, and the general rules of writing, you can create a show. We found that casting was the difference between a popular show and a mediocre production. Do your best to cast believable, awkward, and authentic characters, and the audience will find you.

Why Would Creative Multimedia Storytellers Use the Web as Their Outlet?

Let's say you have an idea for a television show. Do you know the steps it takes to produce it? You would assume the process goes something like this: Idea! Write it down—call an agent—sell it—produce it—it airs!

It is, unfortunately, nowhere near that simple. Here's how it works in traditional media.[21]

You have an idea you want to produce!

Get an *agent*. Hurry—someone else may already have your idea, so you need to protect it. But your agent is probably going to want you to put together a *package*. That means getting an actor or producer who is willing to support your project.

Let's say you know someone who knows someone and you get yourself a package. That's great! This is good news! Now you need a place to create your project. That's called a *studio*. They have the tools to produce your show—it's not a vlog—this is going to be a big camera-and-sound project with lots of crew members. But the studio is going to want to know where it will air, so you and your agent are going to have to pitch a *network* to agree that the project is worth it.

How are you going to get the studio and network on board? Well, you'll need something called a pitch document, or a *pitch doc*.

What's a pitch doc you ask? Well, that's the *outline* of your project, a *beat sheet* (a summary of plot points), and a full *script* for a pilot.

Let's say you successfully did all that. You have the pitch doc, and the studio and network are on board. What's next?

Well, you need your agent to find you a *casting director* who will find the *actors* to perform your script. You'll also need someone with artistic vision to carry out the task and tell the actors how to perform on camera, also known as the *director*. The better the script, the better the cast, the better the director.

Last step: Produce a *pilot* episode—a single first episode to show to the public, but first show it to a focus group. Make some of the fixes requested and air it on television. If it does well in the *ratings*, you get a contract to create a *series*! Congrats!

Or:

Write a script that is brief, packed with emotions, and contains niche beta personalities; get your friends to help shoot it; upload it to YouTube.

New and digital media offer an opportunity for creators that only a few had a few decades ago. This section lets you know how to get in on this new and wonderful industry.

YOUTUBE AND PERSONALITIES

This section is going to focus on the modern history of participatory video content and multimedia storytelling. In their effort to use the web in the savviest way possible, we hope the reader benefits from the several case studies we present in this section. We will focus on the stories of some of the savviest users and multimedia storytellers to give some understanding and context to our current online environment.

WHO CREATES THIS CONTENT?

The term "the under-30 crowd" has always been used when referring to new media. It's as if the youth group is the only set likely to view new media visual content, vloggers, or web series. The web is open to all audiences, but those who influence the content are those who participate. Much of the early era of content participation was coming from the under-30 crowd, but it was much more likely the under-20 crowd was consuming it. The younger generation is more likely to be consuming video media online, and that means those creating content should be considering the younger audience when producing content.

According to the Pew Research Internet Project, creators who upload photo or video have increased yearly.[22] Although young adults and teens are more likely to be content creators, people of all ages are uploading content that they have created. Creators are users who produce their own content, and don't simply repost content from someone else. Video creators span nearly all ages, but more than half surveyed by Pew are in the under-30 crowd. As you read this and the rest of the chapter, we implore you to get involved in the online space. Now is the time!

THE PERSONALITIES

Who is Tyler Oakley? That's the question most asked by non-savvy users when any news media, blog, television show, high schooler, or even President Barack Obama, says his name. Tyler Oakley turned on his web camera and started recording vlogs in 2007, when he was in college at Michigan State University. Tyler is one of the most popular YouTube personalities, or "YouTubers," on the site. He spends a majority of his screen time simply talking about the things he likes (One Direction, Darren Criss) and the things he hates (trolls) and hanging out with other YouTubers (creating "*collabs*," short for collaborations). In his YouTube career, Tyler has gone from college student, to YouTube partner, to gay rights activist, to brand consultant, to consulting the President of the United States on web video.

Tyler Oakley, Jenna Marbles, Shane Dawson, PewDiePie, Bethany Mota, Grace Helbig, and Hannah Hart make up an incredibly small and diverse sample of popular YouTubers, yet they all have something in common: They live their life on camera and stay positive. They produce their content for themselves, knowing full well that, if they produce niche content, someone from the YouTube community is bound to be interested. It isn't just the act of recording that makes them popular: These YouTubers are charismatic, compelling, and authentic. The audience of traditional media is accustomed

to watching characters larger than life, perfect in the way they speak, dress, and act. The people you see on YouTube are the same people you would meet in real life—they are not playing a character.

Grace Helbig, formerly of *Daily Grace* on My Damn Channel, is a perfect example—she produced her show every day from whatever room she was in and wearing whatever she felt like, and she has become incredibly popular among the YouTube viewers. In 2014, she and Hannah Hart hosted the Streamy Awards, the live-streaming event celebrating the best of web series and YouTube personalities, and both Grace and Hannah released books. Grace is now on the E! channel as a late-night talk-show host and she still stays true to her YouTube roots and produces videos.

The following is a quick breakdown of various types of niche vlog on YouTube and an example of a popular YouTube personality in that genre. What you will learn with the following is how different each personality is. We hope we have provided a nice sample of personalities for you to discover and we understand we cannot cover them all. The intent is for you to become inspired to try making vlogs on your own.

WHO ARE THESE VLOGGERS?

Most vloggers have created their own new genres of video, and some do not fit into any traditional mold. Much in the way that Joss Whedon created content outside categorization, you'll find that vloggers are too diverse for classic taxonomy. That said, we'll use the categorization that reporters and news media utilize to explain where these vloggers fit in the environment as best we can. The following are the most popular types of vlog and the most recognizable face in each category.

Pop-culture Vlog—Tyler Oakley[23]

Pop-culture vlogging is the most common type of vlogging found on YouTube. It seems to be what anybody who starts out for the first time on the platform attempts. There are thousands of possible examples to tell you about, but the most popular is Tyler Oakley. Featured prominently on the *Frontline* documentary "Generation Like," Tyler Oakley isn't just an on-screen personality, but also a brand powerhouse. He doesn't just support his content on YouTube, he also has an incredibly strong presence on Instagram and Twitter. His authentic nature has inspired brands to trust him with promoting their product in an honest and sincere manner.

In "Generation Like," Tyler explains that the YouTube channel is the main outlet of his brand, and he puts a lot of work into operating and maintaining his brand. He tells brands that approach him that they "have to play by [the YouTubers'] rules."[24] He takes a lot of pride in the community of YouTubers and says that the sites were built without the help of brands and corporations. When brands now see they want to be part of the YouTube community, they have to work with Tyler and the other personalities. This approach has helped brands negotiate the space, which is still fairly foreign to their sales strategy. Tyler, as well as the other YouTube personalities, attempts to remain as transparent as possible about brand sponsorship, and people know he "has to pay the bills" too. He doesn't just use his viewers to promote products either: He also gets the word out about his favorite non-profits and causes such as Project Trevor,[25] an LGBTQ crisis intervention and suicide prevention group. It's an interesting duality that allows Tyler to be brand promoter as well as an authentic voice to his many millions of viewers. It takes practice, but, more than anything, it requires the YouTube personality to be consistent and stay true to their persona.

In early 2014, Tyler visited the White House to consult President Barack Obama on multimedia storytelling and, later that year, he interviewed Michelle Obama about new education standards. Whether it's a brand, non-profit, the POTUS, or the FLOTUS, Tyler has a way of helping people into the online space.

Entertainment Vlog—Jenna Marbles[26]

Just about everything on YouTube is entertaining in one way or another. To be an entertainer online is to understand how the character of the web works. You can find beta personality traits in Jenna Mourey, who goes by the online name Jenna Marbles. The characters online are a bit awkward and endearing, with a strong sense of self-efficacy. Jenna was a basic YouTube user, unafraid to say her raw thoughts (many NSFW) on camera. She was emotive and entertaining, and users were drawn to her charisma. In 2010, she uploaded her comedic advice video, "How to trick people into thinking you're good looking," where she over-uses makeup and hair dye to prove looks can be deceiving. In addition, her video "How to avoid people you don't want to talk to" made her the de facto online leader of the "anti-grinder" movement and helped people realize you can combat abuse in a public space.[27]

In the years since, Jenna has uploaded hundreds of videos that range from features about her dogs to comedy sketches, makeup videos, relationship advice, and regular vlogs. She releases a video every week and entertains her audience as a one-person variety show.

Comedy and Sketch Vlog—Shane Dawson[28]

In 2008, Shane Dawson got fired from his job because he decided it would be funny to post a video on YouTube of himself pole dancing and stripping while at work. He learned two lessons that day: Companies don't like their employees to abuse the workplace, and he was a natural for the YouTube environment. Since his early uploads on the site, Shane has invented dozens of characters and impersonated Lady Gaga and Miley Cyrus. Shane doesn't just talk into the camera: He highly produces all of his content. He wants to gain viewers. The *New York Times* recognized that his formula for equal parts teen confessional, pop satire, and really great hair attracts young viewers.[29] He talks about his personal life and his struggles through weight loss and entertains with raunchy sketches and parodies (such as a disgusting take on the *50 Shades of Grey* film). He is consistent and continues to release a video once a week.

"Let's Play" Vlog—PewDiePie[30]

Since the beginning of the Internet and the web, console and computer gamers have used the web to find user guides, post tips and tricks in forums, and meet and compete with other players. YouTube has been the display case for gamers to post their progress through games. There is a certain specific genre of YouTube clips called "Let's Play" (or LP) videos. LP videos are not user guides or forum based: They are single-point-of-view game play of different games, usually with the gamer's audio narrative and commentary. There are hundreds of these channels, but, as of this book's time of writing, the most popular by far is the user PewDiePie. His is not only the most popular LP video channel: PewDiePie is the most popular channel on YouTube.

Felix Kjellberg, aka PewDiePie, is a Swedish-born game commenter. Although PewDiePie creates his content for "his bros," a fair number of his audience are female and non-gamers. Felix plays all his games, adds all his personal commentary, and personally edits all his content. In a profile with the *Wall Street Journal*, Felix said his secret for success is making the audience feel like they are hanging around watching their friend play a video game. His YouTube earnings and the endorsements apparently make an economic impact, and he is supposedly earning more than $4 million a year from his work.[31]

Theme Vlog—"My Drunk Kitchen"[32]

When you have a niche skill, you should use that skill to its full potential. Hannah Hart is the author of *My Drunk Kitchen: A guide to eating, drinking, and going with your gut.* The book is a print adaptation of her extremely popular vlog, called "My Drunk Kitchen." Hannah moved to New York from California and decided to make a fake cooking show to make her friends laugh and remember her. The concept is simple: Hannah gets drunk and attempts to cook. It results in humorous outcomes, messy experiments, and pure entertainment. She's collabed with dozens of YouTubers, and, aside from the possible damage to her liver, her production model is very sustainable and consistently creative.

Parody/Sketch/Comedy Vlog—Smosh[33]

Ian Andrew Hecox and Anthony Padilla knew the Internet was the only place for them to tell stories. Since 2003, the duo has created content in the online space. To say the Smosh duo create oddball and screwy content would be a vast understatement—they make people laugh. Ian and Anthony are two of the most recognizable media stars and have continuously produced content on a weekly basis since 2006. They epitomize relentless creators and take story inspiration from original comedy to quirky parodies of games, movies, television shows, and other YouTube entertainment. Smosh is one of the most robust channels on the web, containing a vast network of additional channels and merchandising.

TUTORIAL VLOGS AND PERSONALITIES

Makeup Demonstration Vlog

Have you ever dreaded a photo day at school or at work? Did you ever wonder how to prepare? Much the way you find out how to change a tire on YouTube or learn new Photoshop tricks, there are YouTubers who focus on makeup demonstration. These videos are step-by-step training on everything from just adjusting eyebrows to imitating the makeup style of Lady Gaga.

Search for some of these:

- Michelle Phan (www.youtube.com/user/MichellePhan): Michelle is quite possibly the most popular YouTube makeup demonstration vlogger. She has been featured on YouTube advertisements and she is Lancôme's spokeswoman.
- Zoella (www.youtube.com/user/zoella280390).
- Andrea's Choice (www.youtube.com/user/AndreasChoice).

Haul Vlog

Demonstration vlogs are popular because they are instructional and helpful, but what if you just want to explain your purchases to an intrigued public? Some YouTubers go shopping and show off their purchases, and these videos are called haul videos. The vloggers get home from their day shopping and explain to the audience each purchase and offer reasons for the purchase. The haul vloggers prefer shops where there is a constant variety of clothes to collect.
Search for some of these:

- Bethany Mota (www.youtube.com/user/Macbarbie07): Bethany is featured on YouTube advertisements on New York City subways and was also a contestant on *Dancing With the Stars* in 2014.
- ChanelBlueSatin (www.youtube.com/user/ChanelBlueSatin).
- Meghan Rienks (www.youtube.com/user/meghanrosette).

Hair-style Tutorial Vlog

Where there is makeup demonstration and wardrobe assistance, there must also be hairstyle vlogs, and there is a hairstyle tutorial for every hair type.
Search for some of these:

- Franchesca Ramsay chescalocs (www.youtube.com/user/chescalocs). Franchesca runs a channel for tutorials and inspiration for natural hair. She is a growing YouTube personality with her comedy channel chescaleigh.
- Bebexo (www.youtube.com/user/bebexo).
- Cinthia Truong (www.youtube.com/user/CinthiaTruong).

Cooking Vlog

After Pinterest became popular, users starting collecting recipes and tutorials to post on their pinboards. Pictures only do so well for tutorials, and it helps to have a vlogger guide the viewer through the process. Cooking channels are as abundant as food, but some YouTube personalities have created a niche for their audiences.

Search for these:

- Rosanna Pansino (www.youtube.com/user/RosannaPansino): One of the most popular cooking tutorial YouTube personalities, she is also featured on YouTube print advertisements. She posts new "Nerdy Nummies" every Tuesday, where she makes food based on video games and movies.
- "How to Cook That With Ann Reardon" (www.youtube.com/user/howtocookthat).

Science and Education

"Hey Vsauce!" Michael Stevens exclaims at the beginning of each episode. Michael Stevens runs the main Vsauce channel and gives explanations of real science and philosophy in an attempt to answer our curiosity. The main channel is about our amazing world. On Vsauce2, Kevin Lieber talks about amazing people, and, on Vsauce3, Jake Roper talks about Internet and fiction interests. The three channels make up some of the most popular learning information available on YouTube. The Vsauce channels combined are subscribed to by millions of people interested in different niche topics, and their upbeat approach to science has caused channels to be an addition to in-class learning in many school classrooms.

- Vsauce (www.youtube.com/user/Vsauce).
- Vsauce2 (www.youtube.com/user/Vsauce2).
- Vsauce3 (www.youtube.com/user/Vsauce3).

CAN VLOGGERS MAKE A LIVING ON YOUTUBE?

The aforementioned channels and personalities all have two things in common: Their on-screen performances are almost always presented with an extremely positive attitude, and their content is extremely niche. Robert Kyncl, the global head of business for YouTube, loves niche product, because he feels that, "the experience is more immersive" for the viewer.[34] YouTube has considered profit from niche product since 2007, when the platform invented the Partner Program that allowed users to profit share with YouTube's advertisements. This amounts to thousands of channels profiting in some way, but it also means that over 500 channels on YouTube are earning six-figure incomes from the program.[35]

Robert Kyncl has redefined television in much the way that Zakarin did in the 1990s. These visionaries consider what is next with television media and go for it, with the audience in mind rather than the advertisers. In the end, the audience will decide what it likes best. The method and model are passed down onto the creators, and they are to focus on their subscribers, the people that keep them in business. The more subscribers any given channel has, the more YouTube knows how to advertise to viewers, and the nicher the better. Although the traditional television audience may fluctuate, the online YouTube audience is very loyal and consistent, and this helps pinpoint advertising to become more specific and relatable to the audience.

The goal of a creator is to entertain their subscribers, because they can see, in real time, how many people follow them (or unfollow them) and can tune their product to their specific interests. Comments are extraordinarily valuable to a creator as well. Unlike traditional TV, which vastly separates itself from the viewers, relying on focus groups and ratings to keep going, vloggers must communicate and answer the questions to seem familiar and close. The creators are always positive, because that is what the audience wants to watch—they want to escape to a familiar friend online who will talk to them about their interests.

The Partner Program

YouTube does not release the specific facts and figures for the channels that participate in the Partner Program. Many speculate that the profit share can be as high as 55 percent of the advertising dollars. However, this is a sliding scale and is dependent on the success of the channel, the number of subscribers, and the number of views.

There are more than 1,000 channels that make a six-figure income from the YouTube platform, and some of the top earners make income into the millions.[36]

Create and Participate

Now, it's your turn. There are several ways to start producing content for the online environment and turn your ideas into a web series or a vlog. We have focused specifically on YouTube in this section of the chapter, and so the following lessons are designed for YouTube, but many of the methods can be used on various different online video outlets.

Getting Started

You'll need some tools of the trade:

- camera
- microphone
- editing software
- a brief script
- a sense of humor
- persistence and a willingness to learn
- patience.

Video

The camera part is easy—there's probably one in your pocket. Your cellphone's camera is sufficient, but it will be a bit shaky. You may want to buy a small cellphone tripod for it. There are many models available, but any will do. You can also use your web camera on your computer. Our recommendation for the highest quality with the computer is using QuickTime Player and the New Movie Recording feature. On new computers, that will record in high definition. The highest-quality bet is investing in a small HD camera or a DSLR with a flip out viewfinder, so you can see yourself. Don't forget to look in the lens! Don't look at yourself when you are recording. (This takes some getting used to.) And lastly, *always* remember to make sure the camera is shooting in landscape (horizontal), not portrait (vertical)!

Audio

Don't forget the audio. Many people forget how important audio is to the creation process. Think of it this way: Audio is 50 percent of the production. If your project doesn't sound good, the audience is likely not to watch. The microphone on your headphones actually works well as a recording microphone, before you've saved up some money to buy an external, clip-on lavalier microphone.

Editing

Editing is vastly important to the creation process. It's especially important if you are shooting narrative programming such as web series, but it is just as important when recording a vlog. You will notice, in all the aforementioned examples, that there are a lot of cuts in each of those episodes. They use an editing technique called jump cuts. Jump cuts remove some of the slower material of the video, but leave the edit uncovered by footage that would hide the edit. A jump cut is raw and visible, but also keeps the pace of the product moving forward. It's also a way to add humor and movement to an otherwise static shot—try moving around in the frame and cutting from side to side, like Shane Dawson does. You can have a conversation with yourself!

There are different types of editing software available for your projects, but the editor is in your head, not in the machine. Some of the more expensive, but vastly more intense, software would be Avid Media Composer, Adobe Premiere, or Final Cut for Mac. These all work with various types of video and audio material in one sequence. This helps if you are switching between cellphone, DSLR, and/or computer video on one sequence/edit. Using the editing software that comes with your computer (iMovie or Windows Movie Maker) will also be sufficient when you are starting out, but we also recommend you check out YouTube Editor.

YouTube realized that it should facilitate creativity on its platform, and so it created a basic editing tool at YouTube.com/Editor. It allows you to access your clips in your library and edit them together, adding music, pictures, and text. We recommend you make a fair amount of clips, so it is easier to assemble. In other words, don't be afraid to "cut" often and assemble the clips on the sequence. Try this out—it's free, and, after a few tries, you'll become an expert.

Writing

Although it seems as though many of the YouTubers "wing it," their on-screen performances are planned, with notes or a full script, depending on the project. You should always write down what you will say. Not only will it save you time in production, you will also organize your thoughts and be much more coherent when you are delivering your material. If you are working with a small team, they can hold your cue cards just below the camera, so you can see where you are in the script. If you are working alone, large post-it notes or large text on a computer screen work well too. Just try to make sure it never looks like you are reading off the cards.

A Sense of Humor

We cannot stress this enough! As you've discovered by reading this book, the Internet is a weird place. Now you are becoming involved at the most intense level: putting your video personality online. In a perfect world, all the commenters on your page are there just to support you, but this is not the case. Wherever there is a comment box, there is a critic. Take it lightly and don't engage with those who seem to be posting ignorant comments. As mentioned in several of the previous chapters, trolls are just trying to get a rise out of you. Laugh it off and let it go. They aren't worth engaging in conversation.

Answer those who seem to genuinely care. If you are posting yourself online as a YouTube personality, you have confidence and strength and you are already better than the critics. Don't forget that.

Persistence and Learning

Persistence and learning are parts of the recipe of success in doing anything. It's crucial to the vlogging environment. Your audience, whether that is ten people or 10 million, expects a certain consistency to your projects and expects new episodes regularly. Much like television viewers, online viewers are creatures of habit and will leave if there is an unscheduled gap in production. Make a schedule and do not be too ambitious. Start with once a month or once every two weeks and work your way up. Many first-time vloggers feel that the experience is easy the first few times, but then realize how much work goes into the production, and they begin to slack off. It's better to create a more liberal time schedule and work your way into a routine. This is all part of the learning process. Your technique will become much better as time and experience progress, but you have to be willing to learn and correct mistakes as you go along.

Patience

The most important part of being a YouTube personality: patience. Making these projects can sometimes be frustrating, with technical issues, creative blocks, and the audience participation process. Be patient—not one of the vloggers we have mentioned became professional overnight. Go back to their early work and see how different it was at the beginning. It's a growing process, and your ability to stay cool and patient will reflect in your video.

THE REMIX CULTURE

Participating in Creative Ways

Participation in the online video space isn't limited to scripted performance or vlogging. To participate as a multimedia storyteller, you simply need creativity. If you have access to the web, some fairly easy-to-use editing tools, and imagination, you can combine or edit existing material to make something new—you can remix it.

Digital media in any form, whether, music, sounds, pictures, or video, can be remixed and reshared very quickly. As Kirby Ferguson points out, "you don't need expensive tools, you don't need a distributor, and you don't even need skills."[37] Kirby Ferguson explains, in his online series *Everything Is a Remix*, that the folk art of remixing and the techniques of collecting and transforming material and resharing are the same techniques, used at every level of the creating process.

Before we begin with some examples, we should make sure you are aware that, although remixing is creative and exciting, you can easily get in trouble with copyright and usurping intellectual property.

With these three easy steps, you can remix legally:

1. Attribute material to the original artist.
2. Modify the material enough, or it is not original.
3. Make fundamental changes.

Although that may sound limiting, these rules help inspire creativity.

REMIX EVERYTHING

This section will teach you how to watch and discuss remix, appreciate it as an art, and become a savvy remix creator.

As a cultural observer, you may notice remix everywhere. Every time you recognize something from somewhere else, or feel that some bit of media seems familiar, you are probably recognizing something that is remixed. The remix we'll be talking about in this section is not about the overall culture of remix that has existed for centuries, but new and digital media remixes, available on the web.

To increase your level of savvy awareness, the following are some examples of remix you may come across on the web. The projects range in creativity and style, but all show a style of changing original media into something new.

Remix and Law

In reality, if you analyze any media and discover a reference or a parody of earlier media, you are looking at remix. Lawrence Lessig explains, in his TED Talk, "Re-examining the Remix," that creativity in the multimedia space was enabled by remixing.[38] Disney and Star Wars productions (now one and the same) benefited from remixing content. Disney remixed fairy tales and early filmmakers' content, and Star Wars is the result of remixing the themes from hundreds of different films.

Lessig explains that laws have been put in place to keep copyright in the realm of the creator and prohibiting remixers from using their material. The last law regarding digital media and copyright is the 1998 Digital Millennium Copyright Act, which set up a set of rules to protect the owner of media and intellectual property. The Act was created in an era of low access and has yet to be updated. As a user and creative individual interested in remixing content online, it requires you to get permission from all content holders or face the consequences the distribution platform states—which is often removal of your content or shutdown of your channel.

REMIX STYLES

Machinima

Machinima is a narrative mash-up of video games and cinema—or "machine cinema." Machinima uses multiplayer games, usually first-person shooters (FPS), to create narrative films. Creators attach a video game console to a recording device, such as a computer or a camera, and then carefully script stories to be acted out by fellow players. Far more inexpensive than live-action acting and animation, the creators use the computer graphics from the game as their talent. In multiplayer mode, the on-screen characters are voiced by the players. Sometimes, many players gather several game systems together and connect them, to better organize and act their digital roles.

Red vs Blue is the creation of Rooster Teeth (http://roosterteeth.com). The creative team, lead by Burnie Burns, began creating machinima using the Halo games in 2003. The long running series is a comedy that parodies the serious nature of FPS games.

Fair Use

Wait. How does machinima get away with making videos, if the content used is clearly copyrighted by Bungie, the developer of the game? Web-series remixes such as *Red vs. Blue* or *Cops Skyrim* get around the copyright issue using a loophole in the law known as Fair Use.

This is the actual law from the United States Copyright Act of 1976 Part 17 Section 106:

> Notwithstanding the provisions of sections 17 U.S.C. § 106 and 17 U.S.C. § 106A, the fair use of a copyrighted work, including such use by reproduction in copies or phonorecords or by any other means specified by that section, for purposes such as criticism, comment, news reporting, teaching (including multiple copies for classroom use), scholarship, or research, is not an infringement of copyright. In determining whether the use made of a work in any particular case is a fair use the factors to be considered shall include:

1. the purpose and character of the use, including whether such use is of a commercial nature or is for nonprofit educational purposes;
2. the nature of the copyrighted work;
3. the amount and substantiality of the portion used in relation to the copyrighted work as a whole; and
4. the effect of the use upon the potential market for or value of the copyrighted work.

The fact that a work is unpublished shall not itself bar a finding of fair use if such finding is made upon consideration of all the above factors.

You may notice that this law is intentionally vague—that is on purpose. Fair Use is usually decided upon with a mixture of the four factors. In the case of machinima, the usage of Bungie or Bethesda Softworks material is allowed because the productions do not utilize the storylines of the game itself, but create a parody (criticism/commentary) of the game. Even then, Bungie and Bethesda can raise an issue with the content. Sometimes, if the quality of the content is high enough and benefits the rights holder, they'll often forgive the creator and allow them to use the content.

Auto-tuning

Made famous by the rapper T-Pain, Auto-Tune is an audio processor that corrects and alters pitch. The machine can retune and synthesize any sound to a musical note. Now, with dozens of apps and software devices to be utilized, nearly any sound can be auto-tuned. Auto-tuning as remix was made most famous in the online video space by the Gregory Brothers (schmoyoho),[39] who created a web series called *Auto-tune the News* (originally called *Songify the News*). In order to make news broadcasts fun and entertaining, the team of brothers Michael, Andrew, and Evan and Sarah (Evan's wife), remixed segments and auto-tuned them into music. The team would seek out obscure and odd clips of interviewees all over the country and remix them to songs.

Auto-tune remix broke into the mainstream when the team created the viral hit "The Bed Intruder Song," which auto-tuned and remixed a news report about alleged crime victim Kelly Dodson and her exuberant brother Antoine Dodson. The news report, originally shown on an Alabama newscast, may have remained local news if the Gregory Brothers had never made the remix. The team auto-tuned Antoine's voice to make him sound like he was singing and added music and additional vocals. In 2010, "The Bed Intruder Song" entered the Billboard 100 at #89.

Some of the most popular clips on the Schmoyoho channel are "The Bed Intruder Song," "Winning—a song by Charlie Sheen," "Double Rainbow Song," and "Can't Hug Every Cat." Each of these most popular clips is a remix of an already-viral video mentioned in Chapter 5. The remix of these clips allows the viral videos a second life, as well as creating a new viral that competes with the original video.

Mash-ups

A mash-up is a combination of two or more existing pieces of content to create a new, transformational piece. It's well known that many songs and music videos are edited in a similar formula, and, if you replace one audio track with another song's music video, very often the song images of one video line up with the vocal tracks of a different song.

Aside from mashing up music, many creative users also mash up videos to create a new take on a given film. For example, the YouTube user Brad Hansen (moviemaestroten) mashed up the original audio of *The Dark Knight Rises* trailer with the video of *The Lion King* movie trailer.[40] With some minor re-editing, the video track oddly syncs up with the audio track. This particular mash-up remix attracted the attention of director Christopher Nolan, and Nolan thought the remix was "pretty epic."[41]

Speaking of Christopher Nolan, one of the most creative mash-up trailers online is "Upception," a mash-up of the uncut audio from *Inception* added to the re-edited trailer for Disney's *UP*.[42]

Recuts

Transforming material is one of the most fun ways to remix content online. A recut involves taking an original piece of content and transforming it into something unintended by the original artist or creator. In the early days of YouTube, recuts were very popular, as they encourage high levels of creativity to transform the piece. These are different from mash-ups, because additional material and production experience are utilized in the creation of these edits. For example, in 2006, Christopher Rule had an idea, after rewatching *Mary Poppins* and recognizing it had traits of a horror film. Using horror music from *An American Haunting* and adding sound effects, Chris Rule and his friend Nick Eckert reinterpreted *Mary Poppins* as a horror film.[43] The effect works— users continually post comments on this video saying that, "they'll never look at Mary Poppins the same again."

This trend has inspired hundreds of users to recut trailers on YouTube. Some of the most common involve turning comedies into horrors and horrors into romantic comedies. You can find "Willy Wonka Horror Recut"[44] and "Breaking

Bad as Romantic Comedy Recut,"[45] or *The Shining* as if Cameron Crowe had made it.[46] Nearly every film can be reinterpreted and transformed, if it is done in a savvy manner.

Music Creation

The most intense and beautiful remixes can be found as YouTube projects that most likely take immense amounts of time. The projects of Kutiman's ThruYou and Nick Bertke's Pogo take remixes to the next level. Their creations require an incredible attention to detail, musical talent, and willingness to create art with existing material.

Ophir Kutiel, known as Kutiman, is an Israeli-born DJ and performing artist. In 2009, he started a large-scale art music project called ThruYou and remixed YouTube video clips to create original music. On his site at thru-you.com, Kutiman explains, "What you are about to see is a mix of unrelated YouTube videos/clips edited together to create ThruYou. In other words—what you see is what you hear."[47] Crediting each original video in the description of each clip, Kutiman scoured YouTube for people who were performing songs or giving instrument tutorials. He then used each of those clips as instruments in his new music creation. With savvy editing, Kutiman shows the original clips playing side by side. In the end, the aural result is a new, original piece of music made with the YouTube videos. The new music is fascinating and original and could only be made with everyone involved.

The second music creator we feature is Nick Bertke, who created Pogo.[48] Bertke takes movies and films and remixes the popular phrases of the film with sounds from the film and original music. His most popular remixes are music creations from Disney films such as *Alice in Wonderland, Up,* and *Mary Poppins*. Pogo uses the films and original content to create the music by quickly editing scenes to make new sounds and music cuts. With the dance-pop sounds of his remixes, he completely transforms the ideas and concepts of the original films into catchy and entertaining musical pieces. Pogo does not have the rights to the images, and, although he claims Fair Use, very often the original creator asks for the projects to be removed. Some companies have realized that Bertke's work has become accidental promotion and they appreciate his artwork.

Bending the Rules

ThruYou and Pogo are creative remixes that acknowledge their breach of intellectual property. In Kutiman's ThruYou, he credited all the original creators of the video in his description. For the most part, the uploaders who Kutiman added to his project appreciated their inclusion in his artwork. In Pogo's case, the copyright holder has made several complaints. Because Pogo uses strict content, such as Disney material, the decision comes to the holder. After Sony

Pictures Entertainment had his *Hook* remix removed, dozens of YouTubers continued to upload their own saved copies of Bertke's work. Sony decided it'd rather have the original, high-quality version of the video up, rather than dozens of the lower-quality version. A remix brings a new life to dated content, and Sony soon realized the fight was not worth it. Keep in mind that this outcome is not common.

Many companies are very vigorous in their litigious pursuits online and will not bend their rules for you unless you are pretty well established as an online artist. Some companies are so ruthless that they would accidently shut down their own channels because of the Content ID algorithm that checks for copyrighted imagery.[49] Like the YouTubers who work with brands, you have to remember that focusing on your audience comes first, and then experimenting with different material.

Remixes With an Asterisk—Savvy edits

If you have a good ear and a knack for finding content online, you can create new media out of existing material. Good remixers in this space are often sued or accused of copyright infringement, and their material is removed. Some of the best and most abundant material to work with on savvy edit remixes comes from traditional media. Take Bad Lip Reading for example. This form of remix is very popular and has even been featured on television. An anonymous remix artist from Texas takes clips from films, music videos, sports broadcasts, and political debates and replaces all of the audio with his voice, using seamless lip dubbing—and saying extremely odd things. For example, in the Bad Lip Reading of *The Hunger Games*, he takes the audio of an emotional talk between the protagonists Katniss and Peeta, and he replaces Peeta's audio with "Every night, I want you to hold Marvin the cat."[50] These postmodern remixes explore the audience's desire to see unusual material on the web, and the seamless lip dubs take enormous skill.

The idea of savvy remixes has made its way to the mainstream audience of late-night television as well. The *Late Show with Jimmy Fallon* features savvy remix edits pretty consistently on the show. Fallon understands that, in order to achieve an audience in the online space, even he has to participate in the online trends. Fallon's staff searched through hundreds of Brian Williams's news broadcasts in order to recreate the Sugar Hill Gang's "Rapper's Delight."[51] By searching through all of Williams's and Lester Holt's broadcasts, the remixers isolated each word of the song and edited them together without auto-tune. Fallon's methods get an asterisk because NBC Universal owns the footage, and Fallon also airs on that channel. These remixers have nothing to fear when it comes to copyrighted material in this case.

Remixing for Social Commentary

Social commentary is allowed as Fair Use most of the time, and Elisa Kreisinger, also known as Pop Culture Pirate, remixes for that reason.[52] Elisa's goal is to take existing pop-culture television and media such as *Sex and the City* and *Mad Men* and remix the videos to show hidden subtext and give additional insight into the show. For example, over the course of seven seasons, *Mad Men*'s Peggy Olsen character goes from secretary to copy chief of the company. Elisa recuts the scenes with Peggy to show an enhanced view of how feminism plays a large role in the construct of the show. In her *Sex and the City* remixes, Elisa discovers the subtext of Carrie Bradshaw's character and, using actual footage from the show, recuts the character as a lesbian. This type of social commentary deserves a watch and should be encouraging to those interested in intertextual analysis. Remixing as social commentary helps expose and analyze overlooked scenes in popular media.

The Take Down Notice

YouTube's upload algorithm is extremely advanced. It recognizes sound and motion picture during the conversion process using proprietary software known as Content ID. If it notices copyrighted material, it sends the user a threatening warning to remove the copyrighted material or explain to YouTube how it falls under Fair Use. If the user does not comply, the video is either stripped of its audio or taken down. If the user decides to fight back, YouTube will read the response, but, if it deems the response not to be a sufficient explanation, it threatens to deactivate the user's channel.

Sounds pretty dire, right? Well, you can fight back. Elisa Kreisinger explains that knowing your material well helps. If you feel it falls under Fair Use, not only should you paste the law directly into your YouTube response, but you should also calmly and objectively explain how your content falls into Fair Use. If you feel that it does not, then YouTube is probably right, and you should remove it or re-edit the material. If you feel you are correct, be certain and fight back. YouTube may consider it Fair Use, but then pass the video to the property owner for their decision on how you may use the material.

If it goes to the copyright owner, they get a notice that someone (you) is using their material and they have three choices: Ask the user to remove it; allow the user to use it, but place an advertisement on it so that they profit; or allow the user to use it freely. There is a famous case from the "Harlem Shake" viral trend, where Baauer, the DJ who wrote the song "The Harlem Shake," received thousands of notices that his material was used in other mixes. He chose the second option: He let the videos stay up, but he profits from the advertisement money. Baauer, who wrote the techno song in 2012, made a million dollars from videos in 2013.[53]

SOME PITFALLS—HOW TO REMAIN TROUBLE FREE?

As mentioned in our sidebars, the laws surrounding copyright, Fair Use, and transformational material should be adhered to. As with any type of multimedia storytelling, there are rights and ownership involved in the creation process. The only real way to make sure you have access to copyrighted material is by asking permission and getting a written response; otherwise, you have to justify the use of copyrighted material under Fair Use.

Copyright is a United States law that protects "original works of authorship," including literary, dramatic, musical, artistic, and certain other intellectual works.[54] As a multimedia storyteller, and especially a remix artist, you should read the documents at Copyright.gov and read about Fair Use from Harvard University's Berkman Center for Internet and Society.[55] Although it may seem fun and playful to utilize works other than your own to assist in your creative process, we creators have something that Kirby Ferguson refers to as "loss aversion." In other words, we don't mind using someone's work, but we are offended when someone uses our work. As a savvy creator, keep this thought in the back of your mind while you work.

As mentioned earlier, the three most basic ways to remix without encountering much trouble is to always attribute material to the original artist, modify the original material enough to make it different, and make fundamental changes. When you work, keep a list of what parts of the material you are remixing and where the source material comes from. That doesn't just mean sourcing it on YouTube: It means finding the original creator. For example, if you find a clip of Tyler Oakley on Jenna Marble's channel, you should credit both Jenna and Tyler, regardless of the fact you found him on her channel. The same goes for uploaded content of copyrighted material such as films. You do source and credit the uploader, but also the original material's director or producer. You must go to the source.

Modification of the material cannot just involve a reordering of clips or an edit together of your favorite parts. It has to transform the material into something new. It means the material you use cannot still be confused with its original context. To recut something such as *The Shining* trailer into a comedy film, the film's lines can no longer have a horror connotation, because that is what the director Stanley Kubrick already made; the remix has to be a new context. And lastly, fundamental changes must be made. In other words, if you feel you are using someone's material too closely to how they originally created it, you probably are. Use common sense, put yourself in their minds, and see if you would be offended.

The Creative Commons

Founded by Lawrence Lessig, the Creative Commons is a huge database of copyright-free multimedia content. The Creative Commons offers media creators' sound, image, text, or video content an additional license for creative distribution. The uploader can choose to give their content to the web so that it can be reused or remixed without permission from the original property owner. This outlet is extremely beneficial to students working on projects and in need of free music, video, and pictures to include in their work.

Figure 6.5
Creative Commons logo.
Source: Creative Commons

Create and Participate

After all these caveats and additional information, why should you go to the trouble of remixing? You should, because it can make you culturally savvier and better able to appreciate content. A good remix artist is not just aware of content in its linear form, they are aware of how to analyze and reconsider original media. Additionally, remixes sometimes offer an audience a new and original take on content it has taken for granted. When you watch *Hook*, you never consider that the bites can be reordered and remixed into a catchy song such as Pogo's "Bangarang (*Hook* remix)." Also, when you watch television shows or movies, you may never see the subtle innuendos or double entendre embedded in the material—the savvy remix artist does and helps show others. Be a better viewer and be a savvy creator.

THE BUSINESS OF MULTIMEDIA STORYTELLING

New and digital media do not exist within a vacuum, and, as we learned with memes, when culture becomes shared and popular, it makes its way into the collective consciousness. Since the beginning of multimedia storytelling, the work of creatives in the digital space has been recognized with awards shows such as the Webby's and the Streamys and real-life meet-ups such as ROFLCon and VidCon. While traditional media continue to attempt to co-opt the new media space, the authentic creators–from Scott Zakarin to Tyler Oakley—remain the leaders of the online platforms. If brands and traditional media want to play in the digital field, they have to play by the rules of those who master the space.

Joss Whedon easily crossed into the new media storytelling environment in 2007 on his reputation and knowledge of his fanbase. Whedon's writing embodies the ideals of the beta person. His characters from *Buffy* and *Firefly* are human and recognizable to their fans. When the 2007 Writers Guild of America strike began, Whedon didn't halt his creativity. Like Steven Tsapelas and Matt Sloan, he took to the new platform, one free of restrictions, notes, executives, and advertisers. The door he opened to professionals simultaneously inspired thousands of amateurs to produce in the digital space.

THE DIGITAL PLATFORM

Many traditional television shows were always aware of the web as an outlet, but many believed it was not a platform for profit. What the digital platform is designed for is as a platform to grow a brand—which later turns to profit through the longtail audience. The writers' strike stirred the industry so much that television shows and films created companion material made for the web. *The Office*, *Parks and Recreation*, *Portlandia*, and *Sesame Street* all make companion programming for the web. On the other hand, some web series made the jump from the web to traditional programming. Shows such as *Broad City* on Comedy Central or *Children's Hospital* on Cartoon Network's Adult Swim started as web series.

Today, the lines are blurring even farther, as television slowly moves to broadband delivery. Where do we draw the line between web television and television made for the web? If it is television created for Netflix, is it web TV, or is Netflix another television channel? If a show is sponsored by a company and produced with product profit, is it entertainment or a commercial? This last section of this chapter focuses on the new multimedia storytelling landscape and will make you a media-literate consumer, capable of analyzing new and digital media content.

WEB CHANNELS

In the early days of broadband, there were several web channels that debuted and hosted content and videos from around the web, and many still exist today. The early sites focused on animation and allowed UGC to thrive until the birth of YouTube. Some of the early channels were homegrown sites such as eBaumsWorld, Albino Blacksheep, and AtomFilms, which supported crude animation and short films that could compete in indie markets. After YouTube's launch, these early web channels lost their audiences to the site, which could support much more content. The audience didn't want to seek

Figure 6.6
Rob Barnett.

content from different sites; it wanted to get it from one place. After the success of *Dr. Horrible's Sing-a-long Blog*, many professionals from the traditional industry felt differently and got involved in the web landscape.

Rob Barnett's background is in traditional media. Rob Barnett was once a production and programming executive at MTV and VH1 and the president of programming at CBS Radio. In 2007, Rob Barnett created MyDamnChannel.com—an online web channel to support original and UGC. He found that the online space offered him more creative freedom and a quicker path to production, without any corporate "notes" or bureaucracy. My Damn Channel takes the idea of an entertainment studio and distributor of content from the traditional marketplace and transforms the concept for the online audience. From the outset, the channel created original content and supported independent talent.

My Damn Channel's original programming content is extraordinarily niche, and Rob Barnett is aware of how the audience thinks. His skill set as a programmer aided him in the online space, but really what worked best was his trust in the creative producers who made original My Damn Channel content. One of the original series, *You Suck at Photoshop*, was a fictional narrative web series that can be considered a how-to vlog. The never-seen narrator Donny teaches his audience to use Photoshop while ridiculing the viewer and expressing himself, in a vlog style, as a depressed divorcee. If Barnett had pitched this series to a television network ("think tutorial video meets unseen depressed narrator"), it would never have been aired, but, in the online space, this is perfect content.

My Damn Channel hosts dozens of series and personalities and treats its talent like studio stars. The channels range from branded entertainment such as IKEA's *Easy to Assemble* and SUBWAY's *Fresh Artists* to comedians such as Mark Malkoff, Andy Milonakis, and Adam Carolla and personalities such as Grace Helbig (*Daily Grace*) and Sara Forsberg (Smoukahontas).

My Damn Channel was not the only outlet to create a channel in 2007: Will Ferrell and Adam McKay also became involved and created Funny or Die as an outlet for extra creative work. With original support from Sequoia Capital (the same venture capital firm that helped YouTube), Ferrell and McKay opened a web channel to support original programming in a competitive format. Relying on a Reddit-like voting system, where the user clicks "Funny" or "Die," the site would allow users to choose what stayed on the site. Will Ferrell's

Figure 6.7
Sara Forsberg.

quirky humor and access to his comedic peer group helped the site grow in popularity very quickly. In 2008, Funny or Die partnered with HBO.

Funny or Die has hundreds of pieces of content, all aimed at niche audiences. In opposition to most of the content on My Damn Channel, many of the contributors to Funny or Die are recognizable faces, such as Steve Carell, Judd Apatow, and James Franco (to name a few of the dozens). Their series are irreverent and unique and get a lot of attention from both new and traditional audiences.

Quite possibly the most popular web series on Funny or Die is *Between Two Ferns*, with Zach Galifinakis. The show exploits Galifinakis's already awkward beta character nature as a talk-show host on a poorly made set. It plays as both a comedy and a parody of online programming because of its low-cost approach. Zach interviews a different celebrity (between two ferns) for each episode. The actors interviewed are able to practice their acting as they play on the inside joke of Zach's awkward, crude, and mean interview techniques. The show became so popular that President Obama appeared as an interviewee, to stress the importance of the Healthcare.gov website. After the episode appeared online, the show became the largest referrer to the government healthcare site.

Identifying Branded Entertainment or Sponsored Content

Terms to understand about content created by brands are sponsored content, branded entertainment, "advertorial," and native advertising.

Since the beginning of television, brands have had a say in the way that media were produced. As mentioned earlier, Milton Berle's *Texaco Star Theater* was branded entertainment. In the online space, there are no commercials, and viewers stray from blatant product placement. If a brand is involved, viewers prefer to be entertained by it.

In 2010, IKEA sponsored a web series called *Easy to Assemble*, starring Illeana Douglas and an ensemble cast of actors, such as Tom Arnold, Kevin Pollack, and Justine Bateman, as out-of-work actors working a "real job." The series takes place in an IKEA in Burbank, California. Like *Texaco Star Theater*, this is easily identified sponsored content.

Brands have become savvier at disguising their advertising and have embedded their content in already existing sites. Consider BuzzFeed, for example: The site does not show any advertisements whatsoever, and founder Jonah Peretti vows he will never run a banner ad. BuzzFeed allows brands to sponsor articles and have staff writers create content sponsored by a brand.

Quite possibly one of the savviest examples of sponsored content produced was when President Obama appeared on Zach Galifinakis' Funny or Die show *Between Two Ferns*. As a result of Obama's meeting with Tyler Oakley, Hannah Hart, Michael Stevens, and other vloggers,[56] he realized the best way to get his message to the audience about the Affordable Care Act was through the existing web series. Obama plays along with Galifinakis's awkward humor, throws some jabs at Zach, and, in the end, plugs the Act. It isn't until the episode ends that we get a full-page slate that refers people to Healthcare.gov. As mentioned previously, it worked well, but also showed a possible trend in new media: embedded native advertising.

As a new media viewer, you have to ask questions about what you are watching if you hear a brand name clearly embedded in the content. You have to ask what the story is saying, and why, and consider how effective this model of advertising is. Our ability to discern between original media and branded content helps us maintain a critical eye for message manipulation, bias, and spin. As viewers, we should enjoy the fact that brands are becoming creative enough to entertain us; we just have to be careful we are not being sold a single point of view.

HIGH-END WEB SERIES

When Steven Tsapelas and Matt Sloan created their web series, the idea of making a living from their product was not the first thing on their mind. In our present, web-series creators know that there is a definite possibility of profit, because the web is an open space for multimedia storytelling and allows homegrown producers to professional interlopers to create high-quality new media stories. People who create for both traditional and new media often say they like the online platforms better, because the audience is easier to define.

Professionally produced web series were around from the beginning of broadband video and, like the web itself, they have changed in aesthetic, storytelling, and technique. The earliest foray into the environment was *lonelygirl15* in 2006. Created by a team of producers from California, the fictional series was designed to look like a young woman named Bree vlogging about her experience of being the target of a cult called "The Order." The show was not originally revealed as fiction, but, as it gained popularity, savvy web users identified Bree as a New Zealand actress. At that point, the show's creators opened the narrative to alternative storylines and more action sequences. This show is generally considered the beginning of the professional web series.

Not all high-end web series start with professional producers; sometimes, the homegrown content grows into professional work. Some of the homegrown content that has become very successful includes *Video Game High School*, *Annoying Orange*, and *Epic Meal Time*. There are also professional productions in the online space, such as Jerry Seinfeld's *Comedians in Cars Getting Coffee*, Bryan Singer's *H+*, and Bernie Su and Hank Green's *The Lizzie Bennet Diaries*. And then there are traditional channels interested in the online space and developing original programming online, such as PBS with *PBS Off Book* and *PBS Idea Channel*.

Homegrown

Niche web series such as *Video Game High School* also provide popular viewing among large crowds, because Freddie Wong takes the imagination of gaming and uses the concept as a web series. *Video Game High School* takes the idea of gaming to a new level and interprets the act of gaming as a real-life education environment.[57] The series is considered an action-comedy set in a world where video gaming is the world's most popular sport. The show's Season 2 cost over $1 million to make![58] Although that seems like a fair amount of money, in comparison with traditional television programming, this is very affordable. A sitcom could cost over a half a million dollars per episode.

If you are in the mood to be annoyed—and entertained—the aptly named *Annoying Orange* went from indie series to multimedia and product power-house. It's a fairly simple premise, created by Dane Boedigheimer, the mouth/voice of the irritating fruit who sits on the counter and makes other fruit and vegetables miserable.[59] The immobile fruits in the show are actual fruit, with the mouths and eyes edited in to seem like they are talking, through savvy editing and storytelling. Ben Huh, founder of the Cheezburger Network (Chapter 4), explained the show's success to the *Wall Street Journal* by saying, "the Internet today is like TV was in the 1950s, a new technology that changes the way we view culture."[60] The show's odd humor and morbidity (graphic fruit death) seem to be very attractive to young viewers. Although traditional critics panned the series, its popularity continued to grow, and the show grew into a video game and a series of toys and clothing, and it was picked up by Cartoon Network as a TV series.

In the realm of cooking shows, *Epic Meal Time* is a variation that most definitely could not exist in the traditional space.[61] The show is a parody of the classic cooking show normally seen on a channel such as Food Network, except the meals made by cook Harley Morenstein contain thousands more calories through massive amounts of meat and bacon. Morenstein and his friends experiment with variations of cooking styles in order to create an "epic meal." Some fine examples of their cooking are the 71,000-calorie fast-food lasagna made of layer upon layer of burgers, bacon, cheese, and homemade "sowce," and their TurBaconEpic Thanksgiving meal made of "a bird in a bird in a bird in a bird in a bird in a pig," clocking in at 79,000 calories. These meals are not meant to be eaten, but are a spectacle to watch as they are created by the inebriated cooks. The show has encouraged cameos by Tony Hawk and Arnold Schwarzenegger. It's adult oriented, but enjoyed by anyone with a strong stomach.

The YouTube Creators Playbook

Did you know that YouTube has a playbook available for all users to teach them the basics of channel maintenance? Why would they do that?

YouTube profits because you participate, and the better you participate, the better your content succeeds. The playbook is located on the site at youtube.com/playbook and offers access to the creator hub, which explains the most effective ways of running your channel, when to upload your content, how to optimize your titles, how to create content people want to watch. The goal is to create a strategy of programming for long-term content creation and community engagement.

Recently, YouTube increased its metrics and analytics functions to allow content creators to keep track of their viewers in real time.[62] That means you can see who is watching, and for how long, and if they engage with your channel. In turn, this helps you improve your content to work better with your audience.

Professional

Although professionally made, the style is clearly that of the web when Lizzie Bennet records her blog. Updating the Elizabeth Bennet Jane Austen wrote 200 years ago, *The Lizzie Bennet Diaries* is a reinterpretation of *Pride and Prejudice* made for today's audience—rather than a written diary, Lizzie Bennet records her story on a vlog.[63] YouTube mainstays Bernie Su and Hank Green make the show. The story still includes all the characters from Austen's classic, but now modernized to deal with the same themes (manners, morals, education, marriage) in a twenty-first-century style. The show has won numerous awards, including a 2013 Emmy Award.

It's always interesting to see professional creators attempt experimental projects in the web-series space. Bryan Singer (*X-Men*, *Usual Suspects*) produced *H+: The digital series* by director John Cabrera about the idea of transhumanism—the act of outsourcing our minds to a microchip in our brain—and the possibility of it shutting down.[64] The show utilizes YouTube techniques in its storytelling process by allowing the audience to follow different storylines and seek hidden information in the plot when exploring the videos. The show was produced as a high-budget sci-fi series with Warner Bros. Studios as the distribution platform. The reason the show was on YouTube rather than another outlet was Cabrera's idea. He wanted the viewers to participate in how they watch the series. Cabrera hoped that he would usher in a style of storytelling called "social distribution, where the actual audiences themselves become part of the storytelling process."[65]

In stark contrast to the heavily stylized *H*, Jerry Seinfeld (who played one of the most famous awkward beta characters on television) created a minimalist web series called *Comedians in Cars Getting Coffee*.[66] The plot of the series is exactly the title. Jerry Seinfeld picks up a comedian (Jon Stewart, George Wallace, Aziz Ansari) in a classic car, drives them around a bit while they are recorded by numerous GoPro cameras, and then takes them out for coffee. When asked by the *Washington Post* if he'd ever move the show to television or a subscription streaming model, he said he would never do that. And that brings us back to our point as to why producers such as Seinfeld choose web series over traditional storytelling outlets: no notes, no pressure, no length—just "genuinely fascinating conversation."[67]

Alternative Television

Whereas many television channels use the web as a companion outlet to their standard programming, PBS uses the web to hold a series of alternative television program series. The nature of PBS as a public utility allows storytelling flexibility in the new and digital environment. PBS uploads nearly all its traditional television content to the web and also created PBS Digital Studios—the multimedia arm of the company. Two of the most popular series are *PBS Idea Channel* and *PBS Off Book*.[68,69] *PBS Idea Channel* is a fast-paced vlog-style show hosted by Mike Rugnetta, where he poses an idea ("Here's an idea!") and discusses it, blending pop culture, new media, philosophy, and literature in a 10-minute vlog. Similar to VSauce, Mike encourages user input in the form of comments and conversation. *PBS Off Book* asks a question about something cultural and assembles a short documentary to offer various opinions on niche topics such as Cosplay and emoticons.

What Do We Call Netflix, Hulu, and Amazon Prime Original Programming? Television or Web Series?

Many traditional producers are creating original content on the streaming networks. Shows such as *House of Cards, Orange is the New Black, 11/22/63,* and *Betas* are all original shows on the streaming outlets. Because the shows are delivered via streaming applications, they are technically web series, but are called television by the creators.

We believe this is more of a philosophical question than technical. It's possible that people consider web series "free," whereas television is considered a subscription service or supported by commercials. The differentiation is not new—"It's not television, it's HBO" is a term coined by the premium service. In this frame, it means that original streaming series are just that, Original Streaming Series, a new hybrid of television and web series.

MULTICHANNEL NETWORKS

As more creators take to the online space for creating content for profit, many users have become savvy as to how to make an income from their passion projects. YouTube's Partner Program pays differently, based on a series of criteria, from views, to subscribers, to length of viewing of the content. This means that a variety of different shows—maybe a how-to and a web series and a vlog—all may get paid similarly, regardless of genre. In order to help newcomers to the online platforms, often web producers will assist with collabs or promotions. In some cases, the channels can team up and profit share, similar to a corporation.

In 2009, several YouTube personalities teamed up to profit share on YouTube. The team of channel holders such as Shay Carl, Philip DeFranco, and Lisa Donovan created a YouTube "subsidiary" studio called Maker Studios. Their goal was to ask channels to team up, share profit, and create new projects. Over the course of the next several years, Maker grew to contain over 1,000 channels and had a combined 1.1 billion views by mid 2012.[70] The Maker goal was to push its content to the top viewed shows on YouTube, and this did not go unnoticed by the traditional media executives. Time Warner invested $36 million into Maker to help it produce original content. Later, Disney made an offer to buy Maker Studios, if it met profit thresholds. After succeeding in its goals, Maker was purchased by Disney for $950 million.[71]

Some of the best web series available on the web have been a result of a multichannel network (MCN). The previously mentioned *Video Game High School* was made possible when Freddie Wong's Rocket Jump Studios teamed up with Collective Digital Studio, an MCN that aims to gain a Millennial

Generation audience. Collective also maintains the *Annoying Orange*'s network of channels, as well as *Epic Meal Time*. When YouTube aimed for the channel initiative that helped users become programmers and partners, MCNs also appeared as a result. When the MCNs focus their funds, they have been able to create collective productions such as the bigger-budget horror/sci-fi web series *BlackBoxTV*.

YouTube channels are finally being recognized as formidable competition to the traditional media networks—and they are taking notice. MCNs such as Defy Media (*Smosh*) and Fullscreen get support from several traditional outlets, such as Viacom and NBC Universal, respectively.

YOUTUBE AS NETWORK

As a platform, YouTube was created because a group of young men were in search of missing video content. In the outlet's short life, it has become the inspiration for thousands of beta people to find a place to put their content or has encouraged them to create in the online space. We focused heavily on YouTube in this chapter because the majority of video content can be located on that site, and many of the external web channels cross-post to YouTube as well, in their effort to gain a larger viewing audience. Vimeo, Veoh, Dailymotion, and even Flickr offer video hosting and boast a range of phenomenal features for the user (password protections, higher quality). Our intention, with our focus, is to make you, the reader, a savvier web user and more aware of the platform of the characters online.

In 2014, YouTube made a bold move to pay millions to many of the most popular personalities, such as Tyler Oakley and Bethany Mota.[72] YouTube's intention is to recognize the hard work of promoting YouTube as well as their personal brand. YouTube will pay these personalities to work for the company to make new material and content that is produced by the YouTube studio. In a way, YouTube will compete with the MCNs to create studio-quality work. Additionally, this is a repeat of television networks paying stars to stay and not jump to other networks—like Milton Berle on NBC. The more recognizable Tyler Oakley or Bethany Mota become, the more likely they will be courted by traditional media, and YouTube would rather they stay on its network.

Create and Participate

Start participating now. Start creating and get your idea on the web. Read Tubefilter.com to keep up with the business of multimedia storytelling.

NOTES

1   Seward, Z. (2014). "Netflix Now Has More Subscription Revenue Than HBO." Retrieved from http://qz.com/245763/netflix-now-has-more-subscription-revenue-than-hbo/ (accessed May 7, 2015).

2   *Advertising Age* (2005). "1950s TV Turns on America." Retrieved from http://adage.com/article/75-years-of-ideas/1950s-tv-turns-america/102703/ (accessed May 7, 2015).

3   Yoshida, E. (2013). "Lost to the Ages." Retrieved from http://grantland.com/features/looking-back-game-myst-20th-anniversary/ (accessed May 7, 2015).

4   Geirland, J. and Sonesh-Keder, E. (1999). *Digital Babylon: How the geeks, the suits, and the ponytails tried to bring Hollywood to the Internet.* New York: Arcade Publishing.

5   Ibid.

6   McDonnell, S. (1997). "Behind the Screens at AOL's Entertainment Network." Retrieved from http://partners.nytimes.com/library/cyber/week/102297aol.html (accessed May 7, 2015).

7   Ibid.

8   Timoner, O. (2009). *We Live in Public.* (see www.imdb.com/title/tt0498329/; accessed May 7, 2015).

9   VanDerWerff, T. (2013). "How Homestar Runner Changed Web Series for the Better." Retrieved from www.avclub.com/article/how-ihomestar-runneri-changed-web-series-for-the-b-104146 (accessed May 7, 2015).

10 Fabric of Folloy (2006). "Top 20 Video Sites Rated." Retrieved from www.fabricoffolly.com/2006/08/top-20-video-sharing-sites-rated.html (accessed May 7, 2015).

11 Reuters (2006). "YouTube Serves up 100 Million Videos a Day Online." Retrieved from http://usatoday30.usatoday.com/tech/news/2006-07-16-youtube-views_x.htm (accessed May 7, 2015).

12 Grossman, L. (2006). "You—Yes, You—Are TIME's Person of the Year." Retrieved from http://content.time.com/time/magazine/article/0,9171,1570810,00.html (accessed May 7, 2015).

13 YouTube Press Statistics. Retrieved from www.youtube.com/yt/press/statistics.html (accessed January 26, 2015).

14 Ibid.

15 Rosenbloom, S. (2008). "The Beta Male's Charms." Retrieved from www.nytimes.com/2008/02/07/fashion/07girlfriends.html?pagewanted=all (accessed May 7, 2015).

16 DiGiacomo, F. (2008). "The Game Has Changed." Retrieved from www.vanityfair.com/culture/features/2008/03/lucas200803?currentPage=2 (accessed May 7, 2015).

17 Rosenbloom, S. (2008). "The Beta Male's Charms." Retrieved from www.nytimes.com/2008/02/07/fashion/07girlfriends.html?pagewanted=all (accessed May 7, 2015).

18 Kotsko, A. (2010). *Awkwardness.* Ropley, UK: Zer0 Books.

19 Ibid.

20 *The Guild*, Episode 1: "Wake Up Call." (2007). Retrieved from www.youtube.com/watch?v=grCTXGW3sxQ (accessed May 7, 2015).

21 According to Rob Swartz, former executive of Cartoon Network, as explained at The Academy of Television Arts and Sciences Foundation in 2011.

22 Duggan, M. (2013). "Photo and Video Sharing Grow Online." Retrieved from www.pewinternet.org/2013/10/28/photo-and-video-sharing-grow-online/ (accessed May 7, 2015).

23 Tyler Oakley's channel: www.youtube.com/user/tyleroakley

24 *Frontline* (2014). "Meet Tyler Oakley: YouTube's self-proclaimed Peter Pan." Retrieved from www.pbs.org/wgbh/pages/frontline/media/generation-like/meet-tyler-oakley-youtubes-self-proclaimed-peter-pan/ (accessed May 7, 2015).

25 The Trevor Project: www.thetrevorproject.org/

26 Jenna Marbles' channel: www.youtube.com/user/JennaMarbles

27 Conlin, J. (2011). "Rendering Grinders Toothless." Retrieved from www.nytimes.com/2011/08/14/fashion/with-grinding-an-unwanted-advance-at-the-dance.html?_r=0 (accessed May 7, 2015).

28 Shane Dawson's main channel: www.youtube.com/user/ShaneDawsonTV

29 Considine, A. (2010). "Shane Dawson, YouTube's Comic for the Under-30 Set." Retrieved from www.nytimes.com/2010/04/04/fashion/04youtube.html (accessed May 7, 2015).

30 PewDiePie's channel: www.youtube.com/user/PewDiePie

31 Grundberg, S. and Hansegard, J. (2014). "YouTube's Biggest Draw Plays Games, Earns $4 Million a Year." Retrieved from http://online.wsj.com/articles/youtube-star-plays-videogames-earns-4-million-a-year-1402939896 (accessed May 7, 2015).

32 Hannah Hart (myharto): www.youtube.com/user/MyHarto

33 Smosh: www.youtube.com/user/smosh

34 Seabrook, J. (2012). "Streaming Dreams: YouTube turns pro." Retrieved from www.newyorker.com/magazine/2012/01/16/streaming-dreams?currentPage=all (accessed May 7, 2015).

35 Ibid.

36 Jacobs, H. (2014). "We Ranked YouTube's Biggest Stars by How Much Money They Make." Retrieved from www.businessinsider.com/richest-youtube-stars-2014-3?op=1 (accessed May 7, 2015).

37 Ferguson, K. (2011). *Everything Is a Remix Part 1*. Retrieved from http://vimeo.com/14912890 (accessed May 7, 2015).

38 Lessig, L. (2010). "Re-examining the Remix." Retrieved from www.ted.com/talks/lessig_nyed?language=en (accessed May 11, 2015).

39 The Gregory Brothers YouTube channel Schmoyoho: http://youtube.com/user/schmoyoho

40 *The Lion King Rises*. Retrived from www.youtube.com/watch?v=1NRsPDhyHrc (accessed May 7, 2015).

41   Jensen, J. (2012). *"The Dark Knight Rises."* Retrieved from www.ew.com/ew/article/0,,20587555_4,00.html (accessed May 7, 2015).

42   "UpCeption." Retrieved from www.youtube.com/watch?v=D1CvhkkWK9Q (accessed May 7, 2015).

43   "THE ORIGINAL Scary 'Mary Poppins' Recut Trailer" (2006). Retrieved from www.youtube.com/watch?v=2T5_0AGdFic]) (accessed May 7, 2015).

44   "WILLY WONKA—Recut Horror Trailer." Retrieved from www.youtube.com/watch?v=o9Cby33ZR98 (accessed May 7, 2015).

45   "Breaking Bad as Romantic Comedy" (2013). Retrieved from www.youtube.com/watch?v=KWrRPohom3I]) (accessed May 7, 2015).

46   "The Shining Recut" (2006). Retrieved from www.youtube.com/watch?v=KmkVWuP_sO0 (accessed May 7, 2015).

47   ThruYou: http://thru-you.com/

48   Pogo: www.youtube.com/user/Fagottron

49   Zaidi, S. (2014). "YouTube Briefly Suspends Blizzard's Channel." Retrieved from www.loadthegame.com/2014/11/27/youtube-briefly-suspends-blizzards-channel/ (accessed May 7, 2015).

50   Bad Lip Reading: www.youtube.com/user/BadLipReading

51   Brian Williams Raps "Rapper's Delight." Retrieved from www.youtube.com/watch?v=7CYJ73pVpVc (accessed May 7, 2015).

52   Elisa Kreisinger: www.youtube.com/user/ElisaKreisinger

53   Hampp, A. (2013). "'Harlem Shake': The making and monetizing of Baauer's viral hit." Retrieved from www.billboard.com/articles/news/1539277/harlem-shake-the-making-and-monetizing-of-baauers-viral-hit (accessed May 7, 2015).

54   US Copyright: Copyright basics. Retrieved from www.copyright.gov/circs/circ01.pdf (accessed May 7, 2015).

55   Berkman Center for Internet and Society: http://cyber.law.harvard.edu/

56   Cohen, J. (2014). "Obama Meets With YouTube Advisors on How to Reach Online Audiences." Retrieved from www.tubefilter.com/2014/03/02/obama-meets-with-youtube-advisors-on-how-to-reach-online-audiences/ (accessed May 7, 2015).

57   *Video Game High School* on RocketJump: www.rocketjump.com/VGHS

58   Gutelle, S. (2013). "Here's What Goes Into a $1,339, 558 Web Series [Infographic]." Retrieved from www.tubefilter.com/2013/07/26/video-game-high-school-season-2-infographic/ (accessed May 7, 2015).

59   *Annoying Orange*: www.youtube.com/user/realannoyingorange

60   Fowler, G. (2010). "Now Playing on a Computer Near You: A fruit with an obnoxious streak." Retrieved from http://online.wsj.com/news/articles/SB10001424052748703404004575198410669579950?mod=WSJEUROPE_hpp_sections_tech&mg=reno64-wsj&url=http%3A%2F%2Fonline.wsj.com%2Farticle%2FSB10001424052748703404004575198410669579950.html%3Fmod%3DWSJEUROPE_hpp_sections_tech (accessed May 7, 2015).

61   *Epic Meal Time*: www.youtube.com/user/EpicMealTime

62 Klein, J. (2014). "YouTube Analytics Now Include by-the-Minute Updates." Retrieved from www.thevideoink.com/news/youtube-anayltics-now-include-minute-updates (accessed May 7, 2015).

63 *The Lizzie Bennet Diaries*: www.pemberleydigital.com/the-lizzie-bennet-diaries/

64 *H+: The digital series*: www.youtube.com/user/HplusDigitalSeries

65 Katzoff, T. (2012). "Bryan Singer's 'H+ The Digital Series' Shuts Down Hardwired Humans." Retrieved from www.mtv.com/news/1691380/h-plus-digital-series/ (accessed May 7, 2015).

66 *Comedians in Cars Getting Coffee*: http://comediansincarsgettingcoffee.com/

67 Yahr, E. (2014). "Jerry Seinfeld Has No Plans to Take 'Comedians in Cars Getting Coffee' to TV. This is a good thing." Retrieved from www.washingtonpost.com/blogs/style-blog/wp/2014/06/19/jerry-seinfeld-has-no-plans-to-take-comedians-in-cars-getting-coffee-to-tv-this-is-a-good-thing/ (accessed May 7, 2015).

68 PBS Idea Channel: www.youtube.com/user/pbsideachannel

69 PBSoffbook: www.youtube.com/user/PBSoffbook

70 Cohen, J. (2012). "Maker Studios Gets One Billions Views {.} a Month." Retrieved from www.tubefilter.com/2012/06/30/maker-studios-billion-views/ (accessed May 7, 2015).

71 Barnes, B. (2014). "Disney Buys Maker Studios, Video Supplier for YouTube." Retrieved from www.nytimes.com/2014/03/25/business/media/disney-buys-maker-studios-video-supplier-for-youtube.html?_r=1 (accessed May 7, 2015).

72 Wade, P. (2014). "YouTube Invests Millions to Keep its Top Stars Home." Retrieved from www.fastcompany.com/3036020/fast-feed/youtube-invests-millions-to-keep-its-top-stars-home (accessed May 7, 2015).

CHAPTER 7

The Online Personal Brand

Through the first six chapters of this book, we have discussed ways to create online content with digital tools, and concepts of web literacy, examined visual storytelling with creative online content such as videos and memes, and explained how to post your new and digital material on the web. Today's savvy user creates a plethora of new content daily, with the intent to share on websites, social networking sites, blogs, and other online platforms. Sometimes, the content creator will share solely on the website they have designed (discussed in Chapter 3) or will share on the several social media sites where the savvy user participates. Occasionally, the content creator will take the "all-of-the-above" approach, posting on their website, Tumblr, community boards, comment sections, and countless other social media sites where the digital user–creator interacts with an audience. The options in the digital world are endless. Before we discuss how to create an online brand, the key term that has come up in discussion is the understanding of the word "share" for today's user.

In order to define sharing, emphasis must be placed on the standard definition, followed up by the meaning in a digital context. The word share is a verb meaning to have, to give, or to use something with others. There are two parts to this definition in the context of the digital realm. For example, a content creator may create a meme using the popular "Overly Attached Girlfriend" photograph, putting it through a meme generator, and adding text to create an image macro. As we previously learned, image macro memes require an audience, and digital creators want to distribute content to others for entertainment, interaction, and creative use. Once the intent to share the meme with an audience is established, the user understands the receivers are the online community he or she has cultivated, which includes friends, family, and Internet followers. By sharing, the creator–participant offers their content to be downloaded, viewed, and interpreted by their audience, who finds the meme by a variety of methods—whether by search engines or social media. Also, the user who comes across the digital content (in this case, a meme) is offered an opportunity to participate in remixing and reinterpretation after viewing the material and thus becomes a creator and distributor in digital culture.

A savvy user of digital media does not just consume media, but participates in all of the media tools offered. Media theorist Henry Jenkins considered the theory of participation when discussing traditional media interaction between television fans and their favorite sitcom, drama, or comedy. In a chapter in Burgess and Green's book *YouTube: Online video and participatory culture* (2009), Jenkins states "The emergence of participatory cultures of all kinds over the past several decades paved the way for the early embrace, quick adoption and diverse use of such platforms."[1] Since then, the ideology of sharing has increased, with the audience becoming more connected through social media, smartphones, and other advancements in technology. Therefore, the idea of sharing becomes a "two-way" interaction between the content provider— creating and posting to the web—and the user of digital media (becoming a participant with the idea of continuing to share the content with others.)

In 2012, Laina Morris and her "Overly Attached Girlfriend" meme went viral. As a participant in digital media, Laina created a video titled "Girlfriend" after Justin Bieber announced a contest asking fans to create their own version of his hit "Boyfriend" (2012). The photograph of Laina is a screen shot of the video that is infamously captioned and insinuates Laina as a stalker or jealous girlfriend. The meme has been shared by millions all over social media and was one of the top memes of 2012.

Figure 7. 1
Laina Morris: The "Overly Attached Girlfriend" meme.

Sharing also means to have a common interest or viewpoint with others in crowds or markets. Sharing does not only have to involve content created by a web participant: It may be through a search engine, or when someone visits a video-sharing site and channel. You might visit a site and find a piece of content to be interesting, funny, or enjoyable. After the initial reaction, you might share it on your own social media platform for your digital audience to engage with. Different types of items shared by digital means include news articles, selfies, links, liked pages, or any form of digital media that the user feels their audience will, not only enjoy, but interact with, owing to common interests and relationships on both sides of the platform—you and the audience.

Users have become increasingly aware of how content in the digital space may affect the viewers, and this creates a demand to continue sharing media. The media may cause different reactions, depending on what they are: a viral video on Facebook that may make viewers laugh, or maybe a controversial article that causes readers to add to a stream of commentary among social media connections. It may be possible that sharing is increased by the opportunity to relive your personal experiences, such as spending the day with friends, going into the city to see a concert, or attending a sports game or theatre show.

Online Brand: Participate and create

Sharing Exercise
Locate an article online pertaining to your current or future career or college major. Post and share the article to your followers on either Twitter or Facebook.

Share more than the link and add personal commentary that includes insight into the article. Regardless of where you post, practice writing commentary in 140 characters (120 characters remain after the link is added) about the importance of the article or why it is important to you. Remember to add appropriate hashtags for your article and mention the company or author of the article. It's possible that the writer or brand may like or favorite your post, and this will attract more readers to the link, as well as your posts.

In the social media environment, participants share media and commentary in a social circle of peers. Your social media feed is made up of people whom you follow and find interesting. You are probably aware that other users may have followed you for a similar reason. On Twitter, for example, you may have built an audience of followers consisting of classmates, relatives, communities, brands, and organizations.

Another aspect of sharing concerns how privacy settings are selected and updated throughout the user's social media experience. What do these technology companies do with my information that I post or have online? Do they sell the information I supply to them? What will these companies do with the information I provide to them? Learning about privacy settings is an integral area of becoming a savvy user of digital media and creating an online brand, which will be discussed in the following sections of this chapter.

While the web is still considered young and in its adolescent stages, the answers to these questions are being thoughtfully discussed, by both companies and the society of users, who are figuring out the long-term effects of such valuable information. Although it is important to ask those questions, there are actually different questions you need to ask when discussing privacy and the ideology of online branding. Several questions we now pose to digital media users include: Who is viewing the content I post and share online? Who is visiting my website and viewing my social media profile? If someone is looking at my public website, does this effect the content I post on the pages? Who is viewing the picture albums on my social networking sites, and why would someone be interested? Who is reading my commentary of opinions and my daily activities I tweet to my followers? When I post a photograph on Instagram, who is the person looking at that selfie or short video? In general, what type of content should I be posting online?

Always keep in mind the content you create daily and post on the web. What type of information is online for the world to see as it pertains to *you*? You'll have to go deeper than just thinking about the memes, videos, or pictures you post.

The Online Brand

Without speaking in the context of digital terms, the basic definition of a brand is the assigning of a name to a product. A personal online brand is a focused, structured, and thought-out "plan" for your digital presence that represents *who you are online*. The savvy Internet user has deliberately arranged all their information, content, and digital profiles, organized and connected together. This means that a user's personality, career, goals, and interests are clearly defined by a visit to their personal website and social media pages of Twitter, Facebook, and Instagram. The goal of the online brand is to connect each one of those traits, qualities, and, especially, individuality and authenticity. Although many Internet communities and message boards have anonymous users, an online brand clearly identifies the individual on the web. You are also being upfront and honest with your audience and the brand created. This, in essence, leads to an individual needing to first decide what they want their brand to be.

The Anonymous Online Brand

Differentiating itself from anonymous groups and hacktivist movements such as Anonymous, from 4chan, an anonymous online brand is someone in our society who does not want to share their actual birth name online, to the masses, whether on social media sites or in emails, and sometimes portrays a different identity to the audience of online participants. This person wishes to retain a sense of privacy or utilizes a variation of their birth name (Middle Name, Last Name Initial). Furthermore, there are times when users take a name or a role in the style of their favorite fandom—for example, joining a community message board discussing comic books and taking the name of their favorite Marvel superhero character. A digital user going on this route may not have a clear understanding of how the web works or preconceived notions of privacy issues. It is imperative that college students and people looking to become savvy in digital media understand the impact or effects of keeping an anonymous name will have on their future careers.

When cultivating, starting, or adjusting an online brand, it is vital to note that the product is *your* name. Your name is intertwined in the digital media landscape. Take a moment and think about each social media site where you participate. From Instagram to Pinterest to Facebook and Twitter, each site asks for a user name and profile picture to be associated with the profile, including the text, comments, and content, where the online audience would want to communicate. We will discuss this ideal as the chapter continues, but your given name is associated with all of the content you have created, posted, or shared. Let's review a few possible examples of name association online. Your name is associated with each photo album created on your Facebook profile page, the blog you wrote on the BuzzFeed community page about the top five controversial issues of the presidential debate, and the 6-second time-lapse video of a sunset posted on your Vine account. Your name is also associated with the comment posted to the *Wall Street Journal*'s website on an article about healthcare, an animation video posted on Instagram, or a tweet giving your opinion on global warming.

Online Brand: Participate and create

Discovery Exercise

Look through all of the social media pages in which you currently participate. Locate and examine the URL of each of your profile pages. Your goal is to have all the profile pages have matching URL addresses. Once you have decided which name to use for your brand, go to the settings of each platform and change the address.

Tip

Remember, this URL will be across all sites. Also, we recommend your actual name. If your given name is already taken, select the closest variation. Here are several examples and how each connects to a digital media or social media site:

- Facebook.com/tkenny83
- Facebook.com/jamesncohen
- Twitter.com/tkenny83
- Twitter.com/jamesncohen
- Pinterest.com/tkenny83
- Pinterest.com/jamesncohen
- Instagram.com/tkenny83
- Instagram.com/jamesncohen
- YouTube.com/user/tkenny83
- YouTube.com/user/jamesncohen

In the section on "Online Identity," we will discuss the importance of using your real name for today's savvy digital media user. In this section, we will discuss some deeper implications of your brand in the digital space. If someone were to search your name on the web using an online search engine, what would come up in the search results that are associated with your name? What information is on the web with your first and last name? Lastly, what kind of content is connected to your name?

When you use your real name in various locations, you are acknowledging that your identity is creating a product out of the totality of your online presence. Your brand is the combined messages of all your participation. Once your name and identity are associated as a brand, as a savvy user of digital media, you will be able to figure out how to market yourself across the web, using all the new media tools offered to you and combining skills of design and storytelling on digital platforms. To explain how to make a brand out of the user, let's look into two recognizable examples: Casey Neistat and Kingsley.

As we begin to discuss how to start the process of online branding, digital media management is a key ingredient of this. The first brand to manage is your own. This chapter will explore ways for someone to create their online brand. Through reading this chapter, users will understand how to utilize Google searches and their social media accounts to manage themselves.

BECOMING AWARE OF YOUR BRAND

Ask yourself and your friends how aware you are of what you are posting when using the web. Who is the audience intended for each post? Is it made up of friends, family, colleagues? Who visits your site and your profiles? We take for granted that our profile is open to a large audience. Do a search for your name on the major search engines, starting with Google, Bing, and Yahoo!, and find out what is currently attached to your name. As we go to the next section, we'll help you manage this better.

Create and Participate

As we move forward, you'll need to make sure you have a website as an online presence, in addition to your social media profiles. Make sure you modify your URLs to represent a consistent name across the platforms, so that you are more easily searchable and shareable. And lastly, gather together content that you will be posting online. We'll walk you through the steps of managing this content in the next sections.

ONLINE IDENTITY

Up until this point of the book, we have reviewed all of the approaches in which you are utilizing digital media, in a variety of ways, without thinking about many of the consequences of your social media posts or personal website due to societal actions and involvement with others. We have posed several questions you should ask yourself when beginning an online brand and thinking about the identity you want in the digital realm. First, when posting any content online (text or media), who is the audience viewing it? Specifically, who is the one behind the laptop, computer, or mobile device visiting your personal website and social media profiles? If you ask your average college student about whom they think may be looking at their sites, their mostly likely response would be close family and friends.

Part of your daily activities includes regularly interacting with your loved ones through social media, as we are digitally connected at all times just by having a mobile device in our pocket. We regularly check a social networking site to see if there is a notification of any kind, including a new event, message, friend's post to comment on to start a discussion, or a brand new photo album to relive an engaged or missed experience.

Your life is increasingly connected through the web and social networking sites. Even those who remember experiencing life without collaborating with new technologies and daily developments have become so accustomed to this current social landscape that it may seem impossible to enjoy activities without these components. As technology and social media become adopted by all generations, there is no chance of reducing the value of these online products. Similarly, the value of a developed online brand and identity cannot be decreased. No matter where they are in life at this moment, in terms of education or career status and ambitions, all cultures and groups of people, from teenagers to adults, have to understand the importance of creating an identity online and branding owing to the implications they have for your personal life and professional opportunities.

UNDERSTANDING THE PERSONAL BRAND

What is the goal of creating an online identity and branding? If you wish to be a savvy user of digital media, you will want to take advantage of all of the digital media tools, both software and platforms, in order to create an identity and brand across all digital media, for positive promotion of yourself, your interests, your causes, as well as career and revenue opportunities.

When you thoughtfully consider who views your posted or shared content, you have to think beyond your family and friends. If you are creating a brand that you wish to use for potential career advancement in your profession or as a way to open up new opportunities, then your audience may be future employers. If you are focused on advancing a cause or helping out a business or nonprofit organization, your audience may be activists. Either way, at some point in your life, you will email a résumé and cover letter and fill out an online application. Whether you are an adult looking to utilize today's technology for a career change, a college student looking to gain a foot in the door, or a parent trying to understand the tools your children are using and hoping to learn, your online identity is open to the public, and the opportunity for an employer to view the day-to-day content you post online is available with a click of the mouse, especially once the email comes in, and the employer wants to research who you are. Today, the Internet is your part of your résumé.

Social media management is paramount for a savvy user of the web, and it is important to note that many social media users have never adjusted the privacy settings for visitors to their profile pages. Many first-time digital media users of a platform agree to the terms of service and immediately begin posting thoughts, opinions, and media, without thinking through the potential consequences and ramifications of their actions. You may not realize that a current or potential future employer may visit your website and social networking sites, thus coming across a wide array of your content. How you brand yourself matters when your content is viewed in a professional context.

Is it possible that a brand can be negative? If all of your digital content is poorly managed, without any thought about the audience viewing your work, all of your pictures, videos, comments, and content are open to the public. Potential examples may include if you are a young college student tweeting and posting thoughts and pictures of rambunctious activities, including mentioning each friend, a controversial meme, or a GIF created of you tripping and falling on the ground. All of these forms of created content can be viewed, searched, and found on the web, if an employer has the desire and simply types in your name on the web.

Privacy Settings

As soon as you create an account on many social media sites, you are immediately set up as a public profile. It is up to you to adjust these settings. Over the last several years, Facebook has tried to make the settings easier to understand, owing to varying complaints from users. You should create friend lists on your profile and carefully organize who gets to see what information on your page. Some examples of lists could be "friends" and "co-workers" and "college." Then, go through the steps to filter out certain aspects of your profile for each list. Should your co-workers see all your tagged photos? Your videos? Make sure to look through everything.

You have control over every single piece of media on Facebook, but this may not be the case on other social media sites. We encourage you to read the terms of service and consider how you use each site. As a reminder, regardless of privacy settings, your data are still collected and sold to advertisers.

EMPLOYERS SEARCHING FOR YOUR NAME

Your name is your brand, and therefore, if an employer types your name into a search engine such as Google, it will retrieve everything related to you. With your online brand, you should keep positive information public and keep personal information restricted to the private. As a digitally savvy user, you should be certain that a search for your name would yield positive results. It is up to you to manage, define, and contemplate which platforms to use, which content will be open to the public, and which will be hidden, at your discretion. Having an online brand and identity involves finding a balance for both. A positive example of public content would be a college student designing a website showcasing a blog series from English class and posting examples of their college or professional works on both their website and each social networking site, with links to the blogs on Twitter and pictures of their artwork on Facebook. The rest of their personal pictures, with friends, family, and loved ones, should be set to private. The only content available and found on the searchable web should be the content you would want a future employer to possibly see. Thus, the blog series from your English class could potentially lead to you becoming a professional writer for an online journalism outlet.

Figure 7.2

Why would an employer want to visit your social networking sites and personal website? Today's professional industries and environments have tools never before available and at their disposal. The main sentiment is that an employer can take a glance and inspect your developed content, because you have requested a position at their company, and they are looking for a good employee to represent them publicly. According to a survey by Career Builder.com, over a third of all employers check social media profiles.[2] There are several ways to look at this. You may be a student graduating with a degree that involves having a library full of videos and other media, such as short films and documentaries. You have created a website to post these videos for a potential employer to find, which would be ideal, not only for you, but also for the employer to come across, because they would get a sample of your work and talents and gain an understanding of some of your skills and qualifications, even before meeting or inviting you for an interview. An employer can potentially view content that is poorly or rarely managed and come across risqué photographs, political opinion tweets, or cultural blogs that the company may not agree with, because they do not align with the company's brand.

Another reason why an employer would want to locate information online before an interview or one-on-one is because they can form their own assumptions and basic understanding of your personality simply from the data you have provided online. By viewing pictures, watching videos, and reading comments and conversations you have posted online, the employer can have a point of view of who *you* are as a person. This includes your digital characteristics, traits, and overall qualities. They can make some assumptions about your likes, dislikes, and personality traits by viewing the search results.

Employers could potentially eliminate you from their hirable pool because you have simply left discretionary content online. You may be perfect for the opportunity, but one lapse in judgment could close the doors on new professional directions. In order to be a savvy digital media user, you must control, manage, and organize all content, knowing that someone is possibly making assumptions and comments and coming up with their own viewpoints on your personality from what is posted to the web.

THE PUBLIC YOU

Besides future employees, who else is looking at your content, and why should you care? Frankly, everyone is looking at your content! This means your identity is being looked at by, not only employers, but also teachers, citizens of your community, classmates, co-workers, loved ones, and members of the digital landscape all over the world. Remember, we connect, not only nationally, but globally on the web. If someone cares about you, they'll probably look you up.

The main purpose of the brand is for you to utilize its features for career and revenue opportunities, but, first, figure out who *you* are as a person and share your story to those connected, who, in today's technological society, are everyone around the world. For instance, imagine your own Facebook timeline for a second. You have posted pictures each week capturing the moments of your life. As you get older, your entire story is posted and registered online forever. By the time you are an adult, society has been able to view your entire story, from the beginning, through every single post through the years. Now, as an adult, it is time for you to change the brand and identity to what you want to share with the world, as well as your accomplishments. It is never too late to change, manage, or update your online identity.

Throughout the remaining sections of the chapter, we will define online identity and figure out how you can evaluate your current online identity. Second, you will investigate and analyze your previous digital footprint and establish your new one. As we close out the section, you will understand the use and importance of social media management.

DISCOVERING WHO *YOU* ALREADY ARE IN THE ONLINE SPACE

The first step in creating an online brand is deciding what type of identity you want to have. This includes figuring out which platforms to use, what content to post, and which sites to continually manage. The brand that everyone comes with is their given name. This is the name that will be researched by employers, connected to your content, and represents who *you* are as a person. Now, it is time to decide what type of identity you wish to establish and present to the public. Whichever subject or area you wish to pursue, including the personality you wish to portray, it has to be continually and actively updated and made consistent on all platforms, using your new media tool kit.

It is important to understand your online identity and how it benefits from being made public. Having a public online identity doesn't mean giving out or posting any personal information, including home phone numbers, addresses, and social security or credit card numbers, on social networking sites or individual websites. However, what having a public online identity means is being open to share your identity and your complementary content with other users. For example, if you have chosen an online identity focused on your future in the podcasting industry, your personal website would have a specific page with examples of past audio shows. Your creative content will be split across websites and social media accounts, with your name attached to it. Although having a public identity through a website or social media platform such as Twitter is the key to success, you can have an open identity while keeping personal information restricted to select groups of people. Remember, when you post a video or photograph to Facebook, as the user of the site, you have the option of having the post open to the public, private, viewed only by friends, or viewed by a certain number of individuals, if you individually tag two or three Facebook users to view the picture.

Online Brand: Participate and create

Clean-up Exercise
Sign in to all the social media accounts in which you participate. Also, visit your personal website. Once signed in, visit the "About" section and check the contact/basic information. Make sure that personal information, such as phone numbers, home address, etc., is not open to the public, or delete it immediately. Remember always to save your settings!

Certain forms of personal information are important to keep public for potential future employers and to help spread the brand you have created. For example, leave relevant work history and education. Previous jobs, college majors, or internships that coincide with the created brand can help explain your identity and build a sample résumé through social media sites. Plus, always leave your email address as the method of personal contact, instead of a phone number. Make sure it's the same email address posted on all sites, and that it's a professional address. Use your name (JohnSmith@gmail.com) rather than a non-professional email address (JohnLovesCats@aol.com).

If you were interested in a career in podcasting or radio, you could use discretion to change the settings on photographs, but leave your audio files and playlists open to the public. If a potential employer came across your Facebook page, they would not be able to view your pictures, but would be able to listen to all of the audio recordings posted. There would then be no possible assumptions to be made about your personality from your profile, before meeting in person, if that could potentially occur.

DIGITAL MEDIA PERSONAL REVIEW

Who are you currently online? Odds are, your name is already attached to information on websites, content, or products when you search your name. You're already participating on several social media sites without ever thinking about your brand. The first thing you want to do before starting to convey a new or updated identity is conduct a digital review of yourself. Do your best to review each piece of content you have ever posted and try to determine the definition of your current identity. Don't just Google yourself: Use the social media sites to go all the way back. Facebook allows users to download all the user data they have ever created. The main goal of conducting this review is to locate and review your social media growth, as well as consider reorganizing some of the data. Once you have gathered all of the information, put it all together and consider how you would describe your online identity before you ever tried to create one. What does this information say about you?

While you are conducting this review, think about how you are portrayed through your social media posts. It is vital to read through all of your tweets on Twitter or scroll through all your posts on Tumblr. Does each blog post on Tumblr describe your personality? Would you be comfortable with a future employer reading any of your tweets? Would you be comfortable if an employer came across your latest Vine or Instagram post? Would you be embarrassed by any of the visual storytelling that is posted?

This will take some time, but the benefits are immense. A review is beneficial to perform as an activity before you apply for that next career move and begin building a brand across the web. It is important to see what you have out there.

Online Brand: Participate and create

Exercise
Sign in to all of your social media accounts in which you participate. Review all of your posts from the last year that are on your profile pages, including pictures, videos, opinions, comments, and links. After reviewing the

information, take a notepad and write down three themes and words that best describe your online identity. Write down responses to the following questions: Does your online identity convey to the audience your future goals and ambitions? Does it tell the audience what you do for a living or hope to do for a career? What assumptions would someone make about your personality?

Tip

A savvy user of digital media wants to utilize all forms of social media and make sure that their brand is across all platforms. If you were to visit your Twitter page and find it describes a different brand from your Pinterest page, using the same notebook, write down three strategies through which you can connect and focus the sites so that they better to complement each other.

CREATING YOUR ONLINE BRAND

Once you have reviewed all of your websites and understand what your online identity currently is in the digital space, it is time to decide what *you* want your online identity to become. It is time to take control of your brand. The question is: How do you come up with an online identity, and what should it be? Starting with your name, we'll work our way to your digital identity. Make sure that your name is the heading of each social media platform and website. Then, decide what headline you would want to be associated with your name. For instance, let's say you are a communications student enrolled in a state college and you want to become a video editor for a major film or television company, in New York City or Los Angeles. What should your online identity and brand become? If you are in any creative industry, you should definitely have a personal website. Also, nearly every profession benefits from the use of social media, and you should use Twitter to discuss media topics and retweet articles affecting the industry. You could also incorporate Instagram, to post 15-second short clips of edited films to showcase your work, and leave the link to your website on your profile, so that those interested can visit your site to see the full video.

Casey Neistat's online brand can offer you a great example of how to manage your identity and promote it. Neistat has a career in film and television and regularly discusses his ventures on Twitter (@CaseyNeistat), posting original series and webisodes to YouTube and promoting his videos on Facebook and Tumblr. He uses all social media sites as a marketing tool for his brand, to increase revenue, open up new opportunities, increase awareness of his skills, and build an audience.

This is a bit different from Laina Morris, of the "Overly Attached Girlfriend" meme, who used an opportunity from a viral video and successful meme to begin an online brand, moving toward becoming an entertainer by beginning her own web series on YouTube. She successfully utilized the web and became a sensation, thus changing the way she distributes her content. Now, if you visit her website, Twitter, or YouTube channel, it is all focused on the goal of being an entertainer and branded as a personality. You should select a subject you have passion for to associate with your name. Your passion will come through in the tone of your posts, content, and comments on your website and social media pages.

WHAT IS YOUR DIGITAL FOOTPRINT?

From the moment you turned on your first computer and double-clicked on the icon for the web browser of your choice, you have created an abundance of personal information, available through search engines such as Google or Yahoo! Each day, you use the web for a number of resources. At the beginning of every semester, we have students research their online identity through different search engines. One semester, a student researched their web history and, at the top of the search results, he found his purchase-information history from when he ordered clothes from a particular online retailer—he had not been aware that the site shared his purchase socially. The credit card information was not stored, but the date of when he purchased the products and the specific items were listed. This simply came up when he typed his first and last name into a search engine.

Social media researcher danah boyd recognizes that the web's own architecture affects how your identity is portrayed online. In her paper "Social Privacy in Networked Publics: Teens' attitudes, practices, and strategies" (2011), she finds that your public sociality is reconfigured through four affordances that play a role in identity dynamics: persistence, replicability, scalability, and searchability.[3]

Persistence is your act of using the web in general—all of your expressions and usage are automatically recorded and archived. Replicability is digital content that is easily duplicated, and scalability is where your content's visibility is greater (which we talked about in Chapter 4). Most importantly, searchability relates to the content you have created that is accessible through a search engine.

Each social network releases your data differently to the search engines, and you should understand the various results. Every Facebook profile photograph is required to be made public, and, every time you post a new profile picture, this picture can come up on the image section of search results. If all of your pictures posted online are made public, then there is a good chance someone will stumble upon them in a basic search of your name. If those images show up in the search results, those same images can be downloaded to someone's machine by a simple copy and paste or by dragging them to the desktop and thereby replicating the content. Photos are also sent by email and posted on specific photograph sharing websites, such as Flickr. Think about each time a website asks for a photograph of you, whether it is a community board or a college website asking to associate a photograph with a name. You upload each picture with the knowledge that it is going to be made public for everyone. By no means is this a negative, as part of managing an online brand is being aware of the pictures you upload to any site. You'll need a default image or avatar on nearly every site on the web that requires a profile.

Figure 7.3

Your daily posts, purchases, creative work, and participation all make up your digital footprint, which is available to the search engines. The search results show the entire history, road map, and footsteps you have taken on the web. We like to refer to it as a map, because, when you find any piece of information online, it usually leads to the location of more information along the way. For example, if you type your name into a search engine such as Google, three image results for your name come up on the feed. Clicking on any one of those photographs leads to locating additional information from the source. When you make it to the source, you may find more information about you, such as education information. Your digital footprint is a long trail of digital artifacts.

Online Brand: Participate and create

Digital Footprint Exercise

Use a browser that you never use to do this exercise. If you are using a browser you consistently use, clear out all of the cache and cookies. This means opening up a browser such as Google Chrome and clearing the browsing data history and the cache. If you clear these data, the browser will not remember any passwords or stored information that would ruin possible results. Once you have decided on the web browser, use Google to type in your name. We recommend you start with your first and last names. If no results come up, try different variations by also typing in your college, the city or town you currently live in, or specific detailed information attached to your name. Pretend that you found your wallet on the ground and you have several IDs of information. What can you search with those data?

Check the first three to five pages of both the web and image results that come up. You want to record any mentions of you, but also anything that seems out of place. This could mean that the information should be attached to someone else. You want to find out what data are connected to your name. (For example, a search for Tom Kenny will result in the voice of Spongebob Squarepants, without adding "Molloy College" to the search.) Is your brand consistent on the web? For example, are there conflicting stories or personalities that summarize you? Can you identify your hobby from the results? Remember, you want your main interest and subject of the brand to be the top result. What other interests appear? Was any of the information false or misleading? Was there a photograph of you associated with the wrong contact information or hobby? The final question when doing this activity is: Did someone else with your name dominate the results? If you are a student looking to brand yourself within a certain industry, you would not want a future employer searching your name and finding your brand attached to a completely different person, where the commonality is your name. Your goal should be to start a brand online, with the results you want on top of the search engines, while the misleading information is pushed back to the farther pages of the web results.

SOCIAL MEDIA MANAGEMENT

The goal for any savvy user is to learn to build an online identity as a resource and utility to control search results. An important process in creating your online identity is managing your social media presence. A social media platform can be looked at as a utility and resource for its users, instead of solely for entertainment value. Hopefully, it will not ruin your social media experience, but lead to you incorporating elements of brand management and keeping up with each post, so that there is no misleading, false, or damaging information on any social networking site. A user on any social media site must understand that likes, comments, and posts between friends and followers or on their personal page should be a factor of their online identity and experience, as their social networking profile pages will be one of the top hits in a search engine result. boyd refers to this as scalability, which means social media have a greater potential visibility.

In Erving Goffman's 1959 book, *The Presentation of Self in Everyday Life*, he uses theatre performance as a metaphor and structure to explain human behavior in social situations. Goffman also takes a look at how others view us in social situations, which, in present day terms, would be how the audience views us on social networking sites. How would a fellow user think of you if they read or watched your content? Goffman relates how you present yourself to others, while attempting to control how others react or respond to your social activities.[4]

Posts

Your posts should incorporate a discourse between friends and followers relating to the subject of your brand. If you are a media student, your goal will be to post and share an article from the *New York Times* about the top films to view at the New York Film Festival. This leads to the user controlling the conversation and the way that others react by discussing the conversation in the comments area or retweets. This hopefully starts a discussion with others, who may follow your site for information and want to participate.

Goffman also states, "the performer must act with expressive responsibility, since many minor, inadvertent acts happen to be well designed to convey impressions inappropriate at the time."[5] It is your responsibility, as a social media user, to make sure that your content is not deemed inappropriate in the context of a job or career. A simple picture may seem innocent to you and your loved ones, but an employer may view the same photograph as inappropriate. Always double-check the privacy settings: If a certain video is only meant for your friends to view, make sure that it is only available for them to see. If a subject seems too controversial to discuss over Twitter, use discretion in your act of sharing the content. If you post the content without thinking who is viewing it, you will not be able to control the message and the response of your followers, thus possibly damaging your brand before you even start your career.

Social Media Policies

Goffman also states:

> Unmeant gestures, inopportune intrusions, and faux pas are sources of embarrassment and dissonance which are typically unintended by the person who is responsible for making them and which would be avoided were the individual to know in advance the consequences of his activity.[6]

For every risqué picture or controversial tweet posted, there can always be consequences for the action, and the material you placed has a footprint on the web. An inappropriate tweet can easily get you fired or let go from a company. This has happened many times, for various reasons, since 2008. This is why many corporations institute social media policies in order for their employees to understand what they are allowed to post. Make sure, when you start working in a professional industry, you research and identify their social media rules and regulations. It is in your best interest to create your own social media policies for yourself. Not only will these save you from embarrassment, they will also keep the wrong message from being sent to the audience. Goffman adds, "It will be necessary for all the participants in the interaction, as well as those who do not participate, to possess certain attributes and to express these attributes in practices employed for saving the show."[7] Your attributes are your characteristics and skills that you can bring to the table to further your brand subject and future career path. To do so, always keeps your skills at the forefront of your social media pages, which is what you want to display to your audience.

Online Brand: Participate and create

Exercise
Locate an article or blog or start a discussion on the subject of your field on Facebook or Twitter. See who responds to the post, retweets the discussion, and interacts with you. Does this article showcase your talent and skill, without ruining your social media experience?

Social Media Grammar

Once you have an understanding of being responsible on social media platforms, it is important to note that all social media platforms have different, unique definitions of use. Because you are accustomed to using social media to interact daily, it is hard to realize that social media are still very new in terms of communication devices. For online branding, each social media site needs to have a specific purpose. Your website should be utilized as your "hub" and home base. Facebook should be used as your main site for marketing and visibility, and you can use it to showcase all of your content and work, from videos to pictures to articles to projects. Everything can be attached to the Facebook page, but it is up to you to filter out the information from other social networking sites. The question "Should I connect all of my social media accounts together?" comes up quite often. This means that, when you post on Facebook, your information will automatically appear on Twitter. This is called cross-posting. We do not recommend this method of sharing, because the language and grammar are different on each social media site.

How you word a post on Facebook is vastly different from a post on Twitter. You should be aware of native posting on each site. According to Gary Vanerchuk, in his book *Jab, Jab, Jab, Right Hook* (2013), a Facebook post should include a photograph and short blurb. Twitter, of course, is a sentence containing information and perhaps a link.[8] It is vital to make sure your posts on Twitter are open to the public, so that the content being posted can be retweeted by other Twitter followers. For your brand, Twitter should be used to have a public conversation about topics, issues, and pop-culture references to your subject, while also promoting content that you are creating.

Social Media Editing

Using proper grammar on social media always seems like trial and error, but, as long as you are always considering how the post or tweet will be shared, you will be on the right track. Always remember to delete your link on Facebook after you paste it and try never to post without a short commentary. Leave enough room on your tweets for someone to respond to your tweet and add their commentary. For a tweet to be shared, a good length is around 60–70 characters (with a link or a photo). Another user can use the quote tweet feature and add additional information. If you found something, make sure you credit the source with a "hat-tip" (h/t) or, if you modify a tweet, you can say m/t.

Image and Video Branding

Instagram can be used to display photographs and short videos, giving your brand a timeline and telling a story through visuals. Regardless of your career, pictures and short videos enhance your brand. For example, the student majoring in media will be able to incorporate Instagram to post pictures of them working behind the scenes using a camera or short clips of their upcoming movie. As we learned at the beginning of the book, Vine and Instagram are fairly easy to use, but hard to master. You can create Pinterest boards by incorporating topics relating to your relevant interests. If you are majoring in media studies, you can have boards on television production equipment, Hollywood news, video editing software, and pictures relating to the industry. If you happen to be a journalism major, you can create a board that ties in information on your specific focus, from sports to politics.

How Many Profiles Should You Have?

There are additional social media principles to keep in mind. One of the biggest questions we get asked by students is whether they should create a second, separate profile. To illustrate, an example would be keeping a Twitter page for your friends and family, but creating a second profile on the platform for business purposes. Many journalists do this, when they keep a Facebook page for their fans and a profile user page for their personal use. However, this may cause confusion in brand management, especially when you are just starting out. We recommend you not be afraid of who you are online and represent yourself responsibly. Having too many of the same type of account may lead a future employer to assume that one of your profiles is fake, or that you may be hiding something.

Another important principle in social media management is only sign up for profiles that you will use regularly. It is important to keep your platforms busy and up to date, giving the visitor to your pages the idea that new content is created daily and engagement is being produced with the audience. If you are on a social networking site, and it has been years since you have looked at what is on that particular page, there could be spam messages and inappropriate comments all over your page and connected to your brand.

Online Brand: Participate and create

Exercise
Go through all the social media accounts in which you have ever participated. Delete any accounts of social media profiles you no longer utilize and participate in. Many social media sites allow you to export or download your content to archive the material. If you feel sentimentality about an unused account, then definitely back up your material.

Tagging

When you are a part of any social media platform, the possibility of being tagged in a picture with your name, so that it appears on your profile, may occur. Being tagged in a picture means that someone else took a photograph with you in the picture, then uploaded the media to their social media site, and mentioned your name so that it now appears on your profile. First, make sure that, in your privacy settings, all tags must be reviewed and approved before they appear on your profile. The majority of social media sites will send you an email notification when you are tagged. This way, you can see the picture, comment, or post that could potentially appear on your site, before it actually does. Additionally, make sure that you un-tag yourself in any controversial or risqué photos that you would not want to be associated with.

Online Brand: Participate and create

Tagging Exercise
Go through all of your pictures on Facebook. See which photographs you were tagged in. If there are any pictures that you question, un-tag yourself from the photograph, and it will disappear from your profile. (Note: It will not disappear from your friend's social media page. The only way to remove it completely is to ask your friend to remove the image.)

Keep any pictures that display your personality, creativity, and online brand! Remember, it is not all about your brand. You have to keep a level of interactivity, entertainment, and participation with friends, but check the tone and image you display to the audience.

CONNECTING WITH OTHERS IN YOUR BRAND

Although a social media platform is a great way for you to connect with friends and family, as we have discussed, it is also a great database to connect with those who engage with your personal brand. Although it is important to post and share content matching your profession, it is equally important to follow important figures and industry influencers who play a pivotal role in your professional landscape. This will open up the opportunity for you to connect with someone in your field and possibly interact with one another. This also provides you the opportunity to open a line of communication, to send messages if you have any questions about the field, share content, and find content related to your brand to share on your profile page.

Privacy

Using social media publicly does not mean that you want all of your information to be broadcast to the masses. You can have open discourse with your audience through Twitter and Facebook comments, but some areas can be made private for your personal life. As you become a savvy user of digital media, it is important to know which platforms are being used for your brand, and which platforms are for your personal life. You can combine platforms or keep platforms separate—the choice is yours. If you want to use a site such as Facebook for both, it is up to you to filter out the information. Much research has been devoted to the notion of privacy and whether the youth of America understand digital media rights and privileges when new technologies are introduced. danah boyd defines social media as a networked public where teens have a space to communicate with an audience thanks to new technologies, but there are challenges in the lack of understanding of a clear privacy definition in the online world, leading to issues about whether someone is allowed to have access to your public space or has to respect the world that is your own.[9] Government attempts at policies such as the SOPA and stopping illegal music downloads make it clear that the entire audience does not have an understanding of what is allowed and not allowed on the web. When something is open source on the web and people have the ability to copy, paste, download, edit, post, and share information regularly, it gives the audience an open-door policy on taking or looking at content on other people's social media pages.

CREATING CONTENT AND UNDERSTANDING SEO (SEARCH ENGINE OPTIMIZATION)

It is now time to build and advertise your brand. If you have organized your social media presence and designed a personal website, your brand should now be focused toward your occupation, skills, and individuality. You have researched and analyzed your online identity and decided on a brand to spread across the web, on multiple platforms and distributed throughout your social media pages for your audience, consisting of friends, followers, and fans. In this section, we have designed a step-by-step guide to producing content to be dispersed on multiple platforms in order to establish a brand, for students or anyone looking to showcase their skills for possible career advancement and ambitions.

CREATING CONTENT FOR YOUR BRAND

To maintain your brand appropriately, create new content or post content that directly affects your online identity. We suggest you begin by visiting your website. Take a look at the home page and see how it looks so far. Then, take a sheet of paper and map out the content you would like to add to your site's pages. Think about the potential employer visiting your website for the first time. Which content would you want them to see in order for them to understand your brand and your creative personality? In the center of the sheet of paper, write down your first webpage (which is probably your home page or welcome page). Then, decide what other pages you would need as menu buttons at the top of the site, describing your brand. You want to make sure that each page has distinctly different content, but they connect together, representing your brand.

There are four pages of created content that we feel are vital to building a brand to place all over the web on multiple platforms; however, they are not the only pages to add, as certain occupations will gear particular tools, products, or materials from the skills you have become savvy in. For example, if you

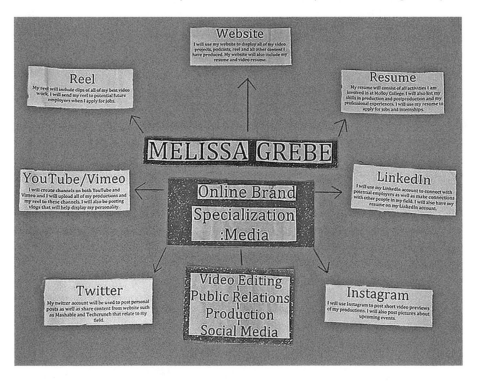

Figure 7.4
Melissa Grebe concept map.

are a teacher, your personal website may look radically different than if you were a lawyer. The website for the teacher may include teaching standards and interactive learning activities for inside the classroom, whereas the lawyer may post example legal documents to download for potential clients. Depending on the occupation, the content will obviously change. The way we have organized content for a personal website is that these distinct pages would be able to showcase skills for all areas—whether occupational or collegiate—utilizing a variety of new media tools and would showcase well-rounded capabilities of the user. For our map and brand management, we recommend adding an online résumé, blog, podcast, and videos.

Figure 7.4 showcases an example digital media concept map. College student Melissa Grebe organizes what she wants her online brand to be. Mapped out is the possible future career she wishes to pursue and what she wants her identity to be online. Connected throughout the map are platforms she wants to use to showcase her brand, with how she will use each one. For instance, Twitter will be used to post articles and discuss issues in the television industry relating to a future career in production.

Online Brand: Participate and create

Design your concept map for your personal website. Take a blank sheet of paper and write home page in the center. In bullets underneath the words home page, write down three important pieces of content that you feel need to be included on that page. Then, in a circle, draw a line connecting to the next webpage, which will also be a menu button. Again, write down three important details of content that is imperative to be seen on the page. Follow the same steps for blog, podcast, and video pages.

Tip

If you have a distinct subject area for your online brand and identity, write down additional menus and pages besides the ones we recommend. For example, a teacher would want to add a page for lesson plans, class examples, and possibly the rules and regulations of the classroom.

CREATING A HOME PAGE FOR YOUR WEBSITE

The first webpage you need to design for your brand is a home page and it is the most important part of the site. Most users spend the most amount of time on the home page, rather than clicking onward, so focus on this page the most. As far as SEO works, the title of your site matters most, then the content on your front page. Your title should be distinct and carry your name and your title, whether that is student or your profession. Choose a theme that best represents you, not the one with the most bells and whistles. Sometimes, a very cool theme is fun to have, but really hard to fill with content and maintain. Consider minimalistic themes at first and, as your material and brand grow, use more advanced themes.

If you are creating a personal website with a more basic, simple, and clean home page design, start out by writing no more than one or two paragraphs describing what your website is about. This will be your introduction to the person visiting your website. You want to explain the importance of the site and why the audience should navigate to other pages.

There are three main points that should be included in your paragraph. First, describe your interests. This can be written in an informal way, to have your personality shine through the pages. By telling the visitor to the site what your interests are, you are directly stating what your brand is, without explaining it or throwing it in someone's face. State your goals for the future. This will help the audience get an idea of where you are going with the website and how you plan on accomplishing your goals. By stating your goals, you will give an employer an idea of how you are displaying your skills throughout the website. Close out your summary by explaining how you plan on using your website. Tell the audience what it will find when it navigates around the site and how this will translate into a career. Explain that you are using the website to display your artwork, animation, or films in order to help further your career or open new opportunities.

After you have written the introduction, make sure that there is a picture of you on the home page. The person visiting the site has to get an idea of the person behind the brand and words on the page, thus it is important to remember that a website is a combination of both text and visuals. It is suggested that the photograph represents your brand, such as a teacher posting a picture of himself in front of the classroom, a broadcast journalist behind a news desk, or an artist in the middle of working on a canvas. It could be a picture in formal attire, such as a suit and tie, but by no means is it required.

Online Brand: Participate and create

Design your website home page. Open your CMS and create a new page. Title the page: HOME or WELCOME. If you have chosen a basic theme, write one or two paragraphs explaining your interests, goals, and plans for the future. Make sure to include a photograph of yourself on the page!

Tip

Remember, when working on a website, it is both design and content. Make sure that the picture is placed in the correct spot, where it looks visually pleasing. First, upload a photograph that is of excellent quality. Then, think about where to place it on the website. Should the picture be between two paragraphs, in the center, or should the picture be aligned to the left, with text wrapped around it. The theme will decide the answer for you.

If your site has a responsive theme, this will change the layout and design of your home page. With a responsive site, there will possibly be animation and effects on the page as someone scrolls from the top of the home page to the bottom. As responsive sites scale the information down to fit, depending on the device, this will affect how much text is displayed on the front page. Your home page must have visuals that showcase both skills and brand. Make sure that the background image is not only clear, but is the main theme of your brand.

If there are multiple images, make sure each one matches the section that it is behind. For example, the home page may have sections displaying what will appear on each page, and thus the picture behind it must match the content. If your home page is geared toward visual storytelling, select images or videos that showcase your best work. For instance, a graphic designer's home page may have two rows, with three boxes on each, totaling six images. Each box contains an animation he drew, and, when a visitor comes to the site, they can click on an image and it will pop up on the page. Another example may be for a videographer of weddings. When someone visits her website, the first page should be showcasing examples of her work. Look through the plug-in section for extensions to build tables or pre-built sections in a theme to design a layout for a video section on the home page. This may be the first time someone is looking at your skills and expertise; therefore, if they enjoy

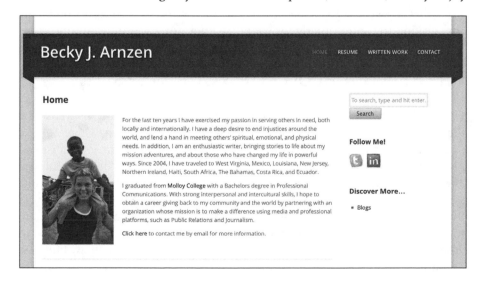

Figure 7.5
Becky Arnzen home page.

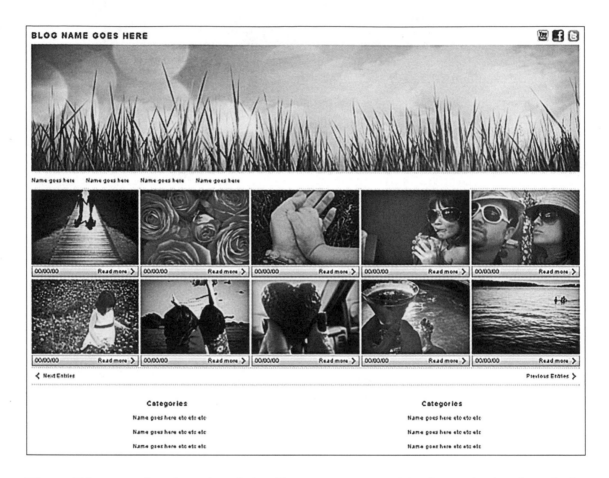

Figure 7.6
Photologger by emmakitchen.
Source: GNU GPL

what they viewed, it will open to opportunities for navigating through the site, visiting the site regularly, or contacting you for a job opportunity.

CREATING A BLOG FOR YOUR WEBSITE

One of the most important skills someone can showcase on their website is the ability to write well. No matter which occupation you will have in the future, having the ability to write crosses all industries, from journalism to film to education to engineering. When it comes to writing, an excellent tool and branding mechanism you can add to your website is your very own blog. Starting your own blog series begins an open discussion with those who have the same passion for your area of interest. This is a way, not only to add content to your site, but also to have regular visitors come to your site daily to read your next post and opinion on the subject they share an interest in. By blogging about a topic in your brand, you are giving the impression to the audience that you are an expert in the field and to employers that you are very knowledgeable on the subject matter. Blogging will open many new doors and opportunities never imagined before.

As dicussed in Chapter 2, blogs have always been an intriguing phenomenon since their inception in the early days of the web, when users moved online to write open, personal diaries to display opinions on different subjects and everyday life. As the web advanced, so did the idea of blogs. Blogs now appear on both personal websites and professional industry ones involved in moneymaking ventures. The intriguing thing about blogs is that they begin as content for your brand and website, but can lead to career fortunes. Once a blog has brought a built-in audience or fan base to your website, this can lead to online journalism as a potential career, with advertisements being placed on your blog or website, or the blog becoming the central idea and product of the site. The blog you will create for your website is a combination of creativity, skills, and proficiencies, and you are expressing yourself by writing your opinions on the subject of your brand. The key ingredient that will make your blog stand out from others is that it will be a combination of both opinion and information on a subject someone can learn from or discuss with you, while the medium is also utilized as a marketing tool. There are three areas to analyze and plan when creating a blog for your website. You must select, first, the topic and, second, the design of how it will appear on your website and components of the blog itself; lastly, you must consider the advantages that having a blog on your website will create.

Oh My Old Soul

Figure 7.7 shows a personal blog by Jessica Schaefer about a young girl in her mid 20s who, after 2 years of graduating college, completing an internship, and starting an entry-level position, married the love of her life and had a baby girl. As a young mother, Jessica started a blog geared toward young adult mothers, discussing and showcasing her journey through marriage and parenthood, while also blogging about personal interests that she will always have, in film, writing, and crafts.

First, begin by selecting the subject matter of your blog. Our advice to you is to select a subject where the focus is geared toward your college major or the industry in which you wish to gain an occupation and is something you are passionate about. What will set your blog apart from others will be that you are not only giving an opinion, but also backing it up with facts and experience, as you have been trained in the specific area. Although having a blog post on your personal website about your love of animals may be a fun and informative read, sharing with the audience your passion and giving it a

Figure 7.7
Jessica Schaefer's personal blog.

new insight, unless you plan on a future career working with animals, such as a veterinarian, your career-branded focus should be on education, for example, and otherwise may lead to brand confusion and an unfocused, unclear website, thus closing potential opportunities.

When trying to figure out what to write about concerning an industry you hope to be in one day, select topics that will generate interest and discussion. For instance, if you hope to have a career in social media management, one direction to go with your blog is to come up with new platform ideas on mobile devices. You are explaining to the reader, who does not have understanding of how to develop a concept for online use, and possibly discussing issues on the social media that they utilize daily. If you are able to inform your audience about what it has never known, you will be showing your skills and proficiencies to a potential employer or fan who may come across your website and that you are a master of the information. If you wish to be an attorney, you can write a blog section focusing on current court cases ongoing through the legal system in New York. Each week, you can take an article published in the newspaper and explain to the readers, who may not be familiar with law terms, what the possible outcomes will be if the person is found guilty and what the law states in New York, explaining the entire legal process of the case for others who do not have a background in and knowledge of the law. This blog may open opportunities with potential employers looking to add a new lawyer to their team, but also with clients who come across the site and feel that you understand the legal system exceptionally and are so knowledgeable that they would want to hire you for their case.

Online Content: Create and participate

Decide what the subject of your blog will be. Take a blank sheet of paper and write down your college major in the center of the page. If you are out of college, select the industry or career area you are currently in. After you write down the main word, come up with different topics pertaining to the area. Try to come up with at least five subjects.

Tip

After you come up with a subject, show your ideas to fellow students, professors, or colleagues. This will give you an indication if it will attract those associated with your brand, as they are the potential readers of the blog.

Writing Your Blog

Now that you have selected the subject matter, it is time for you to start brainstorming the type of information you want to relay to the audience. Will your blog be informational, opinion based, or a how-to guide? If you take any of those choices, how will each post be different from the others, while discussing the same content? This means, how will your blog post from last Monday connect to the blog post being uploaded today to your website? Imagine an educational blog being written by one of your teachers, where she gives fellow teachers and aspiring students advice on ways to engage your class. One blog may discuss using technology as an engagement tool, whereas another blog will focus on collaborative efforts as an engagement tool. Two completely different blogs, but focused on the same subject concerning education. Your goal for the blog on the personal website is to post one that is *both* informational and opinion and is based on the experiences you have had in professional industries and education and the skills developed in your life.

Online Content: Create and participate

Begin planning your first three blogs. Now that you have decided on a subject and main topic, decide what your main points will be in each blog and how each one will connect with, but differentiate from, the others and not repeat any of the same information. Make sure you plan on keeping the blog going and up to date: A dull blog does not look good to readers.

Example

A student majoring in communications is writing a blog about production techniques used in television dramas. Each month, he selects a different television show. This month, he is writing about AMC's *The Walking Dead.* The first blog will be about camera techniques, the second blog will be about lighting techniques, and the last blog will be about special effects.

Tip

Take three sheets of paper and write down the subject of each of the three blogs. Using a bulleted breakdown, write down between five and ten main points you want to cover in each blog.

Even before you start writing your blog, you have to think about the design in two parts. First, where will the blog be located on your website when someone visits? Second, how will each blog post look? In WordPress, you have options to create content in either pages or posts. For a blog, always create the article in posts. There are several advantages to creating a blog in posts. For one, the latest article always appears on top, pushing the older posts toward the bottom of the main blog page and moving the titles down as well, if the headings appear on the home page. In posts, the date and time that the blog was posted are automatically published. This is a feature of all blogs, on

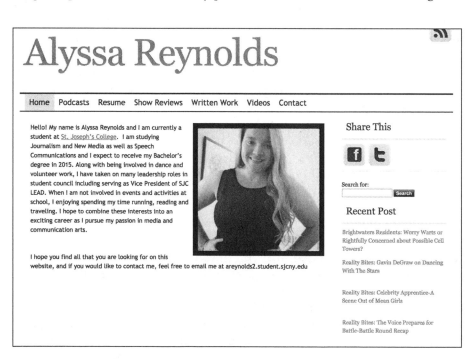

Figure 7.8
*Alyssa Reynolds'
blog.*

personal and professional sites, as it shows how current the events, issues, and topics are that you are discussing.

Keep in mind that, if you begin a blog for your website, you need to be consistent and persistent and publish new articles regularly. If you only post an article once a month, once every 6 months, or once a year, the information will be outdated, losing potential visitors to the website because the impression is given that the rest of the site (such as your résumé!) is outdated as well. As discussed in social media, if you are not going to use a platform, it is better to not join than to have an empty page.

College student Alyssa Reynolds created a blog series on reality television, which appears in posts that the audience and reader can find in recent posts on the right side of her home page (see Figure 7.8).

Starting Out

In WordPress, hover your mouse over Posts and select New post. Here, you will find a section for putting your posts in categories, which means adding a label and describing your posts with a main subject. This helps when you have articles with different topics within your subject. For example, using the earlier subject of your teacher writing an education blog series, one category may be titled "collaboration," and another category will be called "technology." When starting a new blog, make sure you place the post in the related category. This category will appear along with the date and time. Someone can click on the category when visiting your website and see all of the blogs posted on this particular subject matter. This will be labeled next to the date and time, underneath the heading (some themes may have different locations).

As we mentioned the idea of creating a heading in the post title, keep in mind that this is what will be searched through search engines. Remember to come up with a title that someone who has common interests or similar brand concepts would do a search for through Google, and your blog could come up in the possible results. Because of the sheer volume of content produced for the web daily, it's important to optimize the title of your post. The readers on the web want to click on something interesting, so make sure your title is a clickable link. If you are writing about education and teaching strategies, you should optimize the title by wording it as though it's a newspaper headline: "5 Strategies to Help You in the Classroom" or "Valuable Education Tips for Classroom Use." Your title should be unique and optimized enough that, when someone searches for your article, it shows up at the top of the results.

You also have the option of creating tags and keywords, which are also some of the ways your work will come up in search results. If you create a top keyword for your blog post that you or someone you know would type into a search engine, the chances of your article coming up in the results is higher. Tags work the same way as when you place them on a video you have posted

Figure 7.9

Tags.

Source: GNU GPL

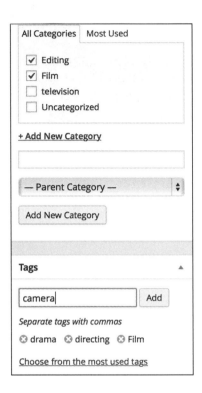

to YouTube. If your blog post is about social media, possible tags are: social networking, Facebook, Twitter, Instagram, Vine, etc. Commas separate tags when you create them in Word Press.

Now, start writing your blog post. Remember, the post is from your point of view and perspective. Make sure to incorporate opinions, but follow it up with resources and facts, with hyperlinks to the source information. Adding links to your article helps SEO and brings additional traffic to your blog. When you write, use examples from your experiences in the industry or the classroom to back up statements. For instance, if your blog is about television production techniques in broadcast dramas, with the first post about the camera operation tricks used on the latest episode of *The Walking Dead* on AMC, the blog can start off explaining what the camera techniques were from the first few scenes of the episode. Then, you can follow it up in the next paragraph, giving your opinions on what you felt the director did right with the camera shots and what you would improve upon. There is no specific rule of thumb for how long the post should be, but keep it to a couple of paragraphs. It should be no longer or no shorter than the content requires. The Associated Press states that short-form, single-byline articles should be between 300 and 500 words,[10] and that is often a nice size for writing. As long as you are writing consistently, you cannot do it wrong. Keep in mind to always bring it back to your brand as you are telling the story. Use strong verbs throughout and keep it in the active voice.

After you have written the article, keep in mind that today's blogs are also visually driven. All you have to do is visit BuzzFeed to see the trend. The BuzzFeed model is heavy picture posting with minimal text, and its influence has affected the way readers consume blog posts. Therefore, for your professional blog, add media content such as pictures and video to keep the reader engaged with the article. Always locate a picture or video example that matches the text. This gives the reader an example of what you are discussing, and we think it works because, if you have written a long article, an embedded YouTube video on the subject gives the reader a break to take in all of the content and comprehend the material. After viewing the video, the reader can finish the blog, gaining well-rounded knowledge on the subject. If you are using WordPress, you are able to caption any photos that you insert in the page or post. If you post a photo that isn't yours, make sure to credit the photographer or source website. Just because you are blogging about your favorite band or television show, you cannot post an image that someone else created, even if it is from Google Images, without permission.

Online Content: Participate and create

Write your first blog post! As it is your first post, keep it short: about 300–500 words (three or four paragraphs.) Make sure to add at least three forms of media (pictures or video) that coincide with the text. Always reread and revise the post before you press the publish button. Remember to add tags and create a category.

Tip

One of the key elements of a blog is the conversation between the author and visitors to the site. Leave the comments on. See what the reactions are from readers and interact with your audience. Reading comments can help you come up with new ideas for your next blog and help you become a better writer, as you might have missed something from your post that someone recommended!

Becoming a Professional

It's intriguing and quite astonishing how quickly blogs changed the landscape of journalism. Starting as opinion pieces by a multitude of early Internet users, with relatively little chance to make money, bloggers found the opportunity to have their voice heard around the world, in hopes of instituting an ounce of change. Today, there are million-dollar corporations appreciating the benefits of blogs and understanding that a blogger doesn't have to be a professional journalist, but someone who has the reach to a worldwide audience. Popular blogs are found on major websites all over the world, including ESPN, *New York Times*, Mashable, and the Huffington Post.

But how does an opportunity to blog for one of those companies come about? Is it only journalists with years of writing experience landing jobs as bloggers, or broadcast journalists being asked to blog on the network's website? The opportunity starts with writing a blog on your website, building an audience, and promoting it all over the web. Following the same protocols as when a video becomes viral or a user-generated web series becomes the latest hit, the goal of creating your blog on your website can generate several opportunities for your brand.

Through employers finding out about or coming across your blog, you have potentially showcased your writing skills, which can be parlayed, and you can become a valuable asset for a blogging website such as Cracked.com or journalism outlets such as *The Washington Post*. You become an asset for an employer who may want you on their team because you have understood how to sell a product to readers, continually grabbing their attention and getting them to come back to your site. As with popular YouTube channels that cultivate a consistent audience on a regular basis, your blog can do the same thing. Your blog may become a success and become the main piece of content on your website; it may become a revenue stream, as advertisers may contact you because you have a massive following that is geared toward their product. It all comes down to how you market your brand by sharing on social media pages and promoting it the best you can. Between your website adding revenue or potential writing opportunities in several areas, this side project just to add to your brand has become a potential new career in the process!

CREATING A PODCAST FOR YOUR WEBSITE

As you are on your way to becoming a savvy user of digital media, you want to explore all of the tools available to you when creating content to post and market all over the web. One tool that is available for you to use to express your creativity and even promote your brand is through audio. In order for you to utilize the power of your voice, you can create your own podcast series.

Podcasts have become very popular over the last decade. If you open iTunes and visit the podcast section, you will find a vast amount of free audio shows to listen to, on subjects including technology, entertainment, education, sports, and health. Each one of those areas contains shows for anyone to enjoy listening to in their spare time or looking to gain knowledge about a subject. But, if you break down each one of those subjects, it would translate into academic majors, which got us thinking when we designed our course for online branding. What would happen if you could create a podcast discussing your college major or industry profession? How would this influence your online brand across all platforms? The results have been nothing but positive and added more tricks to the content creation toolkit for all users.

When designing a podcast, we take three concepts used in television production and bring them over to the audio world: pre-production, interviews, and editing. In podcast pre-production, you organize the show, script, and details needed to produce the show. In the previous step, we asked you to create a blog. As most of our students and industry professionals have never created a podcast before, we decided it would be best to turn your blog into an audio show. Start with the subject and topic of your blog that matches your college major or industry profession.

Next, find someone to interview. Rather than just make a podcast from your point of view, it would be more of a learning experience for you and for your listeners to hear from an expert in your area of research. For a podcast on your site, you will play the role of host. As far as the criteria for a guest, make sure the person shares the same interest and has experience in the subject matter. For example, if you are a college student interested in becoming a police officer, you can interview your criminal justice teacher; if you are a new media student and major interested in becoming a social media manager, you can interview someone who manages the social media account at your internship; or, if you are interested in politics, visit your local town hall and ask to interview the mayor. By interviewing a subject, *you* are learning from an expert and receiving advice from an industry expert you potentially want to navigate by after listening to it, while using the podcast to increase brand exposure of your identity, because you are involved in the conversation with the expert.

Online Content: Participate and create

Find someone related to your online brand to interview for a podcast. Once you have found your interviewee, write up at least ten questions for the show. Some topic points include: Ask about their background and where they grew up; how they got into the business; their journey, including accomplishments and obstacles; important subjects in the area; advice for listeners; and goals for the future.

Tip

If you are having difficulty finding someone to interview, ask a college professor, a colleague at your internship, or a recent graduate with an entry-level position.

After you have scheduled your guest and written up your questions for the interview, the final part of the podcast pre-production phase is developing and writing down your show opening and close. If you write down the show opening and close beforehand, you will be able to record before or after the interview privately, without the subject there. For the show opening, start off by giving the title of the podcast: This could be your blog title or your own creation. Make sure you introduce yourself and your guest and add some preamble right away. Give some basic background information and explain why you are doing this podcast. Next, give a brief overview, describing what this show will cover, leading to introducing your guest. State their name, title, and some accomplishments and highlights of their career.

Online Content: Participate and create

Write your podcast show opening. Remember to write down the following information in one paragraph.

1. Open with the title of your podcast (not required; only if it will be a regular series).
2. Introduce yourself to the audience (listeners).
3. Brief explanation of the conversation and topic.
4. Introduce your guest—include name, background and career highlights.

Tip

This is an audio show! Your personality has to shine through. Try not to speak in a monotone voice. Make sure you have energy and a lively conversation throughout the show, as it will keep your listener engaged throughout the entire podcast!

After you have written the show opening, you immediately want to write and record the closing. For the closing segment, start out by sharing with the audience a place they can visit for more information on the person who is the guest on the show. For example, give the person's website or social media page. Don't forget to sneak in a mention of your website too! Then, give a brief closing statement, with any final thoughts to share with your guest or with the audience. Our advice is to wrap up the key topics discussed as a review. Finally, close out by thanking both the audience and the guest.

Online Content: Participate and create

Write your podcast show closing statement. Remember to write down the following information in a paragraph.

1. Share with the audience where they can find more information about the guest, including contact information (website, social media).
2. Review the main topics discussed.
3. Thank both the audience for listening and the guest for joining the discussion.

Tip

If you have an idea for the next podcast, include a statement explaining what the next show will be about, as a way to bring the listener back to your website.

After the pre-production, it's time to record the interview. If you are recording the show in person, we suggest using a portable audio recorder such as a Zoom microphone. The quality of your work represents your brand, so, if the audio sounds poor or distorted and the quality of the interview is not up to high standards, then visitors may turn off the podcast and perhaps not give you another try. You do have the ability to use more accessible technology, such as your mobile device, and you could use your headset microphone to record the audio. You can use voice memos or any number of recording apps made available through the app stores. Or, you can ask a friend or your college's AV department or communications department to see if they have portable equipment for you to borrow. If your guest lives in a different city, state, or country, there are several apps that record two-way conversations on a phone as well. Make sure you inform the guest that you are recording before you start.

No matter which audio device you utilize, what makes your podcast stand out from a typical radio show is how well you interact with your guest. This is your time to show your personality and your ability to communicate clearly and effectively with another person. Try to put pauses between bites, stay calm, and be a good listener. Don't ever talk over the guest, and, when they answer a question, give your opinions and experiences on the subject as well.

Online Content: Participate and create

Set a time with your guest and record the podcast. Make sure you find a quiet room or spot on campus that has no background noise. If you have an opportunity to borrow or purchase a portable audio recorder, record the show using that device. You can use your mobile device's on-board voice memo app or download one from the app store. If you use your mobile phone, use the microphone that is attached to your headphones as your recording device.

Tip
Do your best to listen to the audio at all times. If it sounds fuzzy, it definitely is; make adjustments on the recorder (such as raising the volume or gain) or find another location.

Once the audio has been recorded, it is time to edit the podcast. We utilize audio editing software such as Apple's GarageBand or Audacity (which is open-source software for either OS Mac or PC). Using this software, you should edit out any long pauses, the word "um," and any details that are unnecessary or drag out the show. Many interviews will run between 15 and 30 minutes. This is a long time for someone to listen to new content for the very first time. We suggest trying to cut down your show to 5–8 minutes or break it up into two separate parts for multiple shows. Also, while in GarageBand or Audacity, check the audio waveforms for audio peaks, adjust the volume, and clean up any background noise you do not want to have appearing on the audio file, before posting to the web. When you have completed editing the audio file, export the file to your computer as an MP3 or WAV file.

After the file has been exported to your computer, it is time to post it on your webpage. Create a new page titled Podcast. A new menu button will appear on the top of your home page once you publish the page; if it doesn't, use the Menus feature and add the page to the navigation bar. In the body of the page, write a one-paragraph description of what the podcast is about, the subject matter, and the main points. Import the media file into the CMS media library. The next step depends on your website theme. There are some themes that have an audio plug-in built into the CMS, where you can automatically select audio files, and the site builds a player for you. If not, you will have to save your current podcast webpage as a draft and visit the plug-in page of your WordPress. When you are in plug-ins, type in "Audio player." Select a player to download and install to activate the plug-in. Very often, plug-in audio players will require the URL to the source file of your MP3 and will ask you to paste the link in the player's short code.

Alternatively, you can use SoundCloud to upload your file and add it to the audio community. SoundCloud integrates with WordPress seamlessly and allows for your audio file to appear on your page. If you are not using WordPress, SoundCloud also provides embed code to post into your webpage to add the audio player.

THE ONLINE RÉSUMÉ

An online résumé is one of the most important pieces of content you can add to your website. If a potential employer is visiting your website for the first time after receiving an email from you, the next link clicked will be your résumé. Having your résumé online has several advantages: One, you do not have to limit your résumé to only one paper page. You can add additional education and career descriptions and as many accomplishments as possible. Two, if you sent an email with an attachment of your résumé, the employer does not have to worry about clicking, downloading, and printing out your résumé. He can easily click the link for your résumé without printing, read the information quickly (which is beneficial for someone with a busy schedule), and look over the rest of your website, consisting of blogs, podcasts, videos, and accomplishments. Basically, you have turned your entire website into an online portfolio of your work.

If you already have a résumé, copy and paste it into a new WordPress page. On WordPress, you will find an option to paste from Word. The formatting is completely different from a Word document. If you have never completed a résumé before, let's go over some basic tips and required sections you should have in order to showcase your skills to potential employers. Remember, there are different formats and styles for writing résumés. Also, depending on your area of study, the format may change, and certain information may have to be included. The format we are going over is a general format to go by for all majors.

Start by putting your name and email at the top of the webpage. Make sure that your email address is a hyperlink where the employer can click on the address and send you a quick message (highlight the email address, press the hyperlink button, and type mailto:youremail@email.com, click OK, and the address is active). Unlike when you hand in a physical copy of your résumé, which includes your address information and phone number, you may want to keep that information private from an online audience. Just make sure to give out the email address that you use regularly.

If you are looking for an internship, the next section should be your education information. If you have prior work history or are currently working within your brand, you should put professional experience first. This can include internships for those in college, because you are taking the skills from the classroom and incorporating them into a professional environment. This depends on the current education and career situation you find yourself in. For education, include your area of study, the college, and expected graduation date. If you have attended more than one college, put the latest one first. In the education category, make sure to included honors and achievements, such as GPA, honor societies, dean's list, or any other educational accolades. Always remember, a résumé is in reverse chronological order, just like your blog posts. Newest first.

We recommend adding related courses and giving the course descriptions. For students still in college who have yet to gain an internship, adding your related courses will show employers the skills you are learning in the classroom and potentially generate conversation during an interview. Add up to three courses that directly affect your college major and add the course descriptions. This will highlight the main points of the courses and also tell the employer the skills and areas you have studied.

Next, add your skills. You want this to be a bulleted breakdown of every skill you have learned in your college majors or completed internships. Highlight the key tools you have studied and have a proficiency such as software, writing, interpersonal, or technology skills. Just make sure you are grouping common themes together, such as keeping the software together and the writing skills together. Don't be bashful—this is the time to show how skilled you are.

After you have posted your skills, add your work experience. For students who have had both internships and retail jobs at the same time, we recommend to break it up into two sections of professional experience and work experience, highlighting both jobs. Add the information in reverse chronological order, making sure to include your job title, city, state, and dates worked. Underneath, add at least three bulleted descriptions of your job duties. Always start with active verbs and, if you no longer work in the position, make sure it is written in the past tense. If you currently work in the area, place it in the present tense. But always try to write actively, not passively.

Close your résumé with a heading for activities if you have done any community service or are involved in any campus activities or sports teams. You do not have to add the statement "references available upon request," as any job position contacting you will ask for that information.

USING LINKEDIN FOR ONLINE BRANDING

Now we have discussed the many ways you can create content, another tool that you should take advantage of as a student or digital citizen is the professional industry social networking site, LinkedIn. LinkedIn is a free platform (with a paid premium option) where you combine the information of your online résumé along with interactive features. LinkedIn is a social networking site geared toward businesses with the idea of creating a professional profile. You are able to connect with industry leaders in the career you wish to pursue, while also sorting through job opportunities listed by companies. Your main goal of using LinkedIn is to compliment your other sites and social media profiles to connect directly with companies. If you do not want to have any companies locate your personal Facebook or Twitter, then you will want to absolutely join LinkedIn. Over 90 percent of companies use LinkedIn to research potential employees,[11] and your LinkedIn profile will usually always come up in the top ten results of a search for your name.

It is important for you to follow companies in the line of work you wish to pursue. Following companies through LinkedIn is important and part of the research process, as possible opportunities will come through on your newsfeed or email or as a new job posting is listed on a group board. Before we discuss the tools LinkedIn has to offer to you, keep in mind that it is preferred that you connect with past employers at internships, teachers, or professors who can help elevate your status and your brand for potential employers by interacting with you through LinkedIn.

There are many highlights for using LinkedIn along with your other social media websites. First, placing the information throughout your profile has never been easier, as most of the information across the profile page will be geared toward your occupation and skills developed through your online résumé. This leads to simply bringing over information and plugging it in where necessary. One of the first pieces of information that you will incorporate into your LinkedIn site is the summary. This section is one that you should take advantage of, as it allows you to put a creative biography that catches the attention of a possible employer. Here, you will want to express your individuality with a clear statement. Without repeating your résumé in the paragraph, work on a statement or bullet points that would make you an ideal candidate for any position. If you only had one sentence to tell the employer why you should be hired, what would you say? Start off with a clear, active statement, followed up with three to five bullet points that highlight who *you are*, indicating that the skills you are putting in the summary are *both* your interests *and* your passion. After posting several bullet points, add a short paragraph below with a brief description of any information that a potential job employer would need to know immediately. It may be wise for you to add your specialties and characteristics that you are proficient in, such as digital media, social media, web design, or online journalism.

Online Brand: Participate and create

Writing a summary on LinkedIn is sometimes a bit daunting, because it requires you to write about yourself while walking the fine line between being tenacious and overzealous. Keeping it short helps, and, if you can, write a summary in the form of an "elevator pitch," or about the length of two tweets. Remember to use "spin" and keywords to amplify your skills, without seeming too egotistical. It's tough and will require several rewrites. Have your classmates and friends read it to see if the balance is appropriate.

Starting Your Profile

There are several key functions when starting your LinkedIn user profile. First, remember to always make sure that your URL is the same as on all of the social media platforms. If your Facebook, Twitter, and Instagram accounts have the same, unique name, then you will want to do the same with LinkedIn. This gives all your social media sites a distinct address for followers and fans to follow you. The next step is making sure that your job position is highlighted underneath your name. This subheading allows the person searching for you to quickly see your industry and your job title.

A profile picture on LinkedIn is essential. Unlike other social media, LinkedIn only allows one photo, so make sure that you are dressed in professional attire. Besides a profile picture, LinkedIn now enables users to have a cover photograph, which is important to promote your brand. In order to do this, make sure the cover photo references your skills. For instance, if you are a media student, have a cover photo of a production camera or studio; if you are a teacher, have a cover photo of a classroom; or, if you are an artist, post a cover photo reflecting a piece of your work. This is an excellent way of showcasing the expression and creativity of the brand.

Now, let's fill in the rest of your profile and digital résumé. The first thing you will want to do is bring over your work experience from your online résumé. As with any résumé, you have the ability to add your job title, the time period you have held this position, along with the skills of the job. One of the highlights of the experience section is that it places the company logo next to the company you have listed. You have the ability to either place honors and awards below each job or create a separate section with your achievements. Follow the same format discussed with creating an online résumé and list all of your accomplishments, including educational or occupational awards.

The next step is where LinkedIn gets more interactive with your profile. This follows the traditional format of a résumé and lists your top skills. These skills include software, subjects, particular areas of expertise, and tools that you have mastered. To illustrate, if you are a student who has studied digital or new media, your list may include: social media, journalism, web design, blogging video editing, WordPress, Twitter, and photography. One of the great parts of having a LinkedIn profile is that you can have fellow students, colleagues, or teachers endorse your skills. When you visit your profile, LinkedIn will usually ask you what skills or expertise your other connections have. Connections can endorse one of your skills by visiting your profile page and pressing the plus symbol next to the skill, leaving their profile picture next to the skill. This is an excellent feature, as a potential employer looking through your skills can view the number of endorsements next to the skill. Another great option for employers is that they are able to hover their mouse over the picture of one of the endorsements, and their name and job title will appear. This is beneficial, because a potential employer can see that you have been endorsed by an industry professional, which shows that you are qualified for this skill and capable for the position.

Beneath the skills is where you will fill in information on your education background. As with the professional companies, logos will appear next to the title of the educational program that you are involved with. Remember to name the major and minor programs you are currently enrolled in or have received a degree in. Keep in mind to also add any activities or clubs you were involved with, as they may have a comparison and link to the brand you have created. Another good idea for students is to add projects, videos or research papers, such as a seminar thesis.

One of the best benefits of LinkedIn is the recommendation feature on your profile. Recommendations are added to your profile page by your other connections, who are current or previous colleagues who have experienced your skills by working with you. Recommendations appear underneath the specific job in the experience category and in a separate category. Potential employers will read first-hand experience of how you function in the work place and how you excel at the job. If an industry professional is recommending you for your skills and the job that you have completed, this shows your exceptional qualities.

LinkedIn also offers what it describes as groups for users to join. Groups are a place for discussion topics and message boards, for professional industries and jobs as well as academic ventures. Examples include groups for college alumni, for members to keep in touch, discuss job opportunities in the field, and stay connected for alumni events. There are also groups for software skills to match your brand, such as Adobe Photoshop or Apple's Final Cut Pro, where members can discuss new skills using the program, ask other members for help on an issue, and interact with others who have the same interest and skills with the software. Interacting with those who have interests in or knowledge of the same software or skill may lead to future opportunities.

OPTIMIZING YOUR CONTENT

Now that you have increased the professional content on your website, cleaned your social media profiles, and joined LinkedIn, it's time to control your search results. SEO plays an important role in Internet marketing industries, as well as your personal brand.

You have now generated content all over the web on social media platforms and built your own website. To start making sure that your brand appears on the top of Google searches for your name, make sure content appears on each of your platforms. Start with sending out the content and posting links all over the place on social media. Let your audience know where to find your brand and the content you are creating. It is important that, if you created a video for your website, the video can be found everywhere. If you uploaded a video on YouTube, embed the video on your website. Follow it up by uploading and promoting it on your Facebook page. Use Twitter to promote it and bring users to your website. Finish up by taking 15 seconds of your video and posting it to Instagram. Through your posting content on each platform, users are continually visiting the sites and clicking on the links. This will be the content that appears on the top of Google searches, with any misleading information attached to your name being pushed farther down the pages.

Your Content Online

It is important to note that Google personalizes the results of each individual using its services by the information it has through your Google Plus account and YouTube, and each one of those accounts works together. As Google owns these products, it will attempt to show these results higher on the search.

Additionally, when you add hashtags or tags to your content, you are essentially allowing your content to be used for public purposes. For instance, your college uses a tag such as #collegelife when asking students to take pictures around campus and posting those pictures through all social media platforms. While on campus, you take a photograph of a group of your friends having lunch and post it to Instagram using #collegelife. The college is then allowed to use that picture for any promotional purposes, such as articles or magazines.

MEASURING YOUR SUCCESS

To track how well you are faring in search results and content views, you should enable analytics and metrics, explained in Chapter 3. YouTube's analytics come with every single video you post and can give you insight into how people are responding to your video content. If you add a digital résumé, you can see how many people are watching all the way through, and this can help you improve your content for future projects. YouTube's analytic section now hosts a real-time view in which you can see the charts move up and down as it happens, live. If someone starts watching your video, you can see how long your viewer has watched your video.

One of the most helpful charts on YouTube is the audience retention chart. This chart will showcase your videos' estimated amount of minutes watched. It will even give you the average view duration and the average percentage viewed. This gives you a clear indication of whether your audience was engaged and watched the entire video through. If the audience did not watch the entire video, you can see where they clicked away. This helps you, as a creator of content, to see what part of the video your audience is enjoying and what type of content it wants to see. You can even get specific engagement reports. This includes information on your subscribers, likes and dislikes (even seeing which country did not like the video), favorites, comments, and sharing. Under sharing, you can get a report to see on which platforms your videos are being shared. All of this information will only improve the videos you create and help you market your branded videos to the audience.

Google Analytics is a place where you can monitor your website traffic. Google Analytics is free to use, and Google also offers a premium service. When registering for the service, you have the ability to set the data sharing options. Once you are signed in, you will receive a JavaScript code that you must copy and paste into every webpage you want to track. Google Analytics will track and give you statistics on your visitors from social media sites and search engines. This gives you insight into how your webpages are performing.

HAVING ORGANIZED YOUR DIGITAL FOOTPRINT

What you most likely found through researching your digital footprint before you branded yourself is that you are a very creative individual who used a vast number of new media tools and technologies before you focused on personal promotion. By creating an array of different content and posting it on your personal website and social media pages, you have essentially cleaned up and organized your digital footprint, which may have originally had a lot of various content and scattered information. You have achieved a clear, focused, and manageable brand, incorporating your creativity, individuality, and definition of yourself, for loved ones *and* employers, without any questions of what you wish to accomplish professionally.

In organizing your digital footprint, what did you leave behind? The information on the top of Google search results that may have been misleading or unwanted is several pages away and moving farther away with each additional piece of content added to your social networking sites and websites. After organization, the top hit when you type in your name will be the created content of blogs, podcasts, online résumé, videos, LinkedIn profile, and other social media accounts where you have negotiated the balance of professional and personal content. Eventually, the dated information will fade into the background. An increase in clicks will provide more results on search engines and equal brand awareness.

How do you maintain your digital footprint? In order to be a savvy user and continue the brand that you have started, you must constantly create. All industries and fields today require you to constantly create and produce products. Do not be passive in creating digital media products if they have direct correlation to your brand. Connect with other new media users and trends and always join discussions in the online world. Building a brand is like a story you place online, with multiple chapters and locations. In order to continue to tell your story, you have to create and post new and digital media. The final goal with a digital footprint should be not just to maintain, but constantly to improve.

THINK FIRST, POST SECOND

Does your entire experience have to be focused on your online brand? No, but always take a second to think about what you're about to post and create. Take a moment to think about the possible outcomes, reactions, and consequences of anything you are about to post online. When you are about to add content to your social media platform of choice or personal website, reread the post and think about the possible outcomes. You should continue to enjoy your Internet experience to the fullest and continue to interact and participate with friends, family, and followers, creating Vines, memes, and GIFs. *Think first, post second.* What this entails is viewing what you write or create before you press the post or share button. Ask yourself, does this tweet, embedded video, or comment affect my brand? Will it become an obstacle that could keep me from advancing in my career? The ideal for using any social networking site is to have a balance between utility and entertainment.

Between using social media and the web for entertainment, use the resources you have available to you. Although Twitter is a fun place to post a joke in 140 characters, it is also an open source for researching and finding articles for college papers. It is also a great resource for locating internships. Facebook is fun for viewing pictures of your friends, but a Facebook group started by your professor in your math class allows you to practice math problems at any time, ask questions of your professor quickly, and study with your fellow class members while keeping a level of privacy. *Let your overall experience be balanced.* Check things such as spelling and grammar when posting on the web. Remember, your website can be viewed by anyone and is a reflection of you. If someone visits your website and there are spelling and grammar issues on the home page, you might have lost the job before the interview. Again, think first, post second. Review your content. Don't be in a rush to press the publish button. The web is a toolkit for creativity and the development of ideas with others. If you use it for all that it has to offer, we guarantee, you will be happy with the results.

SKIPPING THE LINE

After reading this book, you will have created and figured out the importance of forging a strong online creative presence. This chapter on branding and overall text has helped you navigate ahead of peers who are less informed on online brand and message management. Imagine those who never take a class or learn how to create an online brand. It is the same for all parents, grandparents, and adults who do not wish to learn new technologies. Those who do not use or learn to be literate on social or digital media will be left behind, as technology always moves forward, and those users who have become savvy will reap the benefits and rewards of new opportunities and exciting interactivity in today's society. As a motivated user of new media, you should always be aware of new platforms, software, and technologies that are released and can be incorporated to the benefit of your brand. Be aware of what is going on digitally and how it's affecting you. When a new technology or social media platform gets released, ask the question "Why?" Why do we enjoy this technology? Why do we join and interact on this new social media site? If you can answer the question why something affects us culturally and socially, it will put you one step ahead of the rest, thus skipping the line.

NOTES

1 Burgess, J., and Green, J. (2009). *YouTube: Online Video and Participatory Culture.* Cambridge, UK: Polity.

2 CareerBuilder (2013). "More Employers Finding Reasons Not to Hire Candidates on Social Media, Finds CareerBuilder Survey." Retrieved from www.careerbuilder. com/share/aboutus/pressreleasesdetail.aspx?sd=6/26/2013&id=pr766&ed=12/31/ 2013 (accessed May 8, 2015).

3 boyd, d., and Marwick, A. (2011, September). "Social Privacy in Networked Publics: Teens' attitudes, practices, and strategies." Presented at *A Decade in Internet Time: Symposium on the Dynamics of the Internet and Society,* p. 9.

4 Goffman, E. (1959). *The Presentation of Self in Everyday Life.* New York: Anchor Books.

5 Ibid., p. 142.

6 Ibid., p. 133.

7 Ibid., p. 135.

8 Vaynerchuk, G. (2013). *Jab, Jab, Jab, Right Hook: How to tell your story in a noisy social world.* New York: HarperBusiness.

9 boyd, d., and Marwick, A. (2011, September). "Social Privacy in Networked Publics: Teens' attitudes, practices, and strategies." Presented at *A Decade in Internet Time: Symposium on the Dynamics of the Internet and Society.*

10   Wemple, E. (2014). "Associated Press Polices Story Length." Retrieved from www.washingtonpost.com/blogs/erik-wemple/wp/2014/05/12/associated-press-polices-story-length/ (accessed May 8, 2015).

11   Rothberg, S. (2012). "92% of Employers Use Twitter, Facebook, LinkedIn to Hire New Employees." Retrieved from www.collegerecruiter.com/blog/2012/07/09/92-of-employers-use-twitter-facebook-linkedin-to-hire-new-employees/ (accessed May 8, 2015).

CHAPTER 8

Conclusion

We hope you enjoyed this adventure in the new and digital online environment. Your participation and willingness to learn and create help the web become a better place and make you a personal brand that will lead the new and digital media industries.

For a user of digital media, there are many forms of online community to join, whether they are on social media platforms such as Facebook and Twitter, user-generated visual platforms for exciting visual media, image and threaded forums, or gaming communities. Each community is geared toward your interest, benefits from your participation, and changes the way you interact with the chosen digital platform and what content you create. Whatever community you join and contribute to through the digital content you create, you will become a better storyteller. Now that you know the history and importance of the hashtag, you know how to contribute to the conversations and research of the world and help inform users globally on topics and activist movements. In using all of these communities, you are posting and being expressive, letting your personality shine through in one or multiple contexts through sound, writing, photography, and video elements on each platform. To be a part of the full experience an online community can offer, you have become a creator and engaged user and you interact along with being expressive. This short-form creativity connects you to users who will allow you to grow as an artist and share your story to the world.

We hope you have benefitted from learning how the web works, using and understanding the languages the digital environment offers. Language is a shared experience, and the digital media languages will assist in your future success. It is vital for you to know how to read and write web languages in order to advance yourself in the changing industries. Understanding code, such as HTML5, jQuery, and CSS, will help you gain knowledge of how web designers and all those who have successfully created products we engage with daily have created a platform that connects you to everyone. Now that you know how to build and create, your web literacy will make you a better reader of the web, so that you know why certain designs have been published and can help others understand as well.

After you read about memes, we hope you have been inspired to understand how something such as an image can provide meaning and influence a culture. A meme incites a reaction owing to our culture being a visual language that wants to tell stories and send messages through pictures. What makes memes work is that the online world offers a space for users to create and remix a story and share these images with others in their online community. You now have a comprehension of the difference between memes and virals. An understanding of how a piece of content goes viral is an important part of understanding how digital media work through their strong reach, along with our culture of wanting to find videos that we can laugh at, while major companies are looking for the next big hit. After reading this chapter, not only do you have knowledge of the history of virals, you also know what makes a video go viral, through sharing, the backing of major corporations, and trends that relate to popular culture. Through the case studies showcased in the chapter, you too can create a meme or video that can become viral by being spread through the web.

We hope you participate in multimedia storytelling through web television and as a YouTube personality. Knowing the history of web television hopefully inspires you to become a creator, making your own YouTube channel that includes a vlog or web series. From history, to narrative storytelling, to writing the characters that connect with the audience, these are important elements for making a video and for you to become a YouTube and online video user. As you continually have a presence on the web by creating content, joining social media, and having a voice, it is important for you to remember to pay attention to your online presence, which we use as a culminating chapter. As you post information that search engines are collecting each day online, you're creating a digital footprint. Users can search this footprint and discover information about you on the web, and learning to create a brand for yourself and controlling your online identity are important tools to use as you enter the digital space. This is accomplished by managing your space and social media presence, creating content, and putting thought into each piece of data posted online.

It is now time for you to create! Being in new and digital media involves not only reading about its context, but participating and creating in its various forms. Keep this book next to you at your desktop computer, laptop, or tablet, as you enter the digital world. This will be your manual and guide throughout the entire process, as you try out each phase. Look for an online community where you can participate. It can be through social media, on Twitter, where you want to tweet about a television show with fellow fans, or a short-form community on Vine where you connect with fellows who enjoy making short video animation. Finding others on the web who share your interest will not only help you stay engaged online, but will motivate you to start creating. Now that you have the knowledge of how the web works, write a website, customize a WordPress page, create an image macro meme, shoot a vlog. Regardless of what you choose to create, promote yourself on social media platforms that bring out the best in your writing and storytelling abilities. Whether it's writing a blog, producing a podcast, or joining in conversations with communities, by creating content you are a step ahead of those who do not understand digital tools and how to use the web to their advantage. This advantage is to your benefit, as most users do not consider the power of their online presence. The content associated with your name can be used in a variety of ways, such as career advancement, education, information, and being a member of society in new forms.

ALWAYS BE CREATING

As you create, it is not just posting a video of your cat or a remixed meme in hopes of making your followers on Tumblr laugh. After reading this book, you can incorporate knowledge into the theory and use of the web in ways that can bring users together in one space. You can do this as responsible, engaged, online citizens. You can discuss societal and political issues on the web in hopes of gathering individuals together for a cause or a belief that you have. You can use the web to be an activist and for the social good. Savvy users can discuss topics of race, politics, and other important issues affecting society. Therefore, as a savvy user, you will use digital tools to discuss these important issues on the web. Being savvy allows you to notice issues affecting the world and want to make a difference. The digital sphere allows you to make that difference, because we all have a voice through social media.

You can create massive amounts of new and digital media content, have a voice on the web, and a presence. Be innovative and always be creative. Be who you are online. Be yourself. Be authentic. Let your personality shine through and don't be shy. Be inspired and be unique. There are a lot of benefits and rewards in the digital space, if you stay positive and consistently creative. Most importantly, remember, when you are writing a blog or producing your video, keep your digital footprint and what your online identity is in your mind. Think first, post second. You control your digital footprint and how you will be represented online. Not only do you control your identity, but also you control your digital material and culture.

The web is open to all, and those who are savvy will succeed. Be strong, be creative, and, to prepare for success, prepare for criticism. As long as you are a responsible, engaged, and savvy citizen on the web, you will be a new and digital media leader.

Good luck. Have fun down the path you are about to take. Enjoy all the tools and utilities new and digital media will bring to you.

Glossary

.com—The most common extension on the World Wide Web, short for commercial website. Also known as dot-com.

#—The number sign or pound symbol is most commonly known as the "hash" mark or hashtag on social media. In 2007, Twitter user Chris Messina used the hashtag to organize an in-person meeting and inadvertently invented the social media hashtag.

3D printing—The act of using a fabricator that extrudes plastic into a physical space on a platform, creating a three-dimensional product.

4chan—Founded by Chris "moot" Poole, the site boasts dozens of image boards based on Japan's otaku picture boards. It allows users to remain anonymous and post anything they would like on the boards. The forum has no archive, self-regulates, and is often the digital birthplace of many memes. See also **Anonymous** and **Memes**.

Advertorial—A mash-up word meaning a mix of advertising and editorial.

Algorithm—A problem-solving piece of mathematics that allows a computer program to expedite formulas.

Analytics—The system used to measure web and Internet data.

Anonymous—A loosely associated international network of hacktivists and activists who carry out well-publized hacking stunts, protests, and digital attacks on various websites. Also a user who desires not to use his or her own identity when using the web.

API—application programming interface—Software components given to users in order to specify how the platform may be used outside the original program.

ASCII—American Standard Code for Information Interchange—A 7-bit code language where each bit represents a unique character.

Auto-Tune—A tool used to make any word or sound into a musical note. Allows rappers and users to create music from regular sound content.

AVI—Audio Video Interleaved—Never referred to except as AVI, it is a Windows digital video extension.

Beta person—The type of character or individual most likely seen in early web series and vlogs. According to Stephanie Rosenbloom of the *New York Times*, these characters are anti-*Entourage* characters.

Big data—Data in extremely large sets. Referred to as "big data" to be analyzed to reveal how the data were created, including human behavior, interactions, patterns, and trends.

Binary language—The original language of digital media, where there are two digits, a 1 or a 0, meaning on or off, true or false, yes or no. The power button on computers is a symbol combining a 1 and a 0.

Bit.ly—One of the many URL shorteners designed to shrink long web addresses to fit into microblogging platforms such as Twitter. Also used in analytics to discover traffic and link clicks.

Branded entertainment—Also known as sponsored content, this type of entertainment seems like authentic material, but is actually a cleverly disguised commercial. Good examples are the Old Spice guy and OK Go music videos.

Broadband—The transmission of data via high-capacity connections.

Browser—Invented in 1993, this device reads HTML and allows users to access the visuals of the World Wide Web.

Citizen journalism—Any web or social media user using their tools to report information to be shared with the public.

Cloud computing—Also known as "the cloud," this is when data storage is kept in several locations simultaneously over broadband-connected networks.

CMOS chip—complementary metal-oxide-semiconductor chip—Used as the image processor in small camera devices such as cellphones and digital cameras. A more current image-capture device than the charged coupled device (CCD) of older cameras.

CMS—Content management system—An online database that allows content to be organized and managed. WordPress is a blogging CMS.

Codecs—Derived from code/decode, a codec compresses data to be transmitted digitally and then decompressed on the receiving side.

Collaborations—Also known as "collabs," these are a style of YouTube or online video production where two or more personalities team up for a similar theme, video fad, or cross-promotion.

Compression—Using a digital format to remove redundant information to create a smaller file size. Data can be compressed in lossless formats, where the information compressed is unseen, or lossy compression, where compression leaves artifacts and distortions.

Convergence—A term used for the trend of merging multiple theories and technologies for the benefit of advancement.

Cookies—Also known as an HTTP cookie or web cookie, this is a very small piece of data left on a user's computer that allows websites to track web use.

Cord cutting—A trend of discontinuing cable or traditional media subscription services for Internet-based streaming or downloads of media.

cPanel—control panel—A Linux-based control panel for website backends that allow users access to code, files, directories, databases, and host management of websites.

Creator—The term for a content producer in the online space.

Cross-posting—Using a social media post on other platforms simultaneously, through shared services.

CSS—cascading style sheets—Part of the hypertext language that allows for marking up code for the style and the look and interface of a website.

Developer—A programmer who designs, creates, and advances products for the World Wide Web and applications.

Digital footprint—Your overall data impression online, a culmination of all created content and searchable material from search engines.

Directories—Kept inside the root directory to create a more organized system for the web designer. Also known as a folder.

Divs—Part of the HTML5 syntax that allows the coder to write separate website properties into a page with unique CSS.

DNS—domain name server—Setting your domain name to the host, which points the domain to your directory.

Doge meme—A popular meme where the text is written in Comic Sans and the words are part of a dog's internal monologue.

Doge speak—An Internet dialect based on the doge meme vernacular.

Domain name—Also known as a mask. Uses a word-based web address to disguise the IP address and directs users to your root directory.

Embed—To borrow the code from a piece of content (video, image) from another user or website and paste it onto your own digital platform (website).

Emojis—Originally based on emoticons, small iconographic faces and icons that assist in digital messages.

EXIF data—Exchangeable image file format—A digital standard for digital cameras that contains all data from the image such as technical data, GPS information, and settings.

Fair Use—US copyright doctrine that allows some material to be used, under certain circumstances, without permission of the copyright holder.

Fandom—Groups of dedicated fans who collectively create a subculture around a specific topic.

Follower—A user who subscribes and connects with you on social media platforms.

GIF—graphic interchange format—A lossless raster image format that is used primarily as an animated loop.

Google Analytics—A service to monitor your website traffic.

Guy Fawkes masks—Based on the James McTeigue/Wachowski film *V for Vendetta*, the mask is used to disguise Anonymous activists when they protest in the physical space.

Hacktivist—Internet user who uses group tactics and online tools to promote political issues, protests, and human rights campaigns. Often used by the group Anonymous.

Hashtag (see also #)—Created by Chris Messina, using a label or subject to categorize content, it began on Twitter and has followed on other social media sites since. Also used as a research tool for trending topics in the news, events, and other areas.

Hosting—A hard drive that stores all of your content and files for your website. You can rent hosting space online or create your own server to host other people's files.

HTML5—Current iteration of the main web language, it makes websites more responsive as well as offering compatibility across multiple devices.

Hypermedia—Text and media that can be conformed to the user's screen and interacted with.

Hypertext—A software-based system that allows the web to work, showing images and text through a browser interface.

ICANN—Internet Corporation for Assigned Names and Numbers—A nonprofit organization created in 1998 that organized and standardized the system so that users who made websites could potentially rent any domain and extension available.

Image macro—A type of meme where a digital image includes an amusing and entertaining caption or message.

IP—Internet protocol (IP address)—the location of the data and files that hold the website you want to visit.

ISP—Internet service provider—A company that customers pay a fee to in order to have Internet service in their homes (through broadband or DSL connection).

Javascript—A programming language that animates code to display dynamic content on web browsers.

JPEG—Joint Photographic Experts Group—The most common image format used on the web, owing to its use of an advanced algorithm that discards "extra" data and duplicates simple data.

jQuery—Open-source JavaScript language used by thousands of websites, written to help users add extra features to their site with ease.

Jump cuts—The act of editing out unnecessary information on your video without covering up the edits with other footage or b-roll. Usually used stylistically.

Juxtaposition image meme—A remix meme that takes a facial expression or an act out of context and inserts it into an image that deserves the punch line.

Landing page—An introductory page that lets the visitor know who you are and what your site is about.

Lolcats—A popular image macro or meme using one or more cats, with lolspeak text embedded.

Lolspeak—A community-organized language (designed to be coming directly from the cat's mind) that, through the act of the meme, has created its own remixable products.

Machinima—Also known as machine cinema; a narrative mash-up of video games and cinema, often using multiplayer games or first-person shooters, to create narrative films.

Makers—People who are creators in the physical space using digital media tools. Also known as the "Maker Movement," where people are using computer programming to make open-source materials to help advance the way the web works and how we participate. A few examples include 3D printing, Raspberry Pi, Oculus Rift, among others.

Mash-up—Combining two or more existing pieces of content to create a new, transformational piece.

Memes—An idea utilizing an image, video, GIF, or other form of media that spreads between the online audience, changing meanings and messages between users.

Metadata—Parts of web code that remain invisible to the viewer on the web browser or screen.

Microblogging—Short, frequent posts consisting of only a text, image, etc., commonly found on Tumblr, Twitter, and other social media networks.

Microenvironment—A small environment, platform, or community found on the web.

MMORPG—massively multiplayer online role-playing games—Web users form guilds and teams with other players in order to win battles against other teams. An example of an MMORPG is *World of Warcraft*.

Moore's Law—Gordon Moore observed that transistor technology was increasing exponentially in both storage and physical size. He posited that the computer speed and storage would double every 2 years; today, we call it big data.

Multichannel networks—In order to help online platforms, web producers assist with collaborations, promotions, and funding to create content. In some cases, the channels can team up and profit share, similar to a corporation.

Native advertising—A brand name clearly embedded in the content, also known as sponsored content.

New media—Any emerging technologies that affect you both socially and culturally.

Non-fiction communities—Fans of books, television shows, and other forms of content connecting together in online communities to discuss and create additional content of their favorite stories.

NSFW—not safe for work—A commonly used message board on 4chan or a hashtag when viewing an image or video that is not appropriate for viewing at one's job or around others.

Occupy Wall Street—In the fall of 2011, citizens gathering in the physical space as well as on social media networks to protest the economy and income inequality, among many other issues.

Online audience—Creating authentic content that the audience wants to view and share; building an audience that regularly follows your brand.

Online brand—A focused and structured digital presence that represents who you are online by arranging all of your information, content, and digital profiles in an organized manner. A user's personality, goals, and interests are clearly defined online and connected on all platforms.

Online communities—Environments found on the web such as message boards, databases, and social media sites that offer digital interaction with other online users, discussing content through text, images, and sound that capture the imagination of all web users.

Online identity—A name, personality, or subject you wish to establish and present to the public through the web, including social media platforms.

Online participant—An active user of digital media, both as a participant and content creator.

Open collaboration—People who are loosely connected, with a common goal to improve products.

Open source—Code or content that anyone has access to for personal use, when the owner offers the material for free.

OTP—one true pairing—Associated with fandom; after characters have been "shipped" from original stories, fans write and create content in their own narratives.

Permalink—A hyperlink or URL that is associated with your webpage or a blog post on your website and is based on words and easy to search.

Photo fad—An image that becomes a popular meme or a style of photo that becomes a trend, such as a selfie.

PHP—A database web language where a website's files stay on the host computer while you browse on your computer.

Physical memes—A meme that is performed and participated in by the online audience and is usually a strange act, such as owling or planking.

Platform—A website, social media site, or digital environment where users meet to post, create, and build an online community.

Plug-ins—Extensions to your website theme such as audio players, widgets, slide shows, galleries, and other features.

Podcast—An audio file that is typically an interview series found on the web, which users download or subscribe to on their mobile devices or computer, through iTunes or directly from audio companies such as Podcastone.

Popular culture—Content (images, videos) that is greatly influential in our media and popular within our society.

Post—Each time a user of the web writes a blog, adds an image, shares a video, or other pieces of content, to their social media profiles or websites.

Profile—A user's unique page on a social media site, consisting of their personal information, pictures, videos, interests, and activities.

Prosumer—A user who creates short-form video content and posts it on the web with intent to interact with the online audience and community, but in turn creates a successful venture and turns their product into profit.

Public brand—Also known as public identity, where individuals who create an online brand keep all of their social media sites and content public for a variety of reasons, such as attracting potential employers and increasing followers of their pages.

RAW image—JPEG, TIFF, and PNG image files before compression that contain a large amount of data, because they account for all of the information on the chip, including each pixel.

Reblogging—The act of reposting a blog or microblog (tweet) created by another user onto your profile or site, but crediting the original source (creator of the content).

Remix—A type of meme where users manipulate images of original photos, telling their own version and story with creativity and wit. Examples include "Disaster Girl," "Sad Keanu," "Bubbles Girl," among others.

Retweet—A user reposting another user's tweet on their profile.

Rick Roll—A bait-and-switch Internet prank started on 4chan, where users boast about something worth looking at, leading to Rick Astley's "Never Gonna Give You Up" (1987) music video.

Search engine optimization (SEO)—Making sure one's content or website is viewed by as many Internet users as possible by ensuring it will appear high on the list of search engine results. There are companies that help guide websites to optimize their content, such as Google Analytics.

Selfie—When a user utilizes their mobile device camera, flipping it around to take a self-portrait of oneself, showcasing their personality, emotions, and feelings at that exact moment.

Share—A participant or creator offering content to be downloaded, viewed, and interpreted in a variety of ways through social media.

Ship—To create a relationship between two existing characters that were not intentionally paired in the original concept and making them a "One True Pairing" or OTP.

Short message service (SMS)—A short text message commonly used on mobile devices for communication.

Social commentary—Commonly found when remixing video content, exposing and analyzing overlooked scenes in popular media with narration over the content.

Softaculous—Located in the cPanel of your website backend, it enables users to install applications such as WordPress.

SOPA—Also known as the Stop Online Piracy Act, this was a bill introduced by the government in 2012 to enforce copyright laws on the Internet.

SoundCloud—An audio distribution website that allows users to upload and share sounds such as music and podcasts.

Sponsored content—Also known as branded entertainment, produced material (such as a web series) that is supported and funded by an outside company. This company will be mentioned and seen throughout the material. An example would be Acura sponsoring *Comedians in Cars Getting Coffee* by Jerry Seinfeld.

Tagging—Commonly associated with users of social media sites who identify themselves and others in pictures and images.

Tags—Keywords for your blog post or video that are used as search terms, increasing the chances of the content being found on search engines such as Google. Also widely used on images in social media platforms.

TCP—transmission control protocol—A device, most commonly a modem, that increases the size, volume, and speed of the web.

Themes—All the design elements for the layout and presentation of your website.

Transmedia—Storytelling content developed for more than one medium, such as television, websites, social media, among other platforms.

Trolls—Users who post information and use the web in destructive ways.

Trope—A figurative use of an expression or word.

URL—uniform resource locator—The web address or domain name for any website.

Venture capitalism—When major corporations and entrepreneurs invest in start-up companies with the potential to grow into a money-making venture. Digital media have been at the forefront of this, as many social media, mobile, and emerging technologies have been approached by venture capitalists.

Viral seeding—Companies helping brands increase views, shares, and mentions quickly on video-sharing sites.

Vlog—A video blog, popular on YouTube, where a user talks directly to the audience, with creative editing typically using jump cuts.

YouTube Creators Playbook—Explains the most effective ways of running your channel, with thorough details of when to upload your content and how to create content people want to watch. The goal is to create a strategy of programming for long-term content creation and community engagement.

YouTube Editor—Allows users to edit, enhance, and customize their uploaded videos directly within the platform itself. Video creators have the ability to trim, add music, and quickly republish to the site.

Index